THE TURN OF RHYTHM

Victorian Literature and Culture Series

HERBERT F. TUCKER, EDITOR

WILLIAM R. MCKELVY, JILL RAPPOPORT, AND ANDREW M. STAUFFER,
ASSOCIATE EDITORS

The Turn of Rhythm

HOW VICTORIAN POETRY
SHAPED A NEW CONCEPT

Ewan Jones

UNIVERSITY OF VIRGINIA PRESS
Charlottesville and London

University of Virginia Press
© 2023 by the Rector and Visitors of the University of Virginia
All rights reserved
Printed in the United States of America on acid-free paper

First published 2023

1 3 5 7 9 8 6 4 2

Library of Congress Cataloging-in-Publication Data

Names: Jones, Ewan James, author.
Title: The turn of rhythm : how Victorian poetry shaped a new concept / Ewan Jones.
Description: Charlottesville : University of Virginia Press, 2023. | Series: Victorian literature and culture series | Includes bibliographical references and index.
Identifiers: LCCN 2023020363 (print) | LCCN 2023020364 (ebook) | ISBN 9780813950303 (hardcover) | ISBN 9780813950310 (paperback) | ISBN 9780813950327 (ebook)
Subjects: LCSH: English language—Rhythm. | English poetry—19th century—History and criticism.
Classification: LCC PE1559 .J66 2023 (print) | LCC PE1559 (ebook) | DDC 821/.809—dc23/eng/20230501
LC record available at https://lccn.loc.gov/2023020363
LC ebook record available at https://lccn.loc.gov/2023020364

Cover art: Background pattern, freedesignfile.com; spiral, Kloroform

CONTENTS

ACKNOWLEDGMENTS   vii

Introduction: The Turn of Rhythm   1
   1. Stuttering Rhythm   21
   2. Idealist Rhythms   69
   3. Entraining Rhythms   109
   4. Thermodynamic Rhythms   154
   Coda: (Re-)Turn   203

NOTES   211
BIBLIOGRAPHY   237
INDEX   249

ACKNOWLEDGMENTS

This book could not have come together without the encouragement, critical engagement, and kindness of many people. The University of Cambridge has provided me with a dynamic research environment that I only fully appreciated when it fell victim to a global pandemic. A yearlong fellowship at the Swedish Collegium for Advanced Study refined my sense of the relation between poetry and other disciplines, all over *fika*. A Leverhulme Research Fellowship permitted me to put the final touches on the manuscript. My undergraduates at Downing College never stopped teaching me literature.

Several friends and colleagues read and mitigated early drafts. I am especially grateful to Andrea Brady, Peter de Bolla, Jonathan Culler, Lorraine Daston, Anne-Lise Francois, Alex Freer, Ben Glaser, Devin Griffiths, Irmtraud Huber, Michael Hurley, Sarah Kennedy, Barak Kushner, David Nowell Smith, Paul Nulty, Merja Polvinen, Carmel Raz, John Regan, Marion Thain, and Phyllis Weliver. Kalle Axelsson helped me in ways that will become apparent from the opening pages of the manuscript. My brilliant doctoral students, Timothy Anderson, Oliver Goldstein, William Hall, and John Stowell, have allowed me to unlearn my habits of thought. Two people who do not want to be named have helped me more than they could ever know. Andrew Stauffer and Herbert Tucker offered brilliantly perceptive suggestions, as did the anonymous reader for the University of Virginia Press: whoever you are, thank you.

Eric Brandt has remained a model of (prompt) responsiveness, as he has guided the book through its several hoops. Colleen Romick Clark offered brilliantly incisive suggestions: I am fortunate to have found a copyeditor with such expansive knowledge of writing from the period. Ellen Satrom facilitated the cover art and much besides.

Portions of chapter 1 were published as "'Let the Rank Tongue Blossom': Browning's Stuttering," *Victorian Poetry*, 53.2 (Summer 2015), 103–32. Portions of chapter 2 were published as "Coventry Patmore's Corpus," *ELH* 83.3 (Fall 2016), 839–72. Portions of chapter 4 were published as "Thermodynamic Rhythm: The Poetics of Waste," *Representations*, 144 (Fall 2018), 60–88. I am grateful to the University of Virginia Press, Johns Hopkins University Press, and the University of California Press for granting permission to republish this material.

This book is dedicated to my son, Augustin, who came into being as it was coming into being.

THE TURN OF RHYTHM

INTRODUCTION

The Turn of Rhythm

Amazing Grace

I was congratulating myself on having completed this book, when my friend Kalle invited me to the cinema. Showing that evening was the documentary *Amazing Grace*. I was living at the time in Sweden, on a residential fellowship. We squeezed into the tight seats of the charming art deco theater, whose auditorium housed some forty people. The film arrived on the big screen only following a long and circuitous process: In 1972, Aretha Franklin, then at the height of her fame, free to pursue whatever artistic path she chose, decided to return to her gospel roots for two consecutive nights at the Missionary Baptist Church in Los Angeles. The resultant recordings would form the basis for a live album, released later that year; Sydney Pollack was also commissioned by PBS to record a documentary film of the same sessions. Pollack's failure to use clapperboards, however, left his editors unable to synchronize the audio and visual footage; by the time that digital technology came around, Franklin, by then increasingly frail, had mothballed the jarring reminder of her glorious past. Only following her death, in August 2018, could the synchronized footage appear.

Amazing Grace remains ragged at the edges. No amount of digital restoration can smooth out Pollack's jerky transitions and shaky camerawork, nor should it, because Franklin's remarkable performance is a study in organized chaos. As she sings gospel standards and not-so-standard gospel-blues fusions, the distinctions among singer, backing musician, audience, and worshipper begin to dissolve. Choir members and spectators alike take it in turns to leap up out of their seats, or to shout amen, or to start swaying upright, or to burst out in tears. When the camera settles for long enough, we sometimes see the same person move through all these states in the space of a few seconds. At one point the Reverend Dr. James Cleveland, who sets and conducts the music throughout, has to break off conducting so as to weep. A young Mick Jagger loiters in the rear of the church, for once peripheral to the recorded event.

Sinking deeper into my padded seat, I experienced a strange and divided feeling. Franklin's voice did not only dissolve the boundaries between churchgoers. It also carried, through several degrees of technological mediation, to the very different room in which we present subjects sat. While never moving my eyes from the screen, I was also aware, through my peripheral vision, or through the percussive taps on the padded carpet and wooden armrests, that my fellow audience members were, like me, nodding, toe tapping, finger rapping. Oceans of time, space, and cultural privilege separated these two very different communities. Half of the ecstatic historical subjects are now sure to be dead and gone: the same C. L. Franklin, who halfway through the film pays a moving unscripted tribute to his daughter, was twelve years later shot dead at point-blank range during a botched robbery. The Swedish auditorium, by contrast, contained an exclusively white and incomparably more restrained social body. None of us jumped up out of our seats to shout hallelujah, however much we might have felt it. Yet the voice continued to dictate our more subdued response. Aretha Franklin begins to sweat. With tenderness, Reverend Cleveland towels her brow and neck. The camera again loses focus: you might almost fancy yourself watching the scene through your own sweat and tears.

When, staggering dazedly into the early twilight of Swedish midwinter, I tried to account for what I had just experienced, one word sprang to mind: rhythm. This single term designated my body's impulse to tap its toes upon the padded carpet; the percussive vibrations that I felt through the wooden armrests, which connected me to my friend Kalle and the other faceless unknown persons in the Swedish art deco cinema; the peculiar quality of Aretha Franklin's vocal delivery; and the unstable equilibrium of those who danced and sang in her church. In addition to naming these separate entities, rhythm offered me, in the cozy pub to which by now I had relocated, a means of grasping their superimposition. It allowed me to understand their differential unity: just as each worshipper moved in a singular yet coordinated manner, so too did the white Swedish audience occupy a nonidentical yet palpable relation to the predominantly black group that gathered in Los Angeles. Rhythm named the most immediate and individual bodily reflex, in addition to the historical communities that such subjects form, unthinkingly, in the act of dancing.

My happiness at having been able to formulate this experience in propositional terms (in *a* propositional term) was swiftly counteracted by the realization that the book that I had written was not finished at all.

Unlearning Rhythm

The work that finally does follow explores the broader cultural significance of my brief personal experience. For by reaching for the concept of rhythm in a way that I wanted to call "intuitive," I was unwittingly re-creating a much larger cultural history. Societies, like me, employed the term "rhythm" as a necessarily retrospective designation of individual and social experience. The word came so naturally to me that I could scarcely imagine a time when I had never possessed it. Yet such a time certainly did exist. And not only for me: the story that I wanted to tell, I slowly came to realize, was how culture at large came to acquire a new concept whose utility was so powerful that it came to seem like second nature. It turns out that we can date this transition with unusual precision: it overwhelmingly occurred across the nineteenth century.

At first glance, this claim seems unjustifiably large. Subjects have always had (what we now call) rhythmical experiences, however they chose to designate them (or not). In a very real sense, we never failed to "possess" rhythm: we experienced the concept from the first stages of uterine life, the early cycles of feeding, cradling, weaning, the table-tapping that is absent-minded yet meaning-bearing. Yet the complex and nearly instantaneous unifying work that my conceptual usage performed—tying together individual physiology and broader social and historical orders—did not, as a rule, occur.

In order to perceive this historical development, we have to unlearn certain habits of mind, which include the tendency to employ this now-pervasive concept in fuzzy or inexact ways. As the musicologist Curt Sachs observed, rhythm has been employed in so many discursive contexts that it can denote just about anything.[1] I do not wish to offer a conclusive definition so much as describe a general pattern of thinking that my opening anecdote traces. Let me therefore expand upon that phenomenological description by offering five purposefully broad interlocking definitions:

1. *Rhythm names a process or relation that exists in the world.* A minimum of two discrete events in time or space can be incorporated into a rhythmical sequence: a sounding bell, pacing feet, the synchronous flashing of thousands of Guinean fireflies. Different disciplines from across the science-humanities divide apply this basic premise in immediately recognizable ways: "work rhythms," "biorhythms," "musical rhythms," "speech rhythms," and so on.

2. *But rhythm also names something in the head.* Rhythmical aptitude denotes the ability to form punctual stimuli into a meaningful sequence. Guinean fireflies may flash synchronously, but we do not (commonly) take them to possess rhythmical apprehension. The human talent for rhythm, whether intrinsic or learned, enables complex forms of retention and protention: we hear a dropped beat all the more keenly when the beat is established. The sliding scale of rhythmical apprehension has in the past served various ideologies: rhythm has proven a means of driving attempted distinctions between humans and nonhumans, in addition to different human societies.

3. *But rhythm also names something between heads (and bodies).* Individual (human) subjects impose rhythmical sequence upon periodic stimuli. Yet rhythmical sequences also impose themselves upon human subjects, rendering porous the distinction between bodies. We entrain to an external phase: walking through the shopping mall, we find our stride matching the quickening tempo of Taylor Swift's "Shake It Off," piped in through the inescapable loudspeakers.

4. *Rhythm enables measurement of the variable.* Rhythm enables exact measurement of even very variable sequences. The dropped beat does not eliminate rhythm; rather, it reconfigures it ("syncopation"). This basic principle is at the heart of much more complex or turbulent (yet also measur-

able) sequential patterns: the polyrhythmic drumming of some West African cultures, whose divergences in tempo many musicologists attributed to "improvisation" in live performance, but which computational analysis has since revealed to be formalizable (albeit not reducible to Western norms); or arrhythmia, which implies a dangerous cardiac pattern, rather than no rhythm at all; or even "cosmic arrhythmia," nonlinear yet predictable space-time turbulence.

5. *Rhythm expresses variation of regularity.* In a rhythmical sequence, there is no such thing as "pure" repetition. Human subjects naturally impute difference into the strictly identical successive ticks of a clock ("tick *tock*").

The average language user may not have these associations in mind; they nevertheless routinely operate in several discursive contexts. Prior to 1770, this was not the case. The concept of rhythm did not name something in the world for several disciplines; it did not represent a means for relating human agents to other organic forms of life; it did not dissolve the boundaries between individual bodies, or between individual bodies and external phases; it did not describe how subjects generate difference from repetition of the same.

How this semantic halo came to form around rhythm remains one of the great untold stories of intellectual history. But *The Turn of Rhythm* aims to show not only *that* the concept was educed, but *how* it was educed. Grasping this specific process, I claim, helps us to learn something about concept acquisition in general: the means by which embodied, nondiscursive experience qualifies as thinking, quite as much as ratiocination. I did not impose the concept of rhythm upon my experience of *Amazing Grace* through a process of distanced reflection: it rather translated a frustrated intellectual twitch that itself derived from my own bodily tics, along with the larger social bodies to which I dimly sensed that they differentially belonged. Nineteenth-century subjects similarly got rhythm not solely by reflecting upon it; they actuated it, or had it actuated in them. We cannot separate my five generic designations from the nondiscursive experience that gave rise to them: experience is no ladder to be kicked away, having ascended to the good view of high ground. The nineteenth century can remind us of what we have forgotten by knowing too much: the period could only grope toward the concept, and this groping tells us something.

FIGURE 1. Google Ngram Viewer: "metre" and "rhythm," British English, 1600–2000

It is much easier to prove a presence than an absence. To this end, I will avail myself of several quantitative and qualitative demonstrations of the lack of the concept of rhythm prior to 1770. These move from intentional crudeness to increasing granularity. At the former extreme are a series of computational measures of relative word frequency. Figure 1 reproduces the Google Ngram Viewer, which charts the relative frequency of given words or phrases in the given corpus (here the several hundreds of thousands of books that Google has digitized). No serious intellectual history can rely exclusively upon such a measure, whose several limitations are well-established.[2] The sheer scope of the corpus nevertheless effectively reveals large-scale trends. Here the trend is large enough to be incontestable. The graph compares the relative probability of "rhythm" in British English documents from 1600 to 2000. I compare it to "metre," in part given the conceptual disarticulation that I pursued in my five designations; in part because the contrast between the two statistical profiles proves so striking. We might expect the former term to predominate, given the latter's relatively delimited and technical extension (within poetry or music). Yet "metre" exceeds "rhythm" until well into the nineteenth century.[3] The latter, to judge by the graph, appears nearly invisible until the mid-eighteenth century.

The absence of a word does not entail the absence of a concept. Meter, harmony, tempo: all these cognates are familiar to pre-nineteenth-century discourse, and discharge some of the conceptual work that I described above. Yet while "meter" and "tempo" clearly do describe an ordered sequence of periodic stimuli, they hardly permit the other kinds of thinking that I outlined: moving between discursive fields, denoting a cognitive capacity, describing the relations between bodies, expressing complex relations between pattern and variation. No other cognate or phrase performed anything like the same role.

To investigate such trends further, however, we require more robust historical corpora. Gale Cengage's Eighteenth Century Collections Online (ECCO) offers just that: it is far from perfect (the OCR in particular is a familiar source of anguish for historians of the period), yet its 205,000 individual volumes give it a fair claim to historical comprehensiveness. It is not riddled with the many problems of dating and opaque selection criteria that plague Google Books. Table 1 confirms that the term remains conspicuous by its absence throughout the century: over the first twenty years, "rhythm" appears in a paltry three titles, in comparison to 511 texts that feature "metre"; while the former increases more quickly than the latter over the ensuing century, it remains strikingly infrequent in absolute and relative terms. Of the hundreds of thousands of documents that comprise ECCO, a vanishingly small total of 257 feature the word "rhythm." If we move from nouns to adjectives, the same pattern recurs: "metrical" outnumbers the "rhythmic*" stem (which includes the interchangeable "rhythmic" and "rhythmical") many times over.

Similar searches from other datasets yield similar patterns.[4] The Google Ngram Viewer reveals comparable tendencies in French (*rythme*) and German (*Rhythmus*) over the given period. Of the 132,363 texts from 1473 to 1700 that comprise Early English Books Online (EBBO), just 224 texts fea-

TABLE 1. Frequency of "rhythm" and cognates, 1700–1800

	1700–1719	1720–1739	1740–1759	1760–1779	1780–1800	TOTAL (1700–1800)
Rhythm	3	22	21	54	145	257
Metre	511	831	1,061	1,783	2,680	6,854
Rhythmic*	5	10	6	27	49	94
Metrical	80	121	162	334	873	1,562

Source: Eighteenth Century Collections Online (ECCO, Gale Cengage)

ture variants on "rhythm" ("rhythme," "rithime," "rithim"). A large proportion of the few that do clearly designate a much narrower phenomenon, namely rhyme: Alexander Brome's *A Record in Rithme Being an Essay towards the Reformation of the Law* (1670?), written in heroic couplets, is a representative case in point. In short, the word *rhythm*, at least so far as the vernacular languages are concerned, is a strikingly modern invention.

Proportion ≠ Disequilibrium

Word-counting alone cannot take the conceptual historian very far. To get a clearer sense that something new did occur across the nineteenth century, we need to consider the larger conceptual networks in which individual lexical tokens ("rhythm" and its cognates) were embedded. The relatively rare eighteenth-century texts that *did* use or define rhythm prove significant in this regard. Samuel Johnson's *Dictionary* of 1755–76 finds no room for the substantive, in keeping with the trend described above. Johnson does, however, define the adjectival variant, albeit in a manner that strikes modern ears as quite counterintuitive: "RHY´THMICAL. *adj.* Harmonical. Having proportion of one sound to another."[5] No musicologist would now see harmony and rhythm as isomorphic, however related they may be: the vague "proportion of one sound to another" suggests that the less familiar word does little more than elegantly vary its then more illustrious cognate.

"Harmony" is one of the master tropes of classicism. But it is not quite true to say that rhythm had no comparable preexistence. Indeed, the *Dictionary* entry cites what might at first seem to offer a strong challenge to my claim for the modernity of rhythm: the Greek etymology of the term *rhuthmos*, which Johnson, in keeping with several scholars before and since, derives from the verb ῥέω, *rheo*, "to flow." The more we explore this earlier concept, however, the more we see that it meant something very different from what rhythm came to denote. As Martin Heidegger and Émile Benveniste have explored at length, the "flow" derivation is tendentious at best: Heidegger's 1966–67 Heraclitus seminar links the term rather to a stamp, bind, or fetters [*Fetteln*].[6] Aeschylus's Prometheus is—in a phrasing that cannot but sound peculiar to modern ears—*errúthmismai*, literally "en-rhythmed" to the rock. "He, who is held immobile in the iron chains of his confinement," Heidegger glosses, "is 'rhythmed,' that is, joined."[7]

Rhuthmos does indeed fetter far more than it flows.[8] The rhythm of Democritus's atom means its distinctive shape, rather than any more dynamic temporal variation.[9] Archilochus may well have introduced unprecedented metrical liberty to his verse, yet *rhuthmos* itself again means binding or fixing (fragment 128: "the rhythm that controls men's lives"). Benveniste challenged the "flow" derivation only to claim that Plato later liberated the rigid, prohibitive pre-Socratic notion into something more dynamic.[10] But even in his *Laws*, the regulative element predominates: rhythm operates in the sphere of "motion," yet always and only in "orderly" fashion, as a distinctively human achievement. Animals have no rhythm.[11] Rhythm clearly differentiates men and women, free men and slaves, pure and mixed artistic modes.[12] Harmony and rhythm prove isomorphic throughout,[13] just as they do in the surviving fragments of Aristoxenus of Tarentum's fourth-century BC treatise *On Rhythm*, whose geometric approach remained significant until the later Middle Ages.[14] As even the arch-Hellenist (and arch-liberator) Friedrich Nietzsche came to recognize, *rhuthmos* was finally more a matter of Apollonian order than Dionysian transgression.[15]

The other English derivation, from the Latin *rithmus*, tells a similar story. As J. W. Rankin argued some time ago, there is strong evidence to derive the English *rime* from the medieval Latin *rithmus*, itself traceable to the contested Greek root. Grammarians frequently identified *rithmus* with the accentual prosody that increasingly crept into previously syllabic Latin verse: "Thus," writes Rankin, "from the metrical point of view *rhythmus* lacked *ratio*; it was *sine ratione* (sans raison)."[16] There is certainly a hint here of a more dynamic concept: a nondiscursive medium that would not be predicated upon strict and unyielding laws. Over the Middle Ages and early modern period, however, the term lost all specificity, given the general confusion with "rhyme" that we have already had reason to observe.

In short, despite occasional exceptions to the general rule, and despite the most ingenious efforts to detect in Greek culture a more "ek-static" understanding of rhythm, the classical and medieval and early modern extensions of the word remained highly restrictive.[17] We can contrast this with the common early nineteenth-century intuition, shared by prosodists such as Joshua Steele, philosophers such as F. W. J. Schelling, and natural scientists such as William Whewell, that the concept needed somehow to be defined for the very first time—in a manner that, they concurred, would hold consequences for cognition, embodiment, and the cosmos. In his *First Principles of a New System of Philosophy* (1862), Herbert Spencer defined the term in a manner that had become powerfully representative: "It will be seen," Spencer wrote, "that rhythm results wherever there is a conflict of forces not in equilibrium."[18] In little more than a century, the concept has thus undergone a *volte-face:* rhythm, formerly a matter of harmonious proportion, has become conflictual disequilibrium. The "turn" of my title thus marks both the revolution in the concept's meaning, and the moment of its historical vocation.

What Verse Knew

Across the nineteenth century, an eclectic variety of extant and nascent discourses come to conceptualize rhythm for the first time. They did so in large part not through the employment of communicative rationality, but by means of nondiscursive experience. One form of nondiscursive experience proved particularly and repeatedly significant: verse. *The Turn of Rhythm* posits an ongoing dialectic between the propositional discussion of its eponymous concept, and the rhythmical structure and experience of poetry. Speech therapists and idealist philosophers and anthropologists and natural scientists called upon poetry to exemplify or illuminate whatever they took to be rhythmical facts in the world; poetry served this function, but also productively resisted it, through an expressive variability that staved off total or final adequation to a fixed concept. This resistance in turn impelled further attempts at concept formation.

My phrasing, here, is purposefully Kantian: aesthetic judgment involves a sensuous particular that generatively resists conceptual subsumption. We less often stress the complementary part of Kant's formulation, however: aesthetic objects continually call for, summon, incite prospective concepts—as if there would finally be, after so long, an adequate explanation for this most puzzling of phenomena. This is what gives them their productive (as opposed to merely aporetic or apophatic) character. The following pages attempt to demonstrate that this productive a-conceptuality is a historical fact, in addition to an ontological or epistemological claim.

We can speculate as to why poetry was peculiarly able to provide this function. After all, it was and is but one of many para-discursive media. Music, painting, sculpture, fishing, weaving, bread-baking: all these offer instances of extended and enactive cognition. Part of the answer must lie in the changing nature of poetry in the period: the several poets that I will read (Robert Browning, Coventry Patmore, Alice Meynell, George Eliot, A. C. Swinburne, among others) pushed verse rhythm in radically new directions. But this by itself is not enough to account for the disproportionate importance of poetry within the propositional discourse that I have outlined. Music underwent similarly profound rhythmical changes in the period: Beethoven's Fifth Symphony is commonly taken to impel a revolution in this regard. Yet music theory seldom feels a need to conceptualize rhythm, in contradistinction to the twin pillars of harmony and melody. While *Rhythmus* begins to circulate within the late eighteenth-century German musical theory of Sulzer, Forkel and Kirnberger, such work remains a strict and restrictive measure of temporal organization, traveling seldom outside narrowly musical circles.[19] As Catherine Dale observes, a sustained and systematic treatment of rhythm as a distinctive constituent of music emerges only with the late nineteenth-century work of Hugo Riemann.[20]

To observe this contrast between poetry and music more fully, we can dip our toe back into the current of history. Dictionary definitions again offer a good way in. Jean-Jacques Rousseau defines *rythme* for the *Encyclopédie*, where it offers one of many indices of modern decline. The entry adopts wholesale Isaac Vossius's theory of *rhythmopoeoeia*, which analyses music according to the classical conventions of foot-based prosody: "a detached rhythm, like ours," writes Rousseau, with the romance vernaculars in mind, "that doesn't represent all the forms and figures of things, can have no effect." It follows that "we do not have any true *rhythm* in our poetry, and that in making our verses we think only of bringing in a certain number of syllables, without worrying ourselves as to what type of syllable they may be."[21] Rhythm means perfect adherence to syllabic norms, which correspond exactly to preestablished figured content. Lest such a picture seem limited to the incorrigibly syllabic French, we can append Charles Burney's four-volume *History of Music* (1782–89). His section "On Rhythm"—significantly part of a broader "Dissertation on the Music of the Ancients"—follows *doxa* obediently. Rhythm is developed in (and restricted to) antiquity; it represents just proportion (the familiar analogy with sculpture); it is linked to fixed metrical quantity ("Rhythm in Latin was called *numerus*").[22] Its regulative and constraining properties again hold political consequences: "Pythagoras," recaps Burney, "according to Martianus Capella, used to call *Rhythm*, in music, the *male*, and *Melos* the female; and Doni (*n*) has compared *Rhythm* with *design*, in painting, and *Melos*, to *colouring*."[23]

What a difference we observe, when we advert from musical theory to contemporaneous considerations of the structure and experience of poetry! While many authors continued to defend, extend, and practice a restrictive notion of exact classical syllabic quantity, an increasing number of countervailing voices began to formulate a rhythmical variability better suited to the tongue in our mouths. Joshua Steele was the first and most significant figure to call into question the foot-based model that music was continuing to import; ironically enough, he described his drastic rescripting of the human voice in analogy to "music." As my first chapter will explore in greater detail, Steele's *Prosodia Rationalis* (1772) employs the word "rhythmus" not so as to mark slavish adherence to Greek precedent: in fact, it means just the opposite, an unprecedented attention to the slides, hesitations, contours, and stumbles of the human voice. Even the simple expostulation "Oh!" required registration in a complex score (fig. 2). Accent was no longer a binary pattern of thesis and arsis, but a quantum of energy: "rhythmus" inhered not in the poetic object, but in the mind and body of its performer.[24] Despite a pseudo-musical notation that is often opaque, unconvincing, and dogmatic, Steele's notion of linguistic *rhythmus* travelled far beyond the narrow field of prosody. When his follower Jonathan Odell suggests that "man alone is sensible of a rhythmus in his motions,"[25] his clipped phrase proffers the kernel of a huge cultural shift.

Verse remained central to this process. A natural scientist such as William Whewell did not refer repeatedly to individual poems only because those references were likely to be familiar to his readers, or because they offered epigrammatic concision (though they were, and they did). Rather, verse ex-

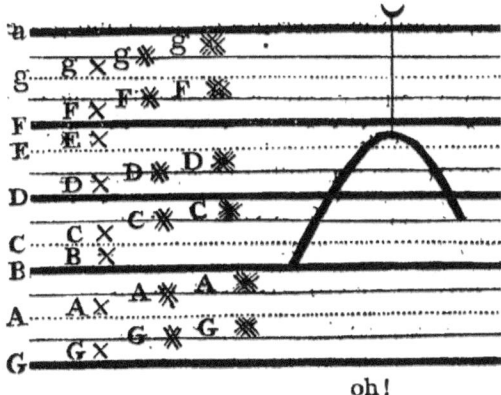

FIGURE 2. Joshua Steele, *Prosodia Rationalis* (1798), 6

emplified, as no other medium could, what he newly took to be an intrinsic human capacity: the rhythmical capacity. (It was not coincidental that, in addition to his work on the inductive sciences, Whewell wrote several technical papers on versification.) Contingent factors such as established cultural prestige and ease of access cannot by themselves explain the scale of the phenomenon. Poetry did peculiar cognitive work through the sum of its intrinsic expressive resources and historical conventions: the constitutive relation (or contention) between non-signifying sound and linguistic reference allowed it both to drive and to resist concept formation in the manner that I have described; the highly composite nature of English provided a range of rhythmical possibilities (accentual, syllabic, other), which enabled the language to slip more readily than other romance vernaculars from the shackles of quantitative classical meter. The resultant divergent plurality could, in turn, model and operationalize other worldly facts.

Körperbegriffsgeschichte

My singular case study can shed light upon the broader cultural process of concept acquisition. To this end, I bring into contact two disciplines seldom on speaking terms: conceptual history and verse phenomenology. The former tends to concentrate upon the *representation* of bodily experience, and with good reason: these are what get handed down to us in the historical record. Yet in an apologetic foreword to *Making Sex,* Thomas Laqueur somewhat tantalizingly suggests another itinerary for historical enquiry:

> I confess that I am saddened by the most obvious and persistent omission in this book: a sustained account of experience in the body. Some might argue that this is as it should be, and that a man has nothing of great interest or authenticity to say about the sexual female body as it feels and loves. But more generally I have found it impossible in all but isolated forays into literature, painting, or the occasional work of theology to imagine how such different visions of the body worked in specific contexts to shape passion, friendship, attraction, love.[26]

It could very well be that Laqueur's status as "a man" impedes his capacity for projective identification with other unalike historical subjects—though this would ironically undercut the subsequent sweep of his argument, which demonstrates the extent to which sexual difference from the early modern period was *not* self-evident. His hedging phrasing ("some might argue") reserves the possibility that *déformation professionelle* (his status as a historian) explains the "persistent omission" of aesthetic experience.

Verse offers one privileged means to account for "experience in the body," rather than the representation of experience in the body. It is not only that we can experience something comparable to what previous readers felt: we cannot *not* experience something comparable, given that the only way to get at a poem is by performing it. (Analytic detachment, silent reading in the dusty archive, remains a performance.) "Comparable" does not mean "identical": we cannot naively or fully re-create whatever a nineteenth-century subject felt when she stumbled through a long poem by Robert Browning and set about trying to describe what it did to her tongue. As a white British man living in the early twenty-first century, with an accent that over time I have learned to flatten in a failed bid to escape class distinctions, I experience verse in a particular manner, particularly when I read it aloud while pacing around, as I like to do. But by tallying our differing singular responses, in the real-time of the present, with the imperfect reports of embodied experience that historical agents have left, we can grasp how certain poems produce productive divergences within different bodies and communities of bodies—and how others generate a surprising commonality of response.

My subsequent readings therefore supplement *Begriffsgeschichte* with an approach foreign to Reinhart Koselleck or nearly any other conceptual historian: recurrent phenomenological descriptions of verse reading, during which I strive to be exact yet not so exacting as to lose the quiddity, immediacy, and obscurity of experience. You could call this approach "interdisciplinary," if you like, but I prefer not even to honor the breach that would be crossed: even ignorant or presentist readers of poetry are practicing history, whether they know it or not. My readings thus seek to actuate what Hans-Ulrich Gumbrecht calls "presence effects," which seldom get much of a look-in within the subfield of conceptual history.[27]

Literary criticism should be in a prime position to supply this embodied yet suprapersonal historical account of rhythmical experience. Yet the many dedicated treatments of poetic rhythm that have informed and sustained this present work tend, for the most part, to concentrate upon only one side of the equation: singular embodiment *or* cultural representations. Several phenomenological or psychoanalytical approaches have considered the primal capacity of rhythm to bind and break bodies.[28] "The energy of rhythm," writes Amittai F. Aviram, "exceeds the limits of the limited moment in cultural knowledge reflected in the poem's images and ideas": the inadvertent repetition of "limits" indicates the eradication of historical specificity.[29] More recently, Vincent Berlatta has intriguingly attempted to excavate a pre-Socratic conception of rhythm that inheres not, as for Aviram, in animating force, but rather existential "dispossession." Berlatta's attention to break and rupture delivers several interesting readings of poems, yet levels the distinctions between his very varied historical settings (classical antiquity, the Portuguese *Século de oro*, Virginia Woolf's London).[30]

By way of contrast, a larger number of works have recently focused upon the cultural representation of rhythm: Michael Golston's *Rhythm and Race in Modernist Poetry and Science* traces the powerful (and dispiriting) ideological work that the concept discharges; Meredith Martin's *The Rise and Fall of Meter* similarly investigates the manner in which foot-based prosody helps to fashion national and imperial subjects.[31] Much of this extant scholarship has greatly shaped the following chapters: Jason David Hall's exploration of the nineteenth-century metronome anticipates my discussions of both elocution (in chapter 1) and isochronous meter (in chapter 2);[32] Jason Rudy's *Electric Meters* has greatly influenced my thinking about the biological and physical body, in chapters 3 and 4 respectively.[33] Such works generally have less to say, however, about how individual subjects might have experienced such ideological entrainment. Even supposing the nineteenth century to have held a "metronomic" conception of meter, could they possibly have experienced poems in such a rigid manner? Could we? Much evidence suggests that subjects did not experience poetic rhythm unilaterally; we recover that history with our own tongues.

By bringing together verse phenomenology and cultural history, I want to supply content to the otherwise merely programmatic assertion that art thinks or even, on a good day, "knows."[34] Absent such concretion, the premise that "art thinks" runs a perpetual risk of devolving into an irrefutable yet unverifiable subjectivity; or a dogmatic insistence upon the nonpropositional that congratulates itself upon its departure from a putatively compromised bourgeois rationality (beautiful soul syndrome); or the reduction of art to perpetual self-commentary; or a series of virtuosic but monadic case studies. I list these perils so readily only because, in one way or another, my past work falls foul of all of them.[35] A commitment to the cognitive purchase of art must at some point demonstrate where, how, and when such thinking occurs—however grave the threat of the travesty of paraphrase.

It matters that this is a nineteenth-century story. *The Turn of Rhythm* challenges the prevailing scholarly conviction that its titular term is above all a modernist phenomenon.[36] Golston's work again proves exemplary in this respect, with its foundational claim that "in many ways, Thaddeus Bolton's 'Rhythm,' published in *The American Journal of Psychology* for January 1904, marks the beginning of Anglo-American investigations of rhythm."[37] Yet Bolton's dissertation (which was in fact published in 1894) refers consistently to the multitudinous studies on the subject that British and German scholarship had produced over the previous four decades. In its entry for the term, *The Princeton Encyclopaedia of Poetry and Poetics* revealingly jumps across the yawning abyss between the contested Greek etymology and modernist practice.[38]

This disproportionate focus on twentieth-century rhythm holds political consequences. Modernist scholars cannot ignore the amenability of the fledgling concept to programs of racial purification and imperial domination. Yet this dismal context encourages Golston to enforce a rigid ideological policing, when the very gravity of the period requires finer discriminations. To elide Émile Jacques-Dalcroze's eurhythmic gymnastics with the Nazi policies of corporeal discipline is to travesty the former's explicit intentions and subsequent influence.[39] Similarly, to equate Nietzsche's conceptualization of rhythm (which while hardly unproblematic was often expressly *anti*-Teutonic) with Wagner's vile racism ("the Jew as an alien, non-native, and soil-less person, can at best only poorly imitate [rhythm]") is to paint in brushstrokes so broad that they whitewash history.[40] The nineteenth century is hardly a more innocent period: indeed, my first and third chapters will chronicle several of the more dispiriting causes in which the developing notion of rhythm was enlisted. Yet this prior moment also reveals the extent to which the still-unfixed concept also provided a means of figuring the gendered, dyspraxic nonhuman and plural body. Caught as it continues to be between a naïve fetishization of rhythm and an unflagging hermeneutics of suspicion, our culture can learn much from a moment of early and provisional thinking, whose political consequences were not set out in advance, however much hindsight tempts us to impute inexorability.

On Not Cutting Skeletons from the Flesh

A brief word on what this book does *not* intend to do. By seeking to bring together intellectual history and aesthetic phenomenology, the word "rhythm" necessarily emerges in two distinct ways: as a concept that was increasingly handled by speech therapists, idealist philosophers, natural scientists, and the rest; and as a technical description for the formal properties of verse. The latter usage has often been employed alongside "meter," sometimes as synonym, sometimes as antonym. On this point, I will be absolutely clear from the outset: I do not intend to provide a technical definition of rhythm in poetry, or to generate a reliable contrast to meter. I have neither the talent nor the desire to intervene within long-standing disputes over accentual and foot-based accounts, or to adjudicate quarrels between timers and stressers, or to graft more branches onto T. V. F. Brogan's prosodic tree.[41] I am interested in rhythm as a description of bodily experience and as a concept that travels in broader culture, rather than as a systematic description of verse (or anything else).

To the extent that I adhere to existing theories, I am inclined to the formulations of thinkers such as Thomas Cable and Christopher Hasty, who in fields as remote as medieval poetry and contemporary musicology understand rhythm as embodied experience rather than as an exact measurement of objective facts in the world.[42] But in practice I am ecumenical in the technical language that I use, which serves the poem at hand rather than a preestablished agenda. In some cases, this involves analyzing and experiencing versification in what is sometimes called a "rhythmical" (i.e., accentual) manner: such an approach, most powerfully associated with the pioneering work of Derek Attridge, involves the counting of beats rather than syllables.[43] At other moments, however, I employ the foot-based terminology whose constituent terms (iambs, dactyls, spondees, and the rest) may well prove chimerical, yet produce, like many chimeras, real corporeal effects. I neither like nor adopt evaluative dichotomies such as "metre is a skeleton, rhythm is the functioning body," or "meter is dogmatic" while "rhythm is critical."[44] (Who, given the choice, would prefer the fleshless body, or uncritical dogma?) Rhythms can indeed be vital, variable, and volatile: we like to call such attributes liberated, by comparison to the staid or mechanical patterns from which they diverge. Yet the simple, repeated, undeviating pattern can produce distinctive rhythmical effects of its own: it can sow disquiet; it can represent a refuge to which the enduring body, tired of its variations, finally returns.

Final Itinerary

Each of this book's four chapters localizes the gestation of the concept of rhythm in a different discursive field; they trace a series of overlapping episodes rather than a linear narrative.

Chapter 1, "Stuttering Rhythms," focuses upon the earliest discursive context in which the new concept gains a foothold: the clinical science of speech therapy. Joshua Steele's reformist prosody unwittingly grounded a coherent theory and elocutionary, which sought to mitigate stuttering through the "rhythm method." Verse was frequently employed as an external stimulus to which the subject could entrain vocal production. Yet the very authors and texts that these elocutionists drew upon most frequently (such as Robert Browning) often resisted the clinical ends to which they were submitted. "Verse stuttering" thus came to represent both a clinical pathology and an expressive resource: this rhythmical phenomenon would hold deep aesthetic, political, and social consequences.

Chapter 2, "Idealist Rhythms," extends this notion of rhythmical competence from the mouth to the subject that owns it (or is owned by it). A range of German poets and philosophers (Hölderlin, Novalis, Hegel) experience a growing need to "establish fully for the first time the supreme theory of rhythm." In their hands, the concept becomes a means of expressing nonidentical selfhood and dialectical process. Such thinking percolates into anglophone discourse in unacknowledged ways: through Coventry Patmore's Hegelianized prosody, long misconstrued as "abstract," and through William Whewell's philosophical definition of rhythm, which sought to reconcile idealism with inductive experimentalism. As with chapter 1, this process of conceptualization both relied upon and inspired verse. Poetic thinking drove and exceeded discursive thinking, as in the experimental odes of Patmore and the deceptively compliant poetry of Alice Meynell, who transfigured the idealist preoccupation with break and caesura into an expression of gendered experience.

The following two chapters chart the developing concept of rhythm as it begins to extend beyond the individual subject, so as to encompass nonhuman organisms, communal bodies, and the wider cosmos. Chapter 3, "Entraining Rhythms," explores the nineteenth century's prefiguration of the concept of entrainment within nascent fields such as zoology and anthropology. The tendency for individual oscillators to synchronize to an external phase troubles the distinctions between human and nonhuman life, with manifold attendant ethical consequences. George Eliot's generally overlooked verse tragedy *The Spanish Gypsy* uses variable rhythms to model a liberal sociality that takes into account the irreducibly physiological nature of human sympathy. The final decades of the century witness the extension of such questions through the anthropological treatment of "primitive" song, which theorizes and curates cultural products, such as the ballad, whose rhythmical variability once again exceeds formal designations.

A fourth and final chapter, "Thermodynamic Rhythms," considers how the intertwined sciences of heat and sound transfigure my titular concept. The dismal consequences of the second law of thermodynamics trigger three complementary efforts to recuperate hope in the face of entropy, all of which formulate the concept of rhythm in a distinctive way, and all of which draw extensively upon verse. The third of these tendencies attempts to incorporate waste and fatigue into a broader rhythmical experience: it holds the most significant consequences for poetry, as I demonstrate via an extended reading of Swinburne's appropriately long poem *Tristram of Lyonesse*. Weariness, I claim, can be a positive resource in our experience of art.

I choose the above poems because they perform real cognitive work. But I also read them because they are beautiful, because they are affecting, and because in many cases they suffer extended unjust neglect. I hope that these readings may prove useful even for readers who remain uninterested in or unpersuaded by the broader historical argument. For each individual poem was and is a little difference engine. The rhythmical variation that it induces cannot be reduced to the nominal "diversity" that neoliberalism likes to advertise for itself—predicated as it is upon a notion of individual identity that remains monadic, voluntarist, incommensurable, and abstract. Individuals sound individual lines in individual ways: yet in so doing, they reveal the historical communities and brutely actual constraints in which their bodies are enmeshed.

My coda considers possible pedagogical consequences of the history that this book will have traced. It thereby seeks to prove that to grasp the concept of rhythm is also to actuate it.

1

Stuttering Rhythms

"An Instinctive Sense of *Rhythmus*"

If anglophone culture by 1779 was yet to possess a developed concept of rhythm, it was not for want of understanding of its nature or effects. In fact, argued Joshua Steele, in the expanded second edition to his *Prosodia Rationalis*, which appeared that year, we grasp the phenomenon so intuitively that we scarcely need name it:

> Our animal existence being regulated by our pulse, we seem to have an instinctive sense of rhythmus as connected with, and governing, all sounds and all motions; whence it follows, that we find all people feel the effects of *rhythmus*, as they do those of light and warmth derived from the Sun; so that, without searching for the reason, it has generally been passed over as a first principle, or self-evident truth. The swing of the arm, and other such motions, made by public speakers, are derived from their instinctive sense of *rhythmus* and are, in effect, beating time to their orations. Also cursing, swearing, and many other unmeaning words, so frequently interwoven in common discourse, are merely expletives to fill the measure, and to round each rhythmical period.[1]

Steele's rhythmical inventory is at first glance hardly novel. Saint Augustine's *De Musica* similarly extended precise *numerus* to the beating pulse, speaking tongue, and breathing mouth: "The soul produces the numbers we find in the beat of the veins."[2] Plotinus, Athanasius Kircher, and Leibniz offer comparable numerological cosmologies.

Yet Steele's appeal to the "self-evident truth" of rhythm ultimately veers from such august precursors. Augustine's numbers sought to transcend the "sensible traces of music," so as to discover "the real places . . . free from all body" [*ubi ab omni corpore aliena est*].[3] *Prosodia Rationalis* instead sketches something like a proto-phenomenology of physical tics and vocal exclamation that includes involuntary bodily processes (the "instinctive" swing of the orator's arm), vulgarity ("cursing, swearing"), and semantic vacuity ("unmeaning words"). This physiological component tends to go unnoticed in the many scholarly accounts that perceive *Prosodia Rationalis,* correctly, as a watershed in our understanding of linguistic structure. T. S. Omond and Paul Fussell have demonstrated the scale of Steele's achievement in liberating anglophone prosody from a hidebound adherence to classical "quantity."[4] David Crystal detects in his vocal "glides" the first systematic elaboration of what linguistics has since learned to call intonational contours.[5] I want to consider what this prosodic revolution meant for the human body—since it was on the level of the human body that Steele's ideas had their first and most significant impact.

Corporeality may at first seem peripheral to the nature and occasion of *Prosodia Rationalis,* which took the form of a learned disquisition over the nature of poetry with James Burnett, Lord Monboddo, author of the mammoth *The Origin and Progress of Language* (1773–92). The 1779 edition interpolates many of Monboddo's comments upon the first edition published four years previously, together with Steele's responses. Their dialogue turns upon the precise degree of contiguity between classical prosody and the modern vernacular. As its title suggests, *The Origin and Progress of Language* offers an Enlightenment version of stadial history; in this respect, however, rhythm counts as an intriguing throwback. Monboddo dutifully rehearses the *doxa* regarding the supremacy of antique rhythm that we recently observed in Rousseau's encyclopedia entry. The heading for the twenty-second chapter of his third volume is telling: "Composition not so difficult in English as in Greek and Latin—This arises from the want of rhythm and melody in our language."[6] Monboddo's later epistolary contributions to *Prosodia Rationalis* similarly argue that only the Greeks succeed in marrying grammar, philosophy, and music. "Our language, on the other hand, is the production of unlearned, popular use, corrupting a better language, out of which it has grown" (PR, 111).

Steele, by contrast, argues for the insufficiency of Greek prosody to account for the distinctive merits of vernacular verse. "As the ancient Greeks, as well as their language, are all dead," he archly remarks, "I do not wish to be drawn into a comparative contest about them" (PR, 89). Neither rhythmical experience itself, nor our conceptualization thereof, were lost with antiquity: "As I consider our sense of *rhythmus* to be much more *instinctive* than *rational*, I am of the opinion, that the ancient Greeks might have been practically as excellent in that part of music, as the moderns; but, from any thing I have read, I cannot think they had so accurate a manner, of describing or noting it, as we have" (PR, 78). While *Prosodia Rationalis* borrows its central term from Greek, it does so only insofar as antiquity commands a prestige beyond "our vulgar terms" (PR, 18). Yet *rhythmus* proves more complex than the regular alternation of arsis and thesis. In place of the classical foot, Steele proposes "cadences": temporal groupings that incorporate a large range of expressive variables ("emphasis," "accent," "quantity," "loudness," and "pause").

Monboddo's very Augustinian notion of disembodied *numerus* ("the natural propensity of the human mind to apply number and measure to every thing we hear" [PR, 94]) certainly possesses the virtue of clarity. His foot-based prosody corresponds neatly to his Lockean conception of mind. By contrast, Steele's complex system frequently contains byzantine complexity and terminological redundancy. When Monboddo grumbles that "I am not able to make the distinction between *light* and *heavy*, and *loud* and *soft* &c." (PR, 60), we can readily sympathize. Significantly, Steele responds to his complaint not with a further disquisition upon the structural properties of the English vernacular, but rather the dramatic re-creation of a concrete situation. He invites Monboddo to imagine "a man speaking to his mistress": the former is about to declare "my dear" with all the emphasis of unabashed love, only to find himself interrupted by an interloper, after having already articulated the possessive pronoun; our gallant lover therefore pronounces "dear" in a softer voice (marked *piano*) that nonetheless retains vocal emphasis (fig. 3).

FIGURE 3.
Notation from *Prosodia Rationalis*, 89

I find Steele's commingling of diacritical pedantry and social melodrama quite irresistible. But this closet drama also exposes a broader tension between the normative and the descriptive. *Prosodia Rationalis* often speaks with prepossessing authority of how English *should* be spoken: "Whoever would pronounce our heroic lines of ten syllables with propriety," he asserts at one point, "must allow at least six cadences, by the assistance of proper rests, to each line, and frequently eight" (PR, 26). Steele's scoring of David Garrick's "To be or not to be" soliloquy similarly declares itself the "correct" declamation (PR, 47). Our surprised paramour, by contrast, suggests only how English *might* be articulated, under certain naturalistic conditions.

This very tension between normative and descriptive would, however, facilitate the most immediate cultural impact of *Prosodia Rationalis*. Steele's frequent appeals to the human body demonstrate an intriguing hesitation between normativity and variability. The analogy between metrical and actual feet was a commonplace long before the composition of *Prosodia Rationalis*: Walter Young's "Essay on Rhythmical Measures" (1786), which similarly subdivides verse into musical bars, modeling the alternation of syllables on the human step, whose "rational, perfect" nature elevates man above all other animals.[7] Yet while Steele similarly takes duple measures to indicate "the sound or perfect man" (PR, 21), other time signatures suggest very different bodies. "The halting of a lame man," he continues, "makes a pace divisible into six, instead of four; that is, the *thesis* or *posing* of one of his feet rests twice as long on the ground as that of the other foot." "Lame" is customarily a term of prosodic disparagement; yet for *Prosodia Rationalis*, triple meter limps distinctively. His immediate discussion of the minuet

(*PR*, 25) renders the discussion still more interesting: triple measures confuse dancing and limping, the performative and the nonnormative body.

This consideration of the limping body helps us focalize what might otherwise seem a throwaway aside. Toward the end of the treatise, Steele and Monboddo are disputing possible performances of *Paradise Lost*, when the former digresses:

> It is notorious, when [stammerers] sing, they never hesitate or stutter; whence it may be supposed, the most early and effectual method of curing them, would be to accustom them to beat time to their reading and common discourse, by which means they might learn to speak in just time to the proper measure of their words and phrases. For it should seem, the cause of their hesitation and stuttering arises from some inaptitude to fall in immediately with the *rhythmical pulsation* or *poize* befitting their words. (*PR*, 190)

Once again, we find a tension between the variable body of the stutterer and the normative conception of fluency that he might hope to attain. Steele's fleeting coupling of rhythmical "*poize*" and stuttering would hold significant historical consequences. For *Prosodia Rationalis* left its first and most telling imprint not in the field of academic prosody, which in any case scarcely existed as an isolated field over the first half of the nineteenth century, but rather in the clinical context of speech therapy. Taking Steele's reformist prosody as its inspiration, elocutionary science became the discursive field in which the concept of rhythm first began to circulate.

Steele's first and in many ways most significant adept was John Thelwall, the political radical and public orator who in 1806 established the Institute for Elocution in Bloomsbury (later Lincoln's Inn Fields), the first institution dedicated to the treatment of speech dyspraxia. While lecturing in Hull, Thelwall encountered a clergyman who informed him of Steele's work:

> Having obtained, from this gentleman, the perusal, and, afterwards, procured a copy of the book (the "Prosodia Rationalis") I was exceedingly interested in perceiving the musical part of my theory completely demonstrated, and a system of notation, for the tones, the qualities, and the proportions of sound, in spoken language, invented and applied. Mr. Steele was, obviously, unacquainted with every thing that relates to the physiology of speech: so

much so, indeed, as to have referred that specific and fundamental difference in the qualities of syllables—(the Thesis D and Arsis \) which results from the pure physical necessities of organic action, to voluntary taste and harmonic invention. He had, accordingly, prosecuted his researches on musical grounds exclusively; and it appeared, at first sight, not a little extraordinary, that we should, nevertheless, have been conducted, thro paths apparently so remote, to the same practical conclusions.[8]

Thelwall's claim for simultaneous discovery is more than a mite self-serving, yet his clinical work certainly did ground Steele's *rhythmus* within a more systematic physical materialism. This leans heavily once again upon the nonnormative body: much of Thelwall's work draws heavily upon the blind physician John Gough, whose focus upon the tactile and auditory senses treats the human organism as a resonant vibrating "drum."[9] In an appendix that borrows extensively from *Prosodia Rationalis*, Thelwall speculates that the deaf can be brought to appreciate the rhythmical "alternations of *Thesis* and *Arsis*."[10]

It is difficult to know precisely how Thelwall sought to apply Steele's musical prosody to therapeutic ends. His *Selections for the Illustration of a Course of Illustration on the Rhythmus and Utterance of the English Language* (1812) offers his most sustained notation of verse, employing vertical bars to mark Steelean "*poizes*" in a sample of texts that include Milton, Akenside, and Allen Ramsey's "The Stammerer: A Comic Illustration," which he permits himself to emend, so as to conclude with an appeal to elocutionary science.[11] In an exemplary study, Julia S. Carlson has explored the embeddedness of this text within nineteenth-century print culture and educational reform.[12] Yet it remains difficult to know exactly how Thelwall intended to connect his poizes to the correction of "impediments," which his prefatory essay enumerates. Once again, the tension between the normative and the descriptive arises: does the vertical bar mark an objective feature of English verse, or a possible pause for the subject struggling to speak? Absent a clear indication on this point, George Saintsbury opted for the former, mercilessly ridiculing Thelwall's scansions in the third volume of his *History of English Prosody* (1906):

To | momentary | consciousness a | woke
A | bominable | un | utterable | and | worse
He had a | fever | when he was in | Spain

Now no one of these can possibly be accepted, as an even possible scansion, by any one who has any correct notion whatsoever of the rhythm of English speech. They are, one and all, heterogeneous bundles of unrelated, unproportioned, unrhythmical doggerel—gasp-bursts of infinitely worse than prosaic non-metre, which could come naturally only to a man out of breath with violent running, or under the pressure of some more strange and unusual physical impediment. They *might* come from one of Mr. Thelwall's worst twenty-guinea stammerers in his most grotesque paroxysms; though I never heard anything quite so bad.[13]

However unconscionable the attitude to what he shortly thereafter calls Thelwall's "company of hopeless and fantastic cripples," Saintsbury is quite justified in casting doubt upon these cumbersome scansions.[14] So far from curing stuttering, Thelwall's prosody would induce it.

Such practical problems did not prevent a large variety of now largely forgotten texts, published on both sides of the Atlantic, from developing Steele's work in clinical settings. James Rush's *The Philosophy of the Human Voice* (1827) rather floridly acknowledges "the labours of Mr. Steele, who was among the first to shriek out at the incubus of ancient prosody which had crouched so close on the bosom of his own and of every modern language."[15] This sprawling and synoptic text enlists reformist prosody so as to combat an increasingly polarized antebellum society: Rush takes "Abolition-preacher" and "Slavery-agitater" alike to disregard "the elegant uses of the voice."[16] As with several of these texts, it is noticeable that *The Philosophy of the Human Voice* relies substantially upon verse that—at least from the perspective of foot-based prosody—has long been understood as difficult to scan, namely, Milton's *Paradise Lost*. (Figure 4 shows Rush's musical notation of Gabriel's metrically ambiguous expostulation.) In part this is understandable: Steele's reformist prosody could not usefully test itself upon standard forms, such as regular ballads or heroic couplets, whose metrical structure is unambiguous. The elocutionist (or stutterer) should rather seek

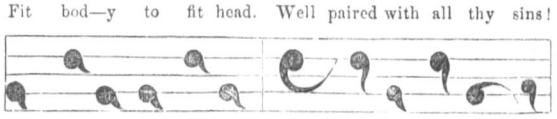

FIGURE 4. James Rush's notation of Gabriel's expostulation, in *Philosophy of the Human Voice* (1827), 333

to impose rhythm upon unrulier material. Yet that unruly material threatens by its very nature to resist such an endeavor; a dialectic to which this chapter will return.

Even Steele's devoted adepts worried that his musical prosody might unwittingly produce the very dyspraxia that it was designed to cure. In his *Essay on the Elements, Accents, and Prosody, of the English Language* (1806), Jonathan Odell imagines notating the various inflections of the human voice still more meticulously than *Prosodia Rationalis,* so as "to preclude all doubt respecting the real sounds intended to be expressed." However, Odell continues, the relation between notation and performance is conventional rather than natural: "Though this were done, what an uncouth appearance must it make to the eye of every one, who has been so far habituated to our present spelling, as barely to be able to read it without stammering and hesitation!"[17] Despite such complications, *Prosodia Rationalis* continued to hold sway within elocutionary circles as the century progressed. Richard Roe's *The Principles of Rhythm, Both in Speech and Music; Especially as Exhibited in the Mechanism of English Verse* (1823) acknowledges Steele's example from its opening sentence.[18] Richard Cull's short pamphlet *Stammering Considered with Reference to Its Cure* (1835) similarly doffs its cap to Steele and Thelwall, demonstrating the increasing fluency of a stutterer who recites initially to a continuous musical note, then to a piece of "defined rhythm," and finally entrains to another reader's simultaneous performance.[19]

Even as the nineteenth century gradually established prosody as a separate discipline, Steele's example predominated overwhelmingly in therapeutic contexts. Algernon Sydney Thelwall hews to his father's line, in his *The Reading Desk and the Pulpit* (1861), another elocutionary text that repeats for a new generation Steele's aside upon stuttering.[20] Charles J. Plumptre's

King's College lectures on the history of elocution, delivered in 1881, return consistently to Steele as the true foundation of the discipline; John Millard's *Grammar of Elocution* still cites Thelwall's example in its section on "Removal of Stammering," in 1889.[21] In short, so far as the establishment of the concept of rhythm is concerned, stuttering came before prosody.

The Rhythm Method

Steele's *rhythmus* grounded a new clinical treatment of speech dyspraxia. Yet the clearest designation of it as such would arrive not from one of its practitioners, but rather from a voluble detractor. The figure in question is James Hunt, perhaps the most celebrated speech therapist of the nineteenth century, whose prominent clients included Lewis Carroll and Charles Kingsley. His survey-cum-treatise *Stammering and Stuttering, Their Nature and Treatment* (1861) would offer one of the most significant contributions to the rapidly developing field of speech therapy. It defined for the first time what Hunt called the rhythm method—in order to reject it.

Stammering and Stuttering charts the etiology both of speech dyspraxia and of the therapeutic regimes that were devised to combat it.[22] Several of these approaches now seem frankly barbaric: the Prussian surgeon Johann Friedrich Dieffenbach's recommendation to cut triangular incisions into a stutterer's tongue enjoyed clinical favor until well into the nineteenth century. While my ethical objections to his project will become clear, Hunt unequivocally rejects such crude interventions: he likens Dieffenbach's surgical practice to popular remedies such as bleeding via leeches, "a good flogging," a prohibition on washing (speech defects arise from excessive moisture), frequent gargling with "woman's milk" (speech defects arises from excessive "dryness"), and the frequent rubbing of a tongue with "salt, honey, and specially with sage."[23]

Hunt contrasts such physical incursions with another therapeutic approach that he calls, simply, "rhythm." The 1861 edition of *Stammering and Stuttering* attributes this method to the French surgeon Marc Colombat de l'Isère, whose *Traité de tous les vices de la parole et en particulier du bégaiement; ou Recherches théoriques et pratiques sur l'orthophonie* (1841) remains untranslated into English. Colombat, explains Hunt, diagnosed stuttering not as a mechanical failing restricted to the tongue, but rather a broader nervous and muscular imbalance. As redress, he "devised a series of orthophonic exercises, in order to restore the harmony between nervous action and the organs of articulation; the most effective agent in these exercised being the application of rhythm in speaking."[24]

Hunt neglects to mention the central innovation that underpinned Colombat's method: the "muthonome" or "orthophonic lyre" (fig. 5), a mechanical spring device that anticipates the modern metronome. The beat of the muthonome is regulated by means of sliding a weight along the length of the pendulum, which in turn strikes the sounding bell; the speaker entrains her vocal productions to this stimulus. (Given the historical tendency to consider harmony rather than rhythm, which my introduction covered at length, it is significant that Colombat's percussive device was dressed up to resemble a harp.)

This rhythm approach—where a subject synchronizes vocal performance to an external stimulus—endured throughout the nineteenth and early twentieth centuries. The pugilistic speech therapist C. S. Bluemel lamented in 1903 that

> the system is particularly rampant in the United States of America, where it is virtually the entire "method" of three of the largest stammering schools. The "metrical" speech of the "orthophonic" method is implied in the names of several American and English "systems" or "speech institutions." Colombat's "muthonome" has ticked its way almost the round of a century. In an American institution it is now a "Word Regulator"; in an English school it is again a metronome: but with its various aliases and guises it still rattles on.[25]

While such clinical practice subsequently fell out of clinical favor, fMRI scans have enabled a resurgence of explicitly or implicitly "rhythmical" treatments of speech dyspraxia.[26] Marcel Wingate has demonstrated the enduring therapeutic utility of metronomes, which intriguingly do not have to follow a strict tempo to deliver clinical benefit.[27]

Having dismissed the surgical interventions of Dieffenbach and others, Hunt appears at first to be more positively inclined to the rhythm method. "Orthophonic gymnastics have the benefit of acting physically and morally,"

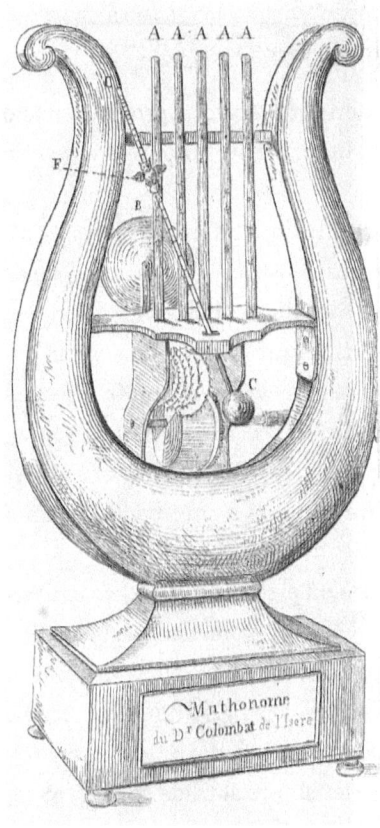

FIGURE 5. Colombat's muthonome, from *Traité de tous les vices de la parole et en particulier du bégaiement; ou Recherches théoriques et pratiques sur l'orthophonie* (1841), plate I

he declares, going on to cite *Les Archives générales de Médicine* (1851) in order to show the efficacy of metronomes or accompanying percussion in curing sufferers of chorea, or St. Vitus's Dance ("Of twenty-two children treated exclusively by gymnastics, eighteen were cured in twenty-nine days").[28] Such tributes only render Hunt's ensuing dismissal more puzzling:

> *Post hoc, ergo propter hoc*—because rhythm is in some uncomplicated cases a very useful adjunct: it has been by most writers cried up as a panacea for stuttering. The real fact is that it is not the rhythm which produces a beneficial effect, but its influence in altering, for the time being, the management of the breath; for the moment the patient begins his ordinary discourse the defect immediately reappears. Unless, therefore, the *fons et origo mali*—vicious respiration be first attended to, so as to establish a synchronous ac-

tion between the respiratory, vocal, and enunciating organs *under all circumstances*, rhythm, alone will produce little or no effect."[29]

Given his earlier interest in the close relation between vocal production and the nervous system, it is strange to find "rhythm" here employed narrowly to refer to acoustic stimulus.

By 1870, *Stammering and Stuttering* had gone into its sixth edition, testifying to the remarkable public appetite for such works. The heavily revised later edition deepens its suspicion of the rhythm method, acknowledging in the process the Steelean provenance that Hunt has previously and curiously overlooked. "As regards the great remedy with which Mr. Thelwall cured stuttering," Hunt remarks disdainfully, "it was simply 'rhythm'; and, as he himself says, 'the rhythm of Milton is the favourite object of my system.' Long, therefore, before Colombat, was rhythm employed as the chief remedy for defective utterance."[30]

If both the surgical and the rhythm method prove defective, what alternative does Hunt propose? *Stammering and Stuttering* remains vague on this question. The work constitutes a sales pitch quite as much as a contribution to therapeutic method: later editions conclude with glowing testimonials of Ore House, Hunt's "educational establishment" in Hastings. To say too much, in this respect, would have been to let slip vital trade secrets, given the growing number of rival practitioners. Yet *Stammering and Stuttering* does give away Hunt's general guiding principles, through the republication in its appendix of an article that Charles Kingsley first published in 1850, under the pen name of "a Minute Philosopher, C. K.," in *Frazer's Magazine*.[31] Kingsley condescends to the hypostatized stutterer in the third person:

> Let him, therefore, eschew all base perturbations of mind; all cowardice, servility, meanness, vanity, and hankering after admiration; for these all will make many a man, by a just judgment, stammer on the spot. Let him, for the same reason, eschew all anger, peevishness, haste, even pardonable eagerness. In a word, let him eschew the root of all evil selfishness and self-seeking; for he will surely find that whensoever he begins thinking about himself, then is the dumb devil of stammering at his elbow. Let him eschew, too, all superstition, whether of that abject kind which fancies that it can please God by a starved body and a hang-dog visage, which pretends to be

afraid to look mankind in the face, or of that more openly self-conceited kind which upsets the balance of the reason by hysterical raptures and self-glorifying assumptions. Let him eschew lastly, all which can weaken either nerves of digestion; all sexual excesses, all intemperance in drink or in food, whether gross or effeminate, remembering that it is as easy to be unwholesomely gluttonous over hot slops and cold ices as over beef and beer.[32]

Kingsley's tribute proves representative of a growing Victorian obsession with stuttering, taken not merely as localized mechanical failing but also as symptomatic of larger moral trends. Speech dyspraxia comes to indicate, among other things, a vitiated, hypertrophied, or troublingly effeminate culture.[33] In Hunt's unusually literal version of muscular Christianity, the single subject imposes top-down control upon the truculent body through will alone. The rhythm method—which he did more than anyone to define—involved by contrast a dynamic and reciprocal relation between vocal production and the muscular system, as between the stuttering subject and an external stimulus. Where Hunt's approach relies upon renunciation of the external world (sex, beef, beer), the rhythm method seeks rather to actively engage cultural products—first and foremost of which was poetry. In practice, as we have seen, this often generated cumbersome scansion and unclear therapeutic process. Yet the growing conjunction of stuttering with the nascent concept of rhythm also told us something *about* those cultural products themselves—however much the verse in question would resist the clinical uses to which it was put.

Browning's Stuttering

The rhythm method, as Hunt defines it, requires the stuttering subject to entrain vocal production to an external stimulus. While Colombat's muthonome offered one instance of how this might be accomplished in a clinical setting, the most common such stimulus was, overwhelmingly, verse. This comes about for obvious reasons: poetry possesses a pronounced rhythmical character, yet its referential aspect also assists the language user in the articulation of individual words. Yet as the concept of rhythm begins to circulate within the discourse of speech therapy, we begin to glimpse two sides of a strange coin. On the one hand, elocutionists employ verse so as to mitigate dyspraxia, often testing itself on materials that resist conventional foot-based analysis. On the other, poetry from the period pushes established metrical repertoires so far as to challenge the very possibility of vocal fluency. It became possible, or in some cases inevitable, to stutter in verse.

The later sections of my chapter will bring together these two sides of the same coin. For now, however, I want to elaborate on what it might mean to "stutter in verse." Let us begin with a negative example. George Crabbe's *The Dumb Orators; or, The Benefit of Society* (1812) offers an acerbic satire of Thelwall's political radicalism and elocutionary practice. The stump orator Hammond provides a thinly veiled caricature; his grand discourse devolves into hiccupping incoherence:

> I seek no favour—I—the Rights of Man!
> Claim; and I—nay!—but give me leave—and I
> Insist—a man—that is—and in reply,
> I speak. (455–58)[34]

Crabbe's morcellated verse resembles nothing so much as Thelwall's own scansions, which Saintsbury would so mercilessly ridicule. Stuttering here derives its disjunctive effect from its violation of the sacrosanct couplet, to which Crabbe remained monogamous throughout his career. The gasping dashes disrupt what would otherwise be smooth iambs; the repeated "I" (456) relinquishes its metrical function, to mark the beginning and end of lines, reduced instead to a series of babbling self-assertions.

Crabbe's verse stuttering travesties sense, yet other poets would willfully exploit dysfluency as a positive expressive resource. The thought is not so strange as it might appear: for every Hunt or Kingsley who takes stuttering to indicate cultural degeneration, there are others who detect in it principled inarticulacy, primitive simplicity, or affective immediacy. Carlyle reports to Emerson "an observation of mine, which indeed I find is hundreds of years old, that a stammering man is never a worthless one"; Coventry Patmore writes that "the holders of the Truth in Verity / Are people of a harsh and stammering tongue!"; Robert and Elizabeth Barrett Browning gloss their epistolary intimacy as mutual stammering.[35]

More than any other poet, Robert Browning embodies this ambivalent nineteenth-century obsession with stuttering. His work was simultaneously taken—sometimes by one and the same person—to mark the ideal of fluency and the nadir of guttural dysfluency. Browning's output proved famously divisive. Yet one peculiar reaction united admirers and dissenters alike: the sense that he was, in some special way, a chronic stutterer in verse. Wildly divergent periods and temperaments espouse the same view so consistently that it becomes almost uncanny: that Browning "stammered" or "stuttered" was apparently as plain to his detractors as it was to his hagiographers, to licensed critics and rival poets, to contemporaries and successors.

These critics often agree on the fact yet not the meaning of the diagnosis. "Was there ever," asked Walter Besant of *Pippa Passes*, "such a stuttering collocation of syllables to confound the reader and utterly destroy a sweet little lyric?" The question proves rhetorical, for here is

> a poem which—if its author had only for once been able to wed melodious verse to the sweetest poetical thought; if he had only tried, just for once, to write lines which should not make the cheeks of those that read them to ache, the front teeth of those who declaim them to splinter and fly, the ears of those that hear them to crack—would have been a thing to rest himself upon for ever, and receive the applause of the world. To the gods it seemed otherwise. Browning, who might have led us like Hamelin the piper, has chosen the worse part. He will be so deeply wise that he cannot express his thought; he will be so full of profundities that he requires a million of lines to express them in; he will leave music and melody to Swinburne; he will leave grace and sweetness to Tennyson; and in fifty years' time, who will read Browning?[36]

In his essay commemorating the centenary of Browning's birth, meanwhile, Rupert Brooke similarly noted that "his ideas were new, for poetry—and for that reason people at first thought them obscure—but they were quite clear. Only he had as it were a stutter in his utterance."[37] (Whether by accident or design, the assonantal corruption of Brooke's formulation ["stutter in his utterance"] enacts what it describes.)

Yet stuttering does not only represent the negative value of obscurity. When Oscar Wilde memorably remarked that "if Shakespeare could sing through myriad lips, Browning could stammer through a thousand mouths," the aesthetic verdict remains somewhat ambiguous.[38] James Douglas's 1903 biography suggests more strongly what Carlyle had postulated as the authenticity of verbal defect:

> Probably his obscurity is due to the fact that he was struggling to express himself in a form antagonistic to his temperament. In prose "Sordello" might have been pellucid, and "Paracelsus" clear. The sense of strain is present in all his work. His poetry is a determined stammer. The irony of his vogue lies in the passionate love which his admirers cultivated for his brilliant stuttering. Browningism was really a disease. Men and women took his poetry as a Chinaman takes opium. He was the fashionable drug of the nineteenth century.[39]

The most thoroughgoing treatment of Browning's stuttering also happens to be by some distance the most ludicrous. In a 1945 *PMLA* article entitled "Browning: Semantic Stutterer," Stewart W. Holmes applies a pseudo-Jungian analytic framework so as to show that psychosomatic blockage rendered the poet unable "to express himself clearly about what we may call metaphysical matters."[40] Browning is resultantly one of those people who "see green snakes or know the TRUTH, or are unshakably convinced that people are trying to hurt or kill them. Stutterers, being usually less sane than the average person, find their trouble increase as they are faced with complicated situations, situations which make them 'nervous.'"[41] His fabled "unintelligibility" is simply "the frenetic note of a man driven to speak when he can only stutter."[42]

It is scarcely worth dignifying Holmes's assertion that stutterers are "less sane" with a response. Yet he and the several others cited above were onto something, I believe, albeit that their common designation of stuttering was both more positive than they imagined, and more specifically keyed to Browning's peculiar use of verse rhythm. For his poetry reconceived Saintsbury's "gasp-bursts" not as inadvertent *fautes de goût*, but as willed expressive resource. Where Crabbe's couplets stuttered to negative and comic effect, Browning's vocal hitches embody personal experience and historical process. There is no fuller or more perverse instance of this than Browning's early long poem *Sordello* (1840), which this chapter reads at length. J. Hillis Miller understands the poem as "a stammering mutter which refuses to commit itself to comprehensible speech, and merely laps back and forth like a sea ungoverned by any moon."[43] I second every word, bar the demeaning "merely."

Sordello generated two incommensurable yet frequently conjoined responses: the conviction that it was unreadable, and the compulsive desire to read it. Dante Gabriel Rossetti confesses his astonished relief, in "On Browning's Sordello," at finally reaching the poem's close, yet nonetheless recited it obsessively before the rest of the Pre-Raphaelite Brotherhood. Swinburne memorized vast swathes. Pound read the work out loud to Yeats at Stone Cottage in 1915, a performance that proved pivotal for the coming *Cantos*. These recitations matter, in part given the history that I have traced above, concerning the interpenetration of prosody and elocution. Browning's verse, however, helps us not to learn but to unlearn normative vocal fluency.

Gasp-Bursts

Herbert Tucker describes the opening to *Sordello* as—what else?—a "self-interfering, tongue-twisting stutter":[44]

>   Lo, the past is hurled
>   In twain: up-thrust, out-staggering on the world,
>   Subsiding into shape, a darkness rears
>   Its outline, kindles at the core, appears
>   Verona. 'T is six hundred years and more. (1:73–77)

The accumulated prepositional portmanteaus ("up-thrust," "out-staggering") and phonemic isolation (the guttural "'T is," where Browning could easily have written the equally archaic "'Tis") indeed qualify this passage as a tongue twister.

We can both extend and clarify Tucker's brilliant observation that "stuttering interruptions, checks, anticipations, and postponements give *Sordello* a stubbornly different meaning. They are its way of meaning."[45] For stuttering emerges in three complementary ways throughout the long poem: as explicit theme; as insistent phonemic reiteration; and as a wider prosodic syncopation or dislocation that violates (but does not cancel) rhythmical experience. These factors establish a range of effects and affects that finally extend beyond Tucker's postulation of deferred gratification ("by postponing a narrative event and its meaning, [Browning] prolongs and savors the pleasure of starting all over again").[46] Forestalled pleasure is certainly part of the story. Yet Browning's stutter also conveys social distress; the apprehension of corporeal decay; a joy in guttural sound or echolalia; and a desire to suspend or to defeat or to escape narrative linearity.

Traces of stuttering as explicit theme lie sedimented within the poem's compositional history. *Sordello* retells the story of its eponymous Mantuan troubadour, whose poetic and political projects unfold against the backdrop of the thirteenth-century warfare between the papal Guelfs and imperial Ghibbelins. (Sordello appears at the entrance to Dante's Purgatory, a place reserved for those who have died violent deaths without having made proper penance.)[47] For broader historical context, Browning relied heavily if liberally upon Giambattista Verci's *Storia degli Ecelini* (1779). One of his several significant amendments concerns the Ecelini family, who under the patronage of Emperor Conrad dominated Lombardy throughout the thirteenth century. This dynastic line extends through several generations: Ecelo is the grandfather to Ecelino I (surnamed "Balbo," or "the stutterer"), who in turn sires Ecelino II ("The Monk"), father of Ecelino III ("The Ferocious").

This welter of similar proper names may well have troubled even the most pellucid poet. In the hands of the unsurpassably circumlocutory Browning, the cause is lost from the beginning: as his telescoped history of the Ecelini (1:237–91) unfolds, it becomes nigh-impossible to tell which generation or individual he is talking about at any given time. *Sordello* slashes a whole branch from the family tree, removing Alberico, the father of Ecelino "Il Balbo"; the latter now descends directly from Ecelin. Browning appended a series of annotations to his manuscript throughout the 1850s, which attempt to clarify matters: at 1:274, for example, he revises the ambiguous "Lombard chief" to read "the stuttering chief." These prospective revisions do not only serve the agenda of narrative exposition, however. Another passage from book 1 returns to the Ecelin family line, in a manner that again stresses dynastic interbreeding, in a manner that here rises to the hint of incest: "–Ecelo, dismal father of the brood, / And Ecelin, close to the girl he wooed" [1:457–58]. A similar revision occurs: Browning inked the word "stuttering" above "wooed." Browning's addition "is of interest," state Jack and Smith; I think they undersell their observation.[48]

Where "stuttering chief" clearly specifies a historical personage, the possible relation of this latest "stuttering" to "wooed" is far less clear. Both words, we might speculate, convey an anxiety concerning self-reproduction, whether on the vocal or actual level (reiterated phoneme or inbred dynasty). This Freudian speculation gains credence from the broader textual context: for by cutting Alberico from the family tree, Browning willfully underscores the phonemic similarity of each generation, as if history itself were eternal recurrence. Ecelo begets Ecelin begets Ecelin begets Ecelin: with such succession, what matter which individual bears the formal title of "Il Balbo"?

While neither of Browning's two manuscript emendations is taken up in the revised 1863 edition, stuttering nevertheless haunts the poem. The literal self-mimetic recurrence of the lemma "stammer" or "stutter" proves inseparable from a range of subtler and ultimately more significant rhythmical syncopations, which do not so much name dyspraxia as compel it. It is through these prosodic stuttering effects that Browning finally communicates the sense of a history subject to mechanical repetition. The tongue-twisting passage represents one of several attempts to make Verona appear:

> I single out
> Sordello, compassed murkily about
> With ravage of six long sad hundred years.
> Only believe me. Ye believe?
>   Appears
> Verona . . . Never,—I should warn you first.— (1:7–11)

This passage flaunts numerous accepted conventions of couplet form. Where the concluding rhyme frequently ties up a self-contained unit, here the couplet pauses prematurely, with the rather histrionic "Ye believe," before pushing into a dangling verb ("Appears"), whose vocal force pushes through into the following line, only to trail off once again into characteristically Browningian ellipsis and self-qualification. Narrative is an engine that splutters into life before giving out: "Then, appear, / Verona!" (1:59–60) demands the speaker soon thereafter, mounting to a pleading apostrophe.

The first eighty lines therefore already contain three truncated attempts to push through the narrative, which fail, ironically, to the extent that the voice is haunted by phantasms from the past: the apparition of Shelley's ghost causes the former to plead, "Verona! stay—thou, spirit, come not near" (1:60). Throughout these early stretches, the speaker is caught between competing desires to force through and to forestall a history whose issue ("ravage of six long sad hundred years") we have good reason to wish to avoid. This prosodic-narrative spluttering launches the first appearance of our eponymous hero, whom Browning, having wandered into a characteristically recondite digression over Armenian marriage customs, suddenly plonks stage-center. Sordello's entrance appropriately marks the first explicit lexical emulation of stuttering:

> The lean frame like a half-burnt taper, lit
> Erst at some marriage-feast, then laid away
> Till the Armenian bridegroom's dying day,
> In his wool wedding-robe.
>   For he—for he,
> Gate-vein of this heart's blood of Lombardy,
> (If I should falter now)—for he is thine!
> Sordello, thy forerunner, Florentine! (1:342–48)

"For he—for he" jump-starts a voice that again, however, immediately splutters out. Vacillation ("(If I should falter now)") and expostulation ("for he is thine!") vie for vocal control. (The exclamatory "thine!" signifies Dante, another forbiddingly fluent poetic ancestor.)

The couplet had already passed through several renovations by the time that Browning set to work upon it with hammers and drills. What for Dryden and Pope had enabled epigrammatic concision, or the felicitous union of prosody, grammar, and sense, became something quite other for the romantics: by loosening prosody's grip on syntax, Shelley's *Alastor* and Keats's *Endymion* generated unprecedented metrical propulsion. These warring yet mutually dependent versions of couplet fluency come into sharper focus through *Sordello*, whose prosody is a self-propelling vehicle that threatens continually to break down. Sordello's poetical and political careers alike move from superfast facility to hobbling incompetence, and back again. Wandering to Mantua, early in the second book, our titular hero chances upon a Court of Love. He need only open his mouth to outperform the rival troubadour Eglamor:

> On flew the song, a giddy race,
> After the flying story; word made leap
> Out word, rhyme—rhyme; the lay could barely keep
> Pace with the action visibly rushing past:
> Both ended. (2:80–84)

In Sordello's fast untutored song, "word made leap / Out word" performs what it describes, with the "leap" of enjambment (Browning is fond of employing the verb at initial or terminal positions)[49] landing to find more of itself, another "word." "Rhyme—rhyme" pushes the self-generative principle further, converting what had been guttural repetition into something more akin to harmonious *epizeuxis*.

Sordello sings fluently, however, only on the condition that he sings vacuously. Having slipped straight into fifth gear, "the lay could barely keep / Pace with the action": we learn not the slightest narrative detail. Browning's sudden tunefulness, far removed from prior convolutions, now lulls us all, singer included, to sleep:

> But the people—but the cries,
> The crowding round, and proffering the prize!
> —For he had gained some prize. He seemed to shrink
> Into a sleepy cloud, just at whose brink
> One sight withheld him. There sat Adelaide,
> Silent. (2:93–98)

Repetition dissolves determination ("the prize!") into vagueness ("some prize"); assonance and internal rhyme multiply within the line, as "crowding round" yawns its long vowel into "sleepy cloud." If Browning's verse be the opiate that James Douglas alleges, this proves one of its headiest moments, as the phonemic energies of "crowding round" fuse into "crowned," repeated and offering a supernumerary rhyme to the couplet in which it is embedded ("his front / Was crowned—was crowned! Her scented scarf around / His neck! Whose gorgeous vesture heaps the ground!" [2:112–14]).

Sordello is drunk on vatic meaninglessness, whose predicament becomes clearer as he considers what public function his effortless verse might conceivably serve. It is in this context that stuttering, from which his fluency had appeared to deliver the poem, recurs, with still-greater disjunctive force. Sordello is travestying the overcooked diction of his rival Plara (Browning always went further than his harshest critics at sending up his own excesses), before another literal stutter interrupts:

> To Plara's sonnets spoilt by toying with,
> "As knops that stud some almug to the pith
> "Prickèd for gum, wry thence, and crinklèd worse
> "Than pursèd eyelids of a river-horse
> "Sunning himself o' the slime when whirrs the breese"—
> *Gad-fly*, that is. He might compete with these!
> But—but—
>   "Observe a pompion-twine afloat;
> "Pluck me one cup from off the castle-moat!
> "Along with cup you raise leaf, stalk and root,
> "The entire surface of the pool to boot.
> "So could I pluck a cup, put in one song
> "A single sight, did not my hand, too strong,
> "Twitch in the least the root-strings of the whole." (2:769–81)

Positioned between two bursts of direct speech, "But—but—" marks a shift from virtuosic pastiche to what Jack and Smith call "the sort of poetry [Sordello] would like to write." If the earlier "rhyme—rhyme" named and performed seamless yet content-less poetry, this more disjunctively reiterative "But—but" conveys the sincere inarticulacy that Carlyle extolled. Sordello's problem is his physical and temperamental unsuitedness for such a project: in the convoluted poem that ensues, his hand "twitches," just as his voice stutters.

The poem henceforth anxiously deliberates over how to do work in the world without falling back upon a native fluency that has lost its efficacy. Sordello's painful coming-of-age at once also marks the historical vantage from which Browning wrote: I think it no exaggeration to assert this work as the first English poem to fully mark and suffer from poetry's estrangement from modernity. Sordello stands riven between two modes of being and speaking: On one side stands the Ghibbelin chief Taurello Salinguerra, to whom he is ambiguously related, and whose name means literally to "leap into war" (he therefore literally embodies Browning's favorite enjambment). On the other are those who seek retirement from the ravages of the world, such as Ecelino II ("The Monk"), who when urged by Salinguerra to protract their anti-papal struggle "stammered; 'let me die in peace—/ 'Forget me! Was it I who craved increase / 'Of rule?'" (2:899–901).

This latest literal intrusion of stammering indicates a practical incapacity from which Sordello too in due course suffers. Having lived his troubadour celebrity far from "the world's concernment" (2:462), Sordello abruptly "resolves to be / Gate-vein of this heart's blood of Lombardy" (3:554–55), forcing through the declaration that had followed the spluttering "For he—for he." Yet we cannot but hear this resolution as a repetition, which thereby threatens to become mechanical. Indeed, when the newly venturesome Sordello seeks an audience before Taurello, he too is described (despite his relative youth) as "lean, outworn and really old, / A stammering awkward man" (4:422–23). Throughout this phase, the prematurely superannuated Sordello appears less likely than anyone to accomplish the hard shift from verse-craft to statecraft. Our suddenly diminished hero, who already twitched at the attempt to write a poem, now stands with "shrivelled hand" (4:19); later, "veins embrace upon his hand" (4:88); we read of "his hand that shook" (4:284) and of his "large tongue, moist open mouth" (4:286); and learn, sadly, that he is "slavering and mute" (4:710).

Given this extended physiological grotesque, it comes as little surprise that Browning's verse now collapses into a guttural dysfluency that exceeds anything to date. The ensuing book 5 has come to stand in the mind of some readers for the obliquity of the whole. The reviewer for the *Atlas* remarked of its opening lines, "Here we have the same pitching, hysterical, and broken sobs of sentences—the same excisions of words—the same *indications* of power—imperfect grouping of thoughts and images—and hurried, exclamatory, and obscure utterance of things that would, probably, be very fine if we could get them in their full meaning, but which, through this bubbling and the tumult of the verse, are hardly intelligible."[50] This diatribe ironically captures much of what is so positively distinctive in Browning's "excisions":

"pitching, hysterical, and broken sobs" actually summarizes pretty well the force and feel of Sordello's sudden disappointment. "Is it the same Sordello," wonders a mordant unnamed voice, "in the dusk / As at the dawn?—merely a perished husk / Now, that arose a power fit to build / Up Rome again?" (5:1–4).

Throughout the opening four hundred lines of this book, Sordello suffers this external voice; is compelled to speak as this external voice; strives to speak as this external voice. Over their course, verse stuttering attains a new pitch. Up until now, my analysis has concentrated upon the emergence of dysfluency either as literal theme (Browning's marginal annotations) or as phonemic repetition ("For he—for he"). At this late stage, however, we witness instances of prosodic syncopation so protracted as to amount to rhythmical stuttering. For all its syntactical obliquity and lexical obscurity, *Sordello* frequently conforms to a broadly iambic pattern, as several of the lengthy quotes above demonstrate. As the "low voice wound into [Sordello's] heart," however, a rash of alliterating sibilants ("strength," "stress," "step") mechanically recur so as to throw the meter off-balance. Take the serial presence of "step" in this representatively, gloriously guttural passage:

> "Sordello, wake!
> "God has conceded two sights to a man—
> "One, of men's whole work, time's completed plan,
> "The other, of the minute's work, man's first
> "Step to the plan's completeness: what's dispersed
> "Save hope of that supreme step which, descried
> "Earliest, was meant still to remain untried
> "Only to give you heart to take your own
> "Step, and there stay, leaving the rest alone?
> "Where is the vanity? Why count as one
> "The first step, with the last step? What is gone
> "Except Rome's aëry magnificence,
> "That last step you'd take first?—an evidence
> "You were God: be man now! Let those glances fall!
> "The basis, the beginning step of all,
> "Which proves you just a man—is that gone too?" (5:84–99)

The "low voice," be it maudlin Sordello himself, or the disabused narrator, or the cynical nineteenth-century poet *in propria persona*, or some other faceless daemon, has a simple moral to impart: Rome, whatever gallant young poets might think, was not made in a day. Yet the distressed rhythmical texture of this passage forces our tongue to undergo what our mind would merely compute: Sordello's fall from unattained grace accordingly feels both more painful and less private. Our tongue trips repeatedly over each successive "step," not only because it recurs in short order in lines 88, 89, and 92, twice in 94, and once again in 96 and 98, but also because it recurs at conventionally "weak" metrical positions (in each line bar 98, Browning places the word at an odd syllable), whose disjunctive force is greatest when (as in 88 and 92) its initial position brutally truncates enjambment's accumulated vocal energy. The "step" is a malfunctioning elevator that so far from letting us ascend throws an obstacle in our way.

Despite this brutal vocal collapse, despite the continuing references to his premature deliquescence ("writhled" tongue and all [5:717–18]), Sordello somehow manages to convince Salinguerra to accept him as the de facto leader of the House of Romano, in a last-ditch effort to intervene on the side of the Guelfs. Yet we might find this sudden coronation hard to credit, not least because Sordello's being "crowned" (5:999) so strongly recalls his misleading triumph over Eglamor in book 2. (Do these echoing—or stuttering—rhymes linger on in our ears or throats?) Indeed, but a single line ensues before "suddenly a sound / Stops speech, stops walk: back shrinks Taurello" (5:1000–1001). The latest interruption of articulate speech finally proves terminal, being, as we will shortly learn, the fall of Sordello's dead body upon the floor above.

The concluding book 6 flashes back to Sordello, still living for the time being, gazing across that day's sunset, whose "tumultuary splendours folded in / To die." (6:15–16). If we have not already come to suspect which way the drama will end, Browning's accompanying marginal gloss ("At the close of a day or life") fairly hammers the point home. Sordello begins this concluding section in characteristically anguished vacillation, wondering whether to wear or discard the badge that Salinguerra has bestowed. Such temporal concerns might seem futile indeed, as the external mocking voice advises him to "'Study the corpse-face thro' the taint-worms' scurf!'" (6:158): a memento mori whose barely veiled mordant irony will be fully exposed when its addressee's corpse is shortly likened to pungent civic musk.

Yet the death sentence under which poem and hero now labor allow both to recuperate the vocal constraints from which they have suffered: the faltering tongue becomes and enables an acceptance of the one thing—finitude—that previously escaped Sordello's capacious purview. The reference to the "corpse-face" sparks a recollection of childhood: "Mantua called / Back to his mind how certain bards were thrilled /—Buds blasted, but of breath more like perfume" (6:175–77). These premature poetic deaths do not, however, induce romantic martyrology: indeed, for practically the first time Sordello now gives over "dreaming how become divine" (6:182). Rather, he and his tongue grope unsteadily toward a humbler version of truth:

> Hence
> Must truth be casual truth, elicited
> In sparks so mean, at intervals dispreads
> So rarely, that 't is like at no one time
> Of the world's story has not truth, the prime
> Of truth, the very truth which, hurled
> The world's course right, been really in the world
> —Content the while with some mean spark by dint
> Of some chance-blow, the solitary hint
> Of buried fire, which, rip earth's breast, would stream
> Sky-ward! (6:184–94)

In his quixotic "exposition" of *Sordello*, David Duff grumbles that "the logic of this passage is beyond recall."[51] Perhaps its metaphysics are indeed nothing much to write to Plato about: so far as we can reconstruct it, Sordello appears meanderingly to suggest that "truth" comes not in simple or unmediated form, but rather is dispersed in chance slivers. This summary, however, is no more than summary, when the whole energy and pathos of the passage stem from the manner in which a tongue that has tied itself in constant knots, finding false fluency only to reject it, now trips newly onward toward a revised knowledge whose constricted nature resembles it. "Truth" recurs, borderline-stutteringly, through a single unwieldy sentence that sprawls across seven consecutive lines that feature no terminal punctuation. Where previously Browning interposed "step" to trip us up with successive stresses at metrically weak positions, this repeated word occurs each time at an even syllable. "Truth" underscores the iambic rhythm to which the voice clings, in the face of syntactical expansion and intellectual obscurity. Its simple repetition feels like relearning to speak.

By the time we reach the initial long dash of 6:191, our tongue has accumulated competing energies: the urge to control, through repetition of word and rhythm; the syntax that compels the voice onward. The long dash absorbs and releases this tension, ensuing with sudden release into four of the most rapid, fluent, beautiful, and stirring lines that Browning ever put into a mouth. We are not merely told of the "mean spark" of truth; rather, we undergo it, through abrupt flurries of molten monosyllables ("some mean spark by dint" / "Of some chance-blow," "fire, which, rip earth's breast, would stream / Sky-ward!"), where the newly secured iambic rhythm embellishes the very words ("rip," "breast," "stream") that underpin it. This turns out to be couplet fluency after all, however little Pope might have recognized it. Browning closes by delicately stitching his monosyllables into portmanteaus ("chance-blow," "Sky-ward"). Yet this language bears the scars that had disfigured it, the dashes that had necessarily carved up the passage of sense. This fluency must gasp in order to sing.

We have seen how previous instances of literal stuttering ("For he—for he," "But—but") cleave the speaking voice; they represented one of Browning's prime means of interposing a clamorous interlocutor, whether the exasperated narrator, the blundering critic Naddo, or Sordello himself. At this late stage, by contrast, Sordello is finally suffered (or finally suffers himself) to speak uninterruptedly. His remarkable extended monologue, which opens "'Make nothing of my day because so brief? / Rather make more'" (6:327–28), does not mitigate language's mechanical repetition; indeed, such repetitions are only more frequent. Yet just as Sordello tripped over "truth," so too does he babble other words whose effect derives more from their repetition than their denotation. We remember, perhaps, that he is about to die. Reiterated "life" thus accrues a signal force: "'Oh life, life-breath, / 'Life-blood,—ere sleep, come travail, life ere death! / 'This life stream on my soul, direct, oblique, / 'But always streaming!'" (6:355–58).

The involuntary reiteration of these Big Words ("truth"! "life"!) makes for a cumbersome metaphysics, in addition to sentences that are difficult for a person to say out loud. But they store a vocal energy that discharges itself in utterance that proves more affecting than native fluency. When the narrator picks up the relay following the close of Sordello's monologue (6:458), it for once does not chide or jibe its hero, but rather with unprovoked generosity protracts both his theme and his words. When this entity speaks of "Sordello's closing-truth evolved / By his flesh-half's break-up" (6:466–67), it no longer seems worth discriminating between character and narrative voice. The latter now babbles "body" just as Sordello had just babbled "life":

> the body was to be so long
> Youthful, no longer: but since no control
> Tied to that body's purposes his soul,
> She chose to understand the body's self—had fain conveyed
> Her boundless to the body's bounded lot.
> Hence, the soul is permanent, the body not.—(6:508–14)

"Soul" strives to dictate terms to the body, whose resistance emerges in large measure through its stubborn lexical recurrence. Once again, this makes for a cumbersome metaphysics, which once again (via the gasping dash) discharges itself into vocal release:

> —lo,
> The minute gone, the body's power let go
> Apportioned o'er earth, he yearned for all it woke—
> From the volcano's vapour-flag, winds hoist
> Black o'er the spread of sea,—down to the moist
> Dale's silken barley-spikes sullied with rain,
> Swayed earthwards, heavily to rise again—
> The Small, a sphere as perfect as the Great
> To the soul's absoluteness. (6:520–28)

The "Small" matches the "Great" not because it too merits an honorific capitalization, but rather because we have already glimpsed it, without being told what it is, through Browning's incomparably beautiful evocation of a field of barley being bent back in the wind and rain. The repeated "body" is finally "let go," to find itself throughout the world.

This new inhabitation of corporeal finitude profoundly revises the phrase "Tumultuary splendours folded in / To die" when now it recurs (6:569–70). But recently, the conceit had mockingly indicted Eglamor's reliance upon pathetic fallacy (1:14–26); now, the same pat phrase names a truth that could not previously have been seen. Only this conversion explicates the narrator's sudden profession of love where previously he mocked and curtailed ("Ah my Sordello, I this once befriend / And speak for you" [6:590–91]). Sordello may well have failed in a task for which he was preternaturally unsuited, "the one step too mean / For him to take" (6:830–31); already with Dante, a generation later, the prospect for a poet to effect meaningful change has, on Browning's reading, evaporated. But by tripping over the curb in his rush to the grand goal, Sordello discovers something that cannot be revoked. "Who would has heard Sordello's story told" (6:886) might feel an anticlimactic closing note to sound: it tells a familiar yet imperfect echo of the inaugurating declaration, "Who will, may hear Sordello's story told" (1:1). Yet the sleight-of hand substitution of "would" for "will" does not only dissolve aspiration in the acid bath of subjunctive mood or past tense. Where language stutters throughout, the non-repetition of "will" proves telling, given that so many of Sordello's problems had stemmed from his preoccupation with volition ("my Will / Owns all already" [3:175–76]). By suffering language to repeat while giving up the claim to mastery, we may find that Sordello's corpse blooms after all.

A colorless summary of the human condition (only at the point of our dying do we learn what our dying words mean) pales in comparison to the ways in which *Sordello* has successively suffered from, attempted to overcome, and learned to inhabit vocal incapacity, as a synecdoche of organic finitude. This personal truth also emphatically conveys the relation that both poems and subjects bear to their temporal situation. History is a nightmare from which we dream of awakening, or better, perhaps, a stutter that we dream of curing. Our failure to achieve fluency wins the consolation of a rhythmical expressiveness new to English verse, which stammers as much as it sings, or—to put the matter in Joshua Steele's terms—limps as much as it dances. To do so requires us to "let," as Browning said elsewhere, "the rank tongue blossom into speech."⁵²

Mechanical Defects

Until this point, my analysis has considered two aspects of a pronounced cultural shift. This chapter's early stretches demonstrated that speech therapy offered the first discursive occasion for a developing concept of rhythm—Steele's *rhythmus*—to circulate freely. The rhythm method enabled subjects to attain vocal fluency through entraining to an external source that in practice was most often poetry. At the same time that this institutional formation developed, Robert Browning wrote verse whose rhythmical and ideational contortions compelled readers to characterize it as expressive stuttering.

These two tendencies might seem incidental or, worse, antagonistic to one another. But I wish now to bring them together, by demonstrating just how central Browning was to the elocutionary tradition, despite (or perhaps because of) his unruliness. For the frequent accusation—or double-edged compliment—that it constituted "stuttering in verse" did not preclude his output from being employed as a therapeutic aid, perhaps more than any other major poet. If early nineteenth-century elocutionary theory receives significant impetus from reformist prosody, the modern institutional formation of literary criticism derives in large part from elocutionary theory. Samuel Silas Curry offers a prominent instance of this historical conjunction: his landmark *Browning and the Dramatic Monologue* (1908) bequeathed its titular term to literary criticism, while also drawing heavily upon Curry's parallel activity with the School of Expression in Massachusetts, an institution that still bears his name.

Literary criticism, like many things, often forgets its own origins. The dramatic monologue has survived as a cardinal genre, however little Browning, Tennyson, or Webster might have recognized their own works by it. Common usage tends to take it as a psychological or narrative term, rather than consider its physical or rhythmical character. Curry, however, considered hermeneutic questions inseparable from vocal articulation: rhythm, as with

Steele and Thelwall, provided the central bridging term. His School of Expression taught that the dramatic monologue was script quite as much as exegetical text: Browning served as exemplum, despite Curry's valiant understatement that the poet "had a very concise and abrupt way of stating things."[53]

Browning only appears obscure, however, so long as we approach one of his poems "as if it were an ordinary lyric": as a collection, that is to say, of more-or-less scattered beautiful images or turns of phrase. We can unite such features into a cogent whole, Curry continues, only if we embody them: through a form of delivery that incorporates posture, gesture, and—above all else—voice. This process entails a more drastic extension of the concept of rhythm even than Hunt's, who had extended it to the nervous system. There is, according to the *Foundations of Expression*, "a rhythm of thinking," which communicates itself through the "touch" of the voice. Correct articulation therefore relies upon cognitive and sensorimotor coordination: "Individualize and intensify," Curry writes, "each successive impression until the rhythm of breathing responds to the rhythm of ideas."[54]

But how do we get the idea of a poem in the first place, except by breathing it into being? Curry's performative conception of the dramatic monologue runs into a logical contradiction: we can know how to recite a poem only once we have grasped its idea or character, but we can know its idea or character only by reading the poem. "We must realize the situation, the speaker, the hearer," Curry says, "before the meaning can become clear."[55] This seems obvious enough. But his several individual readings of verse often suggest the opposite: so far from the "rhythm of ideas" organizing the whole, a smaller variation shapes (or disrupts) the overall sense. Writing of Coleridge's "Hymn before Sun-Rise, in the Vale of Chamounix," for example, Curry glosses the mimetic effect of the word "ravines": it "gives a sudden arrest of feeling almost as if one stood trembling on the verge of a precipice. With mechanical regularity of feet such an impression could not be made."[56] Such rhythmical irregularity poses clear problems for Curry's elocutionary objectives: having defined stammering as "spasmodic hesitations" in *Mind and Voice* (1910), Curry accordingly recommends texts that induce "quiet, confidence, concentration, thinking one idea at a time, taking time to pause, and speak phrase by phrase with great deliberation."[57]

We might counter that stutterers should focus on organized poems, leaving to less dysfluent speakers the "ravines" of rhythmical surprise. Yet Browning troubles this separation. As Curry himself confesses, "The prosaic irregularity of his feet is certainly very expressive of his thinking and feeling."[58] When he claims to have "discovered [a] principle in teaching stammerers" (a promised book on the subject proved unforthcoming), his brief sketch suits Browning less well than any conceivable poet. "The vowel is the soul of the word," Curry grandiloquently declares, "the consonant but a garment." Even a breathy sibilant "demands the immediate support of a vowel or it will become a mere disagreeable hiss; the consonant should glide on the vowel as on a stream of sound." Think of the affricate /t/ in "'T is six hundred years and more": invert Curry's speculations on the gliding vowel, and you have a pretty good description of *Sordello*.

Yet Curry repeatedly volunteers Browning as *the* poet to whom vocal clinician and literary critic alike should resort: significant overlap exists between the former's clinical work and those sections of *Browning and the Dramatic Monologue* that focus upon the poet's prosody.[59] Curry is far from an outlier in this respect.[60] Hiram Corson, another elocutionist with a literary bent, similarly struggles to rationalize or regularize Browning's "grotesquerie of rhythm."[61] The enduring "rhythm method" clearly wished to test itself homeopathically upon resistant materials. It is striking, for example, how frequently critic-clinicians repeatedly recruit Browning's "How They Brought the Good News from Ghent to Aix" to this end. This rather unpromising candidate appears in still another elocutionary manual, George Andrew Lewis's *The Practical Treatment of Stammering and Stuttering, with Suggestions for Practice and Helpful Exercises* (1902), whose practical "exercises" begin as follows:

> There is a certain rhythm in all good speech. It is clearly marked in poetry, and is by no means entirely absent in prose. It is not sing-song, but has an element of variety which is pleasant to the ear. In poetry there are certain accented syllables recurring at distinct intervals, and proper reading of such selections requires a stroke of the voice followed by partial rest. It is like the throb of the heart or the beat of the pulse, like day and night, sleep and work. A period of activity is followed by one of repose. An example or two will be sufficient to illustrate this. The student may add others at will:—

> I sprang to the stir-rup, and Joris and he;
> I gal-loped, Dick gal-loped, we gal-loped all three,
> Be-hind shut the post-ern, the lights sank to rest.
> And in-to the mid-night we gal-loped a-breast
>
> —*Browning*[62]

There is only one problem with this use of Browning's poem: it is not Browning's poem. Lewis surreptitiously omits the central lines of the opening stanza, in order to trammel the pounding triple meter that hyphenation and underscoring further emphasize.

Only this textual trimming secures what would otherwise appear a most unlikely literary comparison, between Browning's racy number and Tennyson's "Sweet and Low," also taken as means for attaining vocal fluency. Lewis is not alone in this curious selection. Having established that "agility of flexibility of breathing may be established by practicing passages of great weight, requiring slowness of movement, in contrast with passages of great excitement," Curry similarly juxtaposes "How They Brought the Good News from Ghent to Aix" with Robert Louis Stevenson's "Pirate Story" and an extract from Carlyle's essay on Boswell's *Life of Johnson*.[63] Like Lewis before him, Curry simply replaces the actual poem's third and fourth lines for the more metrically regular opening to the second stanza.

I earlier described *Sordello* as an unreadable poem that compelled its readers to read it aloud. Can this explain why Lewis and Curry are so drawn to another poem that, so far from inducing fluency, trips up the tongue? No amount of textual editing can mitigate this fact, as Browning's famously stumbling phonographic recitation of 1889 proves. Like Lewis and Curry before him, the poet himself omits (or forgets) the third line that threatens to capsize the triple rhythm; his voice nevertheless still splutters to a halt. To view for a final time how verse rhythms exceed the elocutionary contexts that they establish, I want to set my reading of Browning's poem within a broader history of Victorian media performance. "What we hear in this recording," Yopie Prins summarizes, "is not the immediacy of Browning's voice, but its mechanical mediation. It is difficult to decipher Browning's words, as they are broken up by the very technology that seeks to preserve them: the revolving of the wax cylinder creates a whooshing sound, and the volume of the recording fades in and out of audibility."⁶⁴ Yet mechanical mediation, she continues, predates Edison's phonograph: "The meter is the motor that gives the poem its momentum, and indeed in Browning's recording the words get lost in the thumping of the anapests."⁶⁵

I share Prins's suspicion of voice figured as presence. Yet Browning's poem undercuts this absolute opposition between vocal immediacy and inhuman machinery. So far as we consider Browning's recitation, we might just about uphold the distinction: as the poet's voice splutters and fades, the cylinder's crackling revolutions continue to sound (inadvertently but fittingly suggesting galloping hooves). Yet if we follow Prins's cue to consider meter as a machine, things get significantly more complex than "thumping regularity."

To perceive this complexity, we need to let ourselves hear—or better still, sound—the poem that Browning actually wrote. It is somewhat ironic that Prins, like those speech therapists before her (who certainly *did* believe in vocal plenitude), similarly curtails the poem so as to exaggerate its metrical regularity: she too addresses only the first four lines. Yet this thrumming anapestic motor quickly breaks down. The first significant metrical hitch occurs in the poem's fifth stanza, as the speaker describes his gallant charger Roland:

> And his low head and crest, just one sharp ear bent back
> For my voice, and the other prick'd out on his track;
> And one eye's black intelligence,—ever that glance
> O'er its white edge at me, his own master, askance!
> And the thick heavy spume-flakes which aye and anon
> His fierce lips shook upwards in galloping on. (25–30)

The exclusively monosyllabic line 25 produces a sudden accentual overloading: when we factor in the prior tendency (as Lewis underscored) to stress the second syllable of each line, we can conceivably accentuate a full ten of the twelve separate words, with only the two "and" conjunctions indisputably light. This metrical ballast wonderfully mimes the horse's own painfully straining ear, which bends "for my voice," a direct object that appropriately restores the anapestic rhythm that had been in danger of capsizing. (Here, as throughout, meter and voice prove strictly inseparable.)

But the restoration of this *motorik* rhythm proves short-lived, with the following stanza throwing up a metrical whiplash:

> By Hasselt, Dirck groan'd; and cried Joris "Stay spur!
> Your Roos gallop'd bravely, the fault's not in her,
> We'll remember at Aix"—for one heard the quick wheeze
> Of her chest, saw the stretch'd neck and staggering knees,
> And sunk tail, and horrible heave of the flank,
> As down on her haunches she shudder'd and sank. (31–36)

These six lines offer one of the most moving evocations of animal suffering in literature, caused by—and embedded in—the stuttering tongue. (Browning's poem blurs other distinctions than that between man and machine.) While the stanza's opening clause struggles gamely, through the welter of proper names, to keep its triple rhythm afloat, the third line's abrupt medial caesura interrupts more than just Joris's despairing cries. From this point on, the excess stress that had previously been concentrated within a single disjunctive line now emerges systematically. Browning overburdens his vehicle with assonance ("stretch'd neck"), alliteration ("horrible heave"), and successive accents ("sunk tail") that contrast grotesquely with what has gone before.

Has the voice buckled under the demands upon it by an inhuman machine? Or has the motor of meter spluttered and given way of its own accord? This reasonable question insinuates a meretricious dualism. For "How They Brought the Good News from Ghent to Aix" proves the inseparability of subjects and the various mechanical prostheses that they make a part of their selves, and through which they speak: tongues, prosodies, phonographs. Such machines function, Browning's poem also shows, on the condition that they are liable to break down. As a second steed falls by the wayside, Roland, the last horse standing, assumes an increasingly demonic air: "his nostrils like pits full of blood to the brim, / And with circles of red for his eye-sockets." It is hard to know whether this animal is about to expire, or, alternatively, whether an increasingly mechanical vehicle is now steering its supposed rider. Reduced to a mere passenger, the speaker has recourse to a jarringly ludicrous performance of senseless voice: discarding his clothes and boots, he pats Roland, calls him "by his pet name," praises his excellence as a horse, "Clapped my hands, laughed and sang, any noise, bad or good / Till at length into Aix Roland galloped and stood."

By such desperate expedients, the poem recovers the momentum necessary to carry it to its final destination (the triple measure sounds anew). Yet, as any driver on the hard shoulder knows, the engine no longer sounds quite the same when it splutters back to life. The final stanza relates the triumphal acclamation of Roland and his rider by the inhabitants who receive his "news." We never learn any details of this transmission (Browning treats information as a statistical measure indifferent to content long before Claude Shannon). Whatever other message it carries or conceals, Browning's poem clearly frets over the obsolescence of poetry in the (old) new media world: Roland's sudden arrival restores to verse an instantaneousness that outstrips the fastest telegraph. The burlesque finale, where flagons of wine are poured down the poor horse's throat, might well insinuate comic significance into the name of this strangely anthropomorphic equine—is his enigmatic message a *chanson de Roland*?

Yet this concluding fantasy of instantaneous poetic communication cannot fully forget the hurdles over which the tongue has had to trip, and which endure in the curious litotes of "no voice but was praising this Roland of mine." Browning's phonograph recitation renders audible only what the poem would in any case force upon us; it is not for nothing that nineteenth-century elocutionary science calls stuttering a "mechanical" defect. Browning's voice is, conversely, never more characteristically "his" than when, having failed to read his actual poem, he whoops, "Hip hip, hurrah!" ("Old hippity-hop o' the accents," as Pound called him.) All things considered, "How They Brought the Good News" might well qualify as the worst text imaginable for a speech therapist. So far from curing speech dyspraxia, Browning's verse makes stutterers of us all.

The dialectic of stuttering and rhythm helps to resist the separation between hermeneutics and performance, which came to characterize the early institutional formation of literary criticism. On the one hand, the New Criticism of Wimsatt and Beardsley systematically downplayed singular embodied response, identifying meter rather with "abstraction"; on the other, Curry, Corson, and Lewis insisted that a poem's rhythms be gesturally enacted.[66] To be sure, the New Critics' analytical perspicacity far outstripped the elocutionary tradition, which as we have seen casually mutilated or misset texts in service of its clinical aims. Yet the violence with which the elocutionists excised Browning's verse betrays a rhythmical variability that at better moments they could directly acknowledge. While it tests rather than educes simple fluency, Browning's verse does indeed prove Curry's hypothesized interrelation of the rhythms of speech, breath, and ideas. Poetry, here, is no autonomous and self-contained object, so much as an event. The elocutionary insight usefully counteracts the aversion to embodied performance (even to simple reading aloud) that emerges in even as pragmatic a critic as I. A. Richards.[67] This path not taken remains open.

Musical Syncopation / Semantic Stutter

Rhythm first emerges as a portable and widely sharable concept within the applied context of speech therapy. This nascent field recruits poetry to its clinical ends, yet often selects specific examples (such as Browning) that defy simple fluency. Stuttering rhythm, in turn, moves away from its exclusively clinical setting so as to become a more general aesthetic value (whether positive or negative). We have seen the force of this value in the critical reception of Browning. But the imputation of "stuttering" to verse marks a broader truth regarding the shifting conception of poetry, and in particular a growing resistance to its more obtrusively repetitive devices. The severance of music and verse converts the (harmonious) refrain into a (semantic) stutter. The obsessive returns of Tennyson's "Oriana" come to seem suspect when an increasingly instrumentalized language serves only to get us from A to B. Hesitation becomes impediment, Elizabethan song devolves into jingle, the ballad refrain contracts monomania. Elizabeth Barrett Browning's "The Cry of the Children" turns metrical and lexical insistence into a mimetically appropriate grinding.

The final section of this chapter presses more deeply upon this deepening non-coincidence of verse and music, harmonious refrain and semantic stutter, so as to involve broader historical and political concerns. More specifically, I want to consider how the paradoxical status of stuttering rhythm (as both clinical pathology and expressive resource) develops in a very different cultural domain: the emergence of syncopated ragtime, and the curious and abhorrent subgenre of the "stuttering coon" song. It would be too passive a phrasing to say that such materials were shaped by racist discourse of the late nineteenth century, for the peculiar conjunction of rhythm and dyspraxia itself generated much of this essentializing phobia in the first place.

James Hunt again proves key to this development. We earlier saw how the successive editions of *Stammering and Stuttering* articulated the "rhythm method" as a clinical strategy, which Hunt eventually traced back to the reformist prosody of Thelwall et al. His developing antagonism to this approach proved inseparable from an increasing preoccupation with race. The first edition of 1861 treats such matters only in passing: in his historical-cum-etymological survey of stuttering and its variants, Hunt repeats Herodotus's observation "that Battos meant, in the African language, a king." (The archaic "battology," which indicates needless repetition, derives from the Greek *battolegeo;* this in turn apparently refers to the Cretan who consulted the Delphic oracle concerning his vocal impediment, only to be instructed to found a city in Libya.) Intriguingly—though erroneously—Hunt later observes that the monosyllabic nature of Chinese languages means that its speakers "do not stutter."[68]

Such examples support a striking argument: speech dyspraxia represents a peculiarly Western affliction, attributable at once to linguistic factors, personal frailty, and the debilitating effects of civilization. Hunt does cite Joseph Banks on the purported difficulty with which Polynesians articulate polysyllables, and reproduces the French ethnographer Eugène de Froberville's 1852 account "of a stuttering negro-tribe, the Neambaga."[69] Yet the vast bulk of the anthropological fieldwork apparently supports a contrary generalization: "All travellers, who have long resided among uncultivated nations, and whose authority is of any weight, maintain that they never met with any savages labouring under an impediment of speech. Assuming this to be so, it is not easy to say, whether this immunity be owing to the more ample development of the buccal cavity in savages, to the nature of their dialect, or to their freedom from mental anxieties and nervous debility, the usual concomitants of refinements and civilization."[70] Josephine Hoegaerts, who has written extensively about the late nineteenth-century contexts of stuttering, reads such passages as proof of Hunt's relatively benign attitudes. The diagnosis of stuttering as a bourgeois malady has its economic corollary: "The lower classes did not appear to seek the help of therapists and were considered to be relatively free of the impediment."[71]

We might well question whether the indigenous or lower-class subject considered these generalizations of vocal fluency as a fair recompense for a lack of actual support. In any case, such enlightened attitudes as Hunt did possess swiftly fade. Hoegarts's identification of stuttering with white subjects possessing "high status, privileged character" relies exclusively upon the first edition of *Stammering and Stuttering*. Yet where in 1861 Hunt had concluded his text with a general appeal to physical exercise, the sixth edition of 1870 terminates rather with an extended section entitled "Stuttering among Savages." Hunt endeavors to explain this apparent *volte-face*: "In the first edition of this work, I made a general statement that defective speech was the result of civilisation, and that savages were not thus affected. But from the following it will be seen how necessary it is that exact meaning should be attached to the words 'stammering,' 'stuttering,' 'savages,' and 'civilization' in making such a statement."[72] Indigenous populations are in fact never free from "civilization," Hunt continues; among the various "diseases" that they contract from their colonizers, we find dysfluency. The inhabitants of the West Coast of Africa supposedly stammer after "intercourse with civilised Europeans": indeed, he continues, buttressed by the authority of Robert Clarke, a member of Queen Victoria's Colonial Medical Service, "savages" often stutter in imitation of "*fashionable*" European habits.[73] Anthropological eyewitness accounts now serve precisely the opposite conclusion to 1861: Hunt in short order enumerates "a negro girl stuttering," related to him by "a Turkish gentlemen" (Turks being apparently also constitutionally liable to dyspraxia); the "Niambana Negroes," whose role enlarges from the earlier edition; and stammering "gipsies" and "Abyssinians," who now make their debut.[74] De Froberville's testimony survives only as the exception that now proves a general rule of "savage" dysfluency.

To attribute Hunt's shifting clinical views to developing ethnographic research rather misses the point, when we bear in mind that he himself contributed extensively to the establishment of the latter. In November 1863, Hunt gave a lecture to the Anthropological Society of London (which he had helped to found as an alternative to the more liberal Ethnological Society of

London) entitled "The Negro's Place in Nature."[75] This peroration was greeted with a chorus of boos and hisses; Hunt's commitment to a polygenetic theory of human origin contrasted strongly with what he dismissively called "the preconceived idea of aboriginal unity and essential equality," associated primarily with Darwinians such as Wallace, Huxley, and Burnett Tylor.[76]

I will dwell only briefly on Hunt's text, which often proves unbearably moving in ways that its author would not have foreseen or condoned. A footnote sidelines yet does not quite obscure "a negress [who] underwent the amputation of the right half of the lower jaw with the most astonishing apathy; but no sooner was the diseased part removed, than she commenced singing with a loud and sonorous voice, in spite of our remonstrances, and the wound could only be dressed after she had finished her hymn of grace."[77] Where the 1870 edition of *Stammering and Stuttering* tiptoed around the question of whether "savages" stuttered through intrinsic or contingent reasons (buccal cavities or civilizational corruption), Hunt's lecture more confidently opts for the former. "The larynx in the Negro is not much developed," he declares, "and the voice resembles sometimes the alto of an eunuch. In the male the voice is low and hoarse, and in the female it is acute and shrieking." There is, he continues, "a peculiarity in the Negro's voice by which he can always be distinguished": a "twang" that no amount of "imitation" of civilization can overcome.[78] Non-Western bodies were first immune from speech dyspraxia; then contracted it from colonizers; and finally stutter in an intrinsic and inimitable manner.

Hunt's authority grounds a subsequent pronounced association of stuttering, race, and rhythmical expression, through which pathology and expressive resource again coincide. The musical scores and lyrical scripts of cakewalk and ragtime, genres that rapidly came to prominence following the 1893 Chicago World's Fair, offer compelling and disturbing cases in point. While the almost exclusively white transcriptions of these almost exclusively black practices tended to eliminate or downplay rhythmical variation or improvisation,[79] the later rags of the 1890s feature increasingly prominent use of rhythmical syncopation: accent is redistributed onto conventionally weak metrical positions, tied across two halves of a measure, united within separate halves, or augmented so to exploit the coincidence of treble and bass rhythms. (The "scotch snap" offers one folk musical instance of syncopation, which would increasingly enter into modern classical compositions such as Dvořák's *New World Symphony*.)

Browning's idiosyncratic manipulations of couplet form offered concrete instances of syncopation: his repeated use of "step" in weak metrical positions offers a case in point. Such effects depend upon the contention of sound and sense: a syncopated rhythm clashes against a language that is supposed to get us somewhere (Sordello is struggling and failing to build his new Rome in a day). Ragtime similarly counterpoises syncopated rhythm with lyrics that double as ironic self-commentary. In particular, the subgenre of the "stuttering coon" song portrays the black (or blackface) performer as a chaotic stammerer whose dysfluent utterance corresponds to other physiological grotesqueries (twitching, fussing, grimacing, etc.).

This strange and unsettling genre proved widespread in the late and early decades of the nineteenth and twentieth centuries. Ned Wayburn and Stanley Whiting's "Syncopated Sandy: A Coon That Leads a Really Reckless Life" (1897); Robert Cohn's "Stuttering Jasper" (1899); H. Y. Leavitt's "The Stuttering Coon" (1898), which bears the telling subtitle "A Darktown Impediment" (fig. 6); Hughie Cannon's "Possum Pie, or the Stuttering Coon" (1904); and Vincent Davies's "Sammy Stammers" (1900), all offer but a representative survey of such productions. Similar tropes occur in vaudeville and in films such as *Wooing and Wedding of a Coon* (1905), whose early sequences feature a pair of stammering Afro-American scapegoats.[80]

But it is ragtime that exposes most clearly the fraught relation between (semantic) stuttering and (rhythmical) syncopation. The sleeve notes for "Syncopated Sandy" demonstrate the relish with which white musicians and audiences appropriated and consumed such material: "The authors and publishers," they read, "have succeeded in illustrating for the first time the absolute theory of the now famous 'RAG TIME' music, which originated with the negroes and is characteristic of their people. The negroe in playing the piano, strikes the keys with the same time and measure that he taps the floor with his heels and toes in dancing." This essentializing description sounds svelte enough. Yet while the lyrics address a "dead swell coon with stately tread" (this suave measure coinciding with "ragtime" syncopation), a "Coon Parody" also precedes the music, written, rather incongruously, in the first person of an Afro-American subject who cheerfully confesses

FIGURE 6. H. Y. Leavitt, "The Stuttering Coon" (1898)

himself a "mean" wife-beater.[81] Limping and dancing, the smooth and the rough, the swell and the mean: rhythmical stuttering confutes these apparent antinomies.

Those rags that directly foreground stuttering compound this ambivalence toward the syncopating black body. In "Possum Pie," the stuttering phonemes ("de—de—de—de—de") coincide with simple melodic repetitions that anticipate syncopation; "Stuttering Jasper" concludes with sustained syncopation; "The Stuttering Coon" does much the same (fig. 7). The white minstrel singer Leroy "Lasses" White copyrighted one of the earliest available instances of twelve-bar-blues, which he titled "the Negro Blues," and which employs a distinctively stuttering opening phrase.[82] Such material enabled an overwhelmingly white audience at once to enjoy, sublimate, and demean a rhythmically insistent music that might otherwise have proven disturbingly pleasurable. Musical syncopation becomes semantic stuttering: laughter proves the yield for the conversion of rhythm into (non-)sense.

FIGURE 7. Detail from score of "The Stuttering Coon"

This appalling subgenre thereby enables performers and audiences to channel a profound ambivalence: contemporary discussions resound with eulogies and jeremiads that agree on nothing other than the rhythmical novelty of such songs. Ragtime is alleged to be "decadent" almost as soon as it has emerged: "The fact that the works of Beethoven, Mendelssohn, Wagner and others furnish numerous examples of syncopation," states W. F.

Gates in "Ethiopian Syncopation: The Decline of Ragtime," a 1902 article for *Musician* magazine, "does not excuse the extreme use and extreme perversions to inartistic ends that has marked this craze."[83] The cultural decline is even so pervasive that a forty-year-old "had to advertise for a wife that was not steeped in 'rag-time.'" It is hard to know whether Gates is joking: "Ethiopian syncopation," the bachelor apparently specified, "is my aversion."

Rhythmical syncopation pervades contemporary popular music, so much so that it is difficult to appreciate the force of this perceived moral crisis. When David Bowie sings "Cha-cha-cha-changes," nobody would complain that his song is a stutter. (Although perhaps Bowie was thinking about syncopation in precisely this way: the sleeve notes to *Hunky Dory*, on which "Changes" is the lead track, credits Woody Woodmansey for playing "dr-dr-drums.") We do not hear it as a stutter to the extent that we liberate language from signifying medium into pure sonority. But pure sonority has a history of its own. The affectedly stuttering chorus to The Who's "My Generation" ("people try to p-p-p-p-put us down!") bears traces of the past that belie its putatively definitive *soixante-huitard* break. Within Roger Daltry's vocal hitch lies the "Stuttering Blues" of John Lee Hooker, without whom modern rock and roll would be inconceivable, and who recuperates for positive expressive effect the historical association of dyspraxia, syncopation, and race. Kendrick Lamar's idiosyncratic stop-start delivery offers a contemporary equivalent (Lamar suffered from a childhood stutter). Fluency and dysfluency alike contain sedimented histories of the personal and suprapersonal: it is hard to hear the clarion power of Etta James's voice in quite the same way, when we learn that it came about partly through the routine punches to the gut that her childhood singing instructor administered. Our tongues get tied when they encounter impediments that are historical as much as physiological.

We Never Start from Scratch

We have seen that the antinomies of rhythmical stuttering (clinical pathology and expressive resource; semantic stammer and musical syncopation) emerge in a variety of cultural material. Such instances lend historical precision to a variety of generally poststructuralist accounts of language, which have seized upon stuttering for its a-signifying character, and which have otherwise guided my analysis in significant ways.[84] Deleuze's brief essay "He Stuttered" has proven pivotal for such work. Mechanical failure here reveals a truth that eloquent speech cannot: "It is no longer the character who stutters in speech," states Deleuze, "it is the writer who becomes a stutterer in language. He makes language as such stutter: an affective and intensive language, and no longer an affectation of the one who speaks."[85] This characteristically provocative suggestion relies upon a similar emphatic binary to that which guided Deleuze's distinction between "critical rhythm" and "dogmatic meter," as we witnessed in the introduction. The effect, too, is largely the same: a-signifying language triumphantly breaks free from the prison house of language.

I share Deleuze's desire to recuperate the noninstrumental or redundant elements of language. Yet these do more than simply disrupt logical development; they possess a concrete history of their own. Susan Howe steers us further in this direction, through both her poetic and critical writing.[86] *My Emily Dickinson* develops a sense of stuttering that—in addition to its expressive effects—reflects upon the historical experience of gender. Dickinson, states Howe, "audaciously invented a new grammar grounded in humility in hesitation. HESITATE from the Latin, meaning to stick. Stammer. To hold back in doubt, have difficulty speaking. . . . Starting from scratch, she exploded habits of standard human intercourse in her letters, as she cut across the customary chronological linearity of poetry."[87]

But did Dickinson really "start from scratch"? Once again, we perceive the poststructuralist fantasy of a total deliverance from both linguistic signification and historical process. Yet the various technical devices that Howe enumerates as instances of Dickinsonian stuttering—"repetition, surprise, alliteration, odd rhyme and rhythm, dislocation and deconstruction"—hardly come about ex nihilo. They rather constitute rediscoveries or disfigurations of earlier verse repertoires. "Odd rhythm" certainly figures prominently in this regard. Dickinson's "broken ballad" form is an obvious instance. On other occasions, she uses the same couplet form as did Browning, precisely in order to subvert its historical reputation for fluency. Take poem 372:

> After great pain, a formal feeling comes—
> The Nerves sit ceremonious, like Tombs—
> The stiff Heart questions 'was it He, that bore,'
> And 'Yesterday, or Centuries before'?
>
> The Feet, mechanical, go round–
> A Wooden way
> Of Ground, or Air, or Ought—
> Regardless grown,
> A Quartz contentment, like a stone—

We begin with a heroic couplet that just about maintains itself despite the half-rhyme of "comes" and "Tombs." The ensuing stanza might seem to cast this prosodic convention to the winds. Yet in reality it gives us something far more interesting than liberation. We could typographically re-present the stanza as iambic couplets:

> The Feet, mechanical, go round—
> A Wooden way Of Ground,
> or Air, or Ought—Regardless grown,
> A Quartz contentment, like a stone—

Metrical convention lives on, in the shadow of a holographic presentation that wrenches it out of shape. Meter, however, proves both a tractable and a resistant metal, as the poem recovers its buried couplets: "As Freezing persons, recollect the Snow—/ First—Chill—then Stupor—then the letting go—." Coming home has seldom felt so unsettling a deliverance.

Earlier, I claimed that the nineteenth century catalyzes the separation between instrumentalized language and "pure" sonority. Rhythmical stuttering emerges as a negative evaluation through this process. The poststructuralist appropriation of vocal dyspraxia that we find in Deleuze and Howe *seems* to reverse this tendency, by converting stuttering from a term of opprobrium into positive release from the signifying chain. Yet in reality such judgments only extend the splitting tendency of the nineteenth century, by accepting the opposition of sound and sense. Dickinson's verse proves the shortfall of this view: her syncopated couplets do not break from convention so as to start life all over again; they rather intuit that every rhythmical turn involves a return. What holds true for the short poetic line applies also to the long historical duration. "Syncopation" has never held so clear a technical meaning for poetics as it has for musicology. Literary critics, myself among them, often use it metaphorically or impressionistically, to mean something like "break." Poem 372 shows us that we should perhaps develop a more exact sense of its implications for verse form: in the collision of rhythmical patterns; in the war between visual line and aural pattern; in the loving disfigurement of metrical convention.

Browning internalized such tensions more fully and profoundly than any poet before or since. It is appropriate, then, that one of the latter's many unjustly neglected late masterpieces offers what may well be the first-ever English-language poem to employ the word "syncopation." It does so not as pretty trope, but as exacting self-description. "Flute Music, with an Accompaniment," written in 1888, performs precisely what it names:

> So, 'twas distance altered
> >   Sharps to flats? The missing
> Bar when syncopation faltered
> >   (You thought—paused for kissing!)
> Ash-tops too felonious
> >   Intercepted? Rather
> Say—they well-nigh made euphonious
> >   Discord, helped to gather
> Phrase, by phrase, turn patches
> >   Into simulated
> Unity which botching matches,—
> >   Scraps redintegrated.

Until this point, Browning's interlocking *abab* rhymes have generally matched short lines with grammatical clauses, producing an uncharacteristic fluency. This virtuosic passage, however, mutilates such integrity with the parentheses, violent internal caesuras, and heavy accents ("Say—"), to which the young Browning was so addicted.

We could compare this work to the syncopations that we find in Schumann, a composer of whom Browning was extremely fond.[88] Yet what this late work aptly calls "euphonious / Discord" emerges quite differently in verse, to the extent that rhythmical interruptions disrupt not only musical conventions (harmonic proportion or resolution), but also the whole status of language as communicative medium. By making stutterers of us all, Browning actuates a historical truth regarding the new status of verse within an instrumentalized society. As such, he both extends and challenges Joshua Steele's influential suggestion that prosodic variability could be put in the service of therapeutic ends. Stuttering verse represents our first compelling instance of where poetry drives conceptualization through its non-discursive nature.

2

Idealist Rhythms

Embryonic Concepts

My first chapter demonstrated how the therapeutic treatment of stuttering persistently recruited verse that paradoxically resisted its instrumental ends. Over the course of this historical dialectic, "rhythm" came to stand for an entire and consistent clinical methodology. Yet this growing body of medical literature seldom reflected upon the broader nature of the concept that it had helped to spawn: Samuel Silas Curry's reference to "a rhythm of thinking" remains representatively vague and undeveloped. My second chapter locates a more sustained and reflexive process of conceptualization, which began in Germany at around the time that Joshua Steele was speculating upon how reformist prosody might treat stuttering, and which subsequently percolated into anglophone discourse from the 1840s. The discursive field in question is idealist philosophy—a form of thinking frequently dismissed, then as now, for being "abstract" and disembodied. This chapter claims, however, that both German idealism and its subsequent anglophone emulators recruit the developing concept of rhythm, so as to produce a powerful and moving account of embodied selfhood, temporal apprehension, and desire. This process relies upon the same historical dialectic as did elocutionary science: idealist philosophy draws upon poetry for several of its central claims, and in turn enables the composition and experience of rhythmically innovative verse.

This German context allows me to spell out how my account both consolidates and departs from the only existing scholarly work that I know to advance a similar argument, namely, that a distinctive rhythmical episteme emerges somewhere around the year 1800. Janina Wellmann's *The Form of Becoming: Embryology and the Epistemology of Rhythm, 1760–1830* offers a brilliantly syncretic account of the ways in which activities as distinct as fetal gestation and military exercises cumulatively come to suggest a new conception of dynamic process. My book, like Wellmann's, not only investigates a trans-discursive emergence of the concept of rhythm, but also stresses the constitutive significance of nondiscursive experience: in Wellman's case, this most prominently takes the form of the visual illustrations of embryonic development that played an increasingly pivotal role within scientific literature from the period.

Yet the present work also significantly diverges from *The Form of Becoming*, in ways that enable me to clarify its argument. Some of my contentions are comparatively minor: I do not agree, for example, that the word *rhythm* is "conspicuously present" within (English or German) culture by 1800, or that "it was not until around 1900 that 'rhythm' became a technical term in medicine and biology."[1] (My third and fourth chapters explore the concept's prevalence in nineteenth-century biology and physics, which traversed geographic boundaries.) Other departures prove more substantive. It is not always clear, for example, whether or how Wellmann takes the nineteenth century to mark a decisive break with precedent. Her claim that modernity rediscovers what the concept meant for antiquity runs directly counter to my own introductory assertion.[2] In what respect does the nineteenth century truly count as a *Sattelzeit*, when a military training manual from 1615 already "follow[s] complex laws of rhythm?"[3]

The welter of historical examples also blurs causality. How do individual subjects and discursive spaces come to internalize the concept of rhythm? Wellmann accords explanatory priority to embryology. Yet very often the link between this technical field and other areas of cultural enquiry proves analogical rather than causal: Karl Ernst von Bauer "describes the formation of the embryo through the layering and relayering, bending and folding of membranes in the same way that seventeenth-century and sixteenth-century dancing masters and masters of arms had described the execution of a movement on the dancing and fencing floor or that military writers had depicted the formations and evolutions of troops in the field."[4] The rather vague claim that "August Willhelm Schlegel, Goethe, d'Alton, Pander, Döllinger, and von Bauer were at the very least aware of one another's work" suggests a contingent process of simultaneous discovery rather than a pattern of influence that might connect biology, music theory, philosophy, literature, and botany.[5]

I believe by contrast that verse offers a more specific and demonstrable instance than embryology of where discursive conceptualization comes to rely upon nondiscursive materials. Joshua Steele's *"rhythmus"* proved a case in point; so too does idealist philosophy, as it strives against an "absolute" conception of self-identity, so as to understand experience as a matter of unfolding temporal differentiation. Such otherwise disparate figures as William Whewell and Coventry Patmore would ground this new concept of rhythmical apprehension within the understanding and practice of verse. When, a generation later, Alice Meynell posited a "rhythm of life," punctuated by the caesuras of female experience, she demonstrated all over again how the negativity that characterized idealist thinking could be put in service of sensuous immediacy.

Counter-Rhythmic Rupture

If Deleuze was right to define philosophy as the creation of concepts, then the *Frühromantiker* of Jena certainly qualify as philosophers. It is not surprising that we can add rhythm to the list of their terminological innovations and inflections.[6] Like many nascent terms, the concept is at first often applied in a vague or oblique manner. Friedrich Hölderlin's declaration, in his fragmentary observations upon *Oedipus Rex*, that "in the rhythmic sequence of the representations wherein *transport* presents itself, there becomes necessary *what in poetic meter is called caesura,* the pure word, the counter-rhythmic rupture," has for instance generated much head-scratching exegesis.[7] Walter Benjamin identified this "counter-rhythmic rupture" with a "sublime violence" that morcellates the work of art into fragments, or sets the passage of time at a (dialectical) standstill—in the process removing Hölderlin's comment from the specific context in which it originally occurred (*"poetic meter"*).[8]

Other idealist poets and philosophers would, however, develop a notion of rhythmic interruption that does not so much abolish time as function as a (negative) condition of its continuation. Novalis's *Fichte Studies* (1795–96) represent a significant document in this regard. This series of scattered reflections upon Fichte's *Wissenchaftslehre* proves as fragmentary as any of the works that Benjamin analyzed (or himself produced); yet as it proceeds, the text comes to rely with increasing force and precision upon a concept of rhythm that would guarantee a differential identity across its separate entries. Novalis does not do this all at once. His earlier fragments often employ rhythm in a vague or euphemistic manner, to mean just about anything at all. (A concept often emerges in confusion, matures into clarity, then dies into vacuity.) "Poetry is for human beings," he grandly declares early on, "what the chorus of the Greek theater is—conduct of the beautiful rhythmic soul—the voice accompanying our developing self—entry into the land of beauty—ubiquitous light trace of the finger of humanity—free rule—victory over raw nature in every word—its wit is the expression of free, self-reliant activity—flight—humanization."[9] All this!

Yet later entries begin to flesh out the bare-bones contention that "in the temporal world being is a rhythmical relation."[10] Increasingly, rhythm serves to describe a form of selfhood whose endurance paradoxically depends upon temporal differentiation. This notion opposes what Novalis takes—whether justly or unjustly—to be the absolute or tautological character of Fichte's absolute idealism: its insistence upon the logical copula of the subject ("I am I," a motto modeled upon Leibniz's law of noncontradiction).[11] Differential fragments, which exist in a discrete yet continuing form, oppose the work of systematic philosophy. In this process, Novalis strives to convert Fichtean self-identity from a logical postulate to a temporal unfolding, in which the equals sign becomes an apprehended break, or the blank space between separate entries in a life. This approach may be anti-systematic, yet Novalis nonetheless takes it to deserve the status of method: "All method is *rhythm*. Remove rhythm from the world and you remove—the world." The result is not the ruin of the *Wissenchaftslehre*, so much as a vindication of it in other terms than its author might have countenanced: "Fichte did nothing but discover the rhythm of philosophy and express it verbalacoustically."[12] What Hölderlin called "rupture" now does not abolish time: it alone enables the subject to reflect upon discontinuous selfhood. As such, it offers a practical application of what my introduction described as the distinctively new concept of rhythm: a form of measurement that proceeded through (rather than despite) variation.

Novalis's philosophizing remains constitutively fragmentary. Other contemporaneous thinkers would, however, seek to extend the applications of this newfound concept of rhythm, without falling back into absolute idealism. F. W. J. Schelling announced a representative ambition, in his *Philosophy of Art* (1802/3), "to establish the ultimate significance of rhythm, harmony and melody."[13] Much scholarship understands such thinking as essentially abstract: Tomas Macauley has for instance understood Schelling's idealist appropriation of rhythm as essentially in keeping with the established German eighteenth-century musical theory of *Akzenttheorie,* which defines the concept as "nothing other than a periodic division of a row of homogeneous things." Schelling, Macauley continues, produces a working definition of rhythm that is "practically identical."[14]

This verdict drastically undersells the extent to which German idealism breaks with extant theories of rhythm. Schelling's *Philosophy of Art* does indeed articulate a notion of rhythm as "homogenous" periodic division, only, however, so as immediately to complicate it:

> If for the sake of this proof I may employ the most general concept of rhythm, then rhythm in this sense is nothing more than the periodic subdivision of homogeneity whereby the uniformity of the latter is combined with variety and thus unity with multiplicity. For example, the emotion that a piece of music arouses as a whole is a completely homogeneous, uniform one. It is, for example, cheerful or sad. Through the various rhythmic subdivisions, however, this single feeling that alone would have been completely homogeneous acquires variety and diversity. Rhythm is one of the most wonderful mysteries of nature and art, and no human invention appears to be more immediately or directly inspired by nature.[15]

Rhythm, here, is no empty container, no "unity" that would be combined with a "diversity" that arrives from without. Diversity springs rather from "the various rhythmic subdivisions" themselves. Schelling goes on immediately to state, still more emphatically, that "uniformity of the intervals within the sequence" represents only "the lowest level of rhythm."[16] Schelling's conception of affective variability thus departs significantly from what Christopher Hasty has shown to be the abstract and regulative conception of time that we find in eighteenth-century music theory.[17]

It is at this stage that we observe the first glimmerings of anglophone interest in such discussions. Henry Crabb Robinson took a series of notes in response to Schelling's lectures in the winter of 1802–3, when a student at the University of Jena. "Rhythm," he transcribes, "is the music within music; for particularity is based on the fact that it is informing-into-one of unity in multiplicity."[18] Such statements are certainly numinous enough, in their Russian-doll formulations ("music within music"), their easy reconciliations of subject and object, unity and multiplicity. But at its best, Schelling's postulation of rhythmical instinct enables a profound consideration of temporal apprehension, which makes good upon Novalis's early description of interruption as a paradoxical condition of self-endurance:

> The human being, however, driven by an impulse of nature, seeks through rhythm to impose variety or diversity onto everything that in and for itself constitutes *a pure identity* of activity. In every activity that is by nature meaningless, such as counting, we do not endure long within that uniformity. We divide it into units. Most mechanical workers make their work easier this way. The inner pleasure of that—not really conscious, but rather unconscious—counting enables them to forget the work, and the individual comes in at his appointed place with a kind of pleasure, since it would pain him to see the rhythm interrupted.[19]

Rhythm, then, represents a means to insinuate difference within otherwise unlivable self-identity. While we might quibble over details (does the interruption of rhythm necessarily induce pain?), Schelling's "unconscious counting" vividly anticipates contemporary psychological interest in "flow" states.

Hegel's *Lectures on Fine Art* offer the fullest summation of this idealist articulation of rhythmical phenomenology. It does so in large part through the return of Hölderlin's caesura to its originary context, namely, poetic meter. In the process, he historicizes the experience of rhythmical apprehension that Schelling explores, so as to provide a detailed account of the development of poetry, in addition to an evocation of dialectical progression more generally. Despite all this, Hegel continues to stand for "abstraction," particularly among new historicists, for whom he represents a bogeyman of totalizing unity.[20] Virginia Jackson and Yopie Prins's *The Lyric Theory Reader* reads Hegelianism as crucial for the ideological establishment of "the abstract literary lyric," a baggy monster that cannibalizes generic variety.[21] Dennis Taylor's otherwise faultless *Hardy's Metres and Victorian Prosody* similarly insists that Hegel bequeaths disembodied abstraction to the Victorian "new prosody."[22]

This fatally impoverishes both Hegelian philosophy and its several afterlives. As a preliminary, we should note that *abstrakt* always is a complex (and frequently pejorative) term for Hegel (for proof see his 1807 essay "Who Thinks Abstractly?").[23] "Abstract" is only the first stage in the *Phenomenology*'s abstract-negative-concrete triad; "rhythm" engages it in a dynamic fashion. Hegel does, it is true, on occasion refer to "the rhythm of the bar" to indicate (among other things) an isochronous entity. Yet this is only one form of rhythm, whose various incarnations come (as they did for Schelling) into sustained tension: "The counter-thrust between the rhythm of the bar and that of the melody comes out at its sharpest in what are called syncopations."[24]

Rhythm, in other words, is at once abstract law *and* the animating force that decomposes it: a form that asserts itself, paradoxically, by departing from its own example. (A reductive account of Hegel's prosody may well represent both a symptom of, and a contributing factor to, readings of the Hegelian system as "closed," or "totalizing"; the notion of rhythm as self-departing phenomenon, for which I am attempting to argue, has something in common with what Catherine Malabou calls "plasticity"; indeed, Hegel writes explicitly that "we may compare the principle of rhythmical versification with plasticity" [*L*, 1022]).[25] Throughout its treatment of music, the *Lectures on Fine Art* press home this notion of rhythm as internal variation: "If . . . the melody keeps strictly in its rhythm and parts to the rhythm of the beat," Hegel writes immediately following the above citation, "then it really sounds humdrum, bare and lacking in invention. What may be demanded in this connection is, in brief, freedom from the pedantry of metre and the barbarism of a uniform rhythm" (*L*, 918). Hegel even goes so far as to make the interplay between time and rhythm central to the dialectical emergence of the subject. In order to recognize the self as self, the subject must break up "undifferentiated duration" into a series of intervals: "Its self-concentration interrupts the indefinite series of points of time and makes gaps in their abstract continuity" (L, 914). Such phrasings convert Novalis's fragmentary suggestions into programmatic assertion.

Measure, then, is the means by which the self unfolds, negatively; far from essentially "abstract," it transfigures the temporal material upon which it operates. Hence Hegel goes on to insist that "the satisfaction which the self acquires, owing to the bar, in the rediscovery of itself is all the more complete because the unity and uniformity does not pertain either to time or to the notes in themselves; it is by the self for its own self-satisfaction. For in nature *this abstract identity does not exist*" (L, 915; emphasis mine).[26] Unlike the fixed proportions of architecture (which can be perfectly realized in space), this negative work of measure proceeds truly "from the spirit." As such, meter hardly shares the unchanging and immaterial essence that we customarily impute to pure mathematics: it is rather a specific act, constituted by (and constitutive of) the subject, at a particular historical situation. And this determinative act itself invariably produces variation, which proceeds not from some allegedly external sphere ("performance"), but is rather fully intrinsic: "However strictly the specific beat has to govern the variety of duration . . . nevertheless its domination is not to extend so far that it dominates the variety quite abstractly" (L, 916). Far from rhythm being limited to the bar, this unfolding dialectic of law and variation "is brought about by means of rhythm which alone brings proper animation to the time and the bar" (L, 917).

All of the above examples derive from Hegel's consideration of music. Yet just as "music begins in recitative to liberate itself from the motionless sameness of the beat," so poetic meter operates according to a still more dynamic principle (L, 1018). Hegel gives short shrift to modern attempts to emulate the putatively unvarying norms of quantitative, classical verse: "When Voss wants to read even alcaic and Sapphic stanzas in these abstractedly uniform time-intervals, this is only a capricious fancy and means doing violence to the verse" (L, 1018). While Hegel is acutely aware of the differences pertaining to classical and vernacular prosody (of which more in a moment), both systems of organization have this self-variation in common: "The classical iambic trimeter acquires its beauty especially from its not consisting of six similarly timed iambic feet . . . and in this way the continual repetition of the same time-measure and anything like the beat is avoided" (L, 918); similarly, "in modern times Reichardt and others seem to me to have brought a new rhythmic life into song-composition precisely by abandoning . . . iambic sing-song" (L, 919).

Given all the above, it is hard to see how Hegel's philosophical account of prosody could be entertained for any length of time as uncomplicatedly "abstract." Isobel Armstrong's "Metre and Meaning" offers a salutary corrective, noting "that Hegel's idealism did not abnegate the 'body' of corporeal language, as has often been thought."[27] Of the four conceptions of prosody common to the nineteenth century (meter as "empty container," "correspondence" of sound and sense, productive "noncorrespondence" of the same, or complex "polyrhythm"), Armstrong identifies Hegel with the third and fourth, noting that the "spiritualization" involved in the transition from classical to romantic art has often misled readers in this respect.[28] *The Lectures on Fine Art* do indeed sometimes posit, in keeping with Rousseau, Burney, and Monboddo, that rhythm is an exclusively antique phenomenon: the subsection entitled "Rhythmical Variation" wistfully observes that, in modern vernaculars, "there is little room for rhythm, or the soul has little freedom any longer to spread itself in it, because time, and the sound of syllables outpoured uniformly with the movement of time, is surpassed by something more ideal, i.e. by the sense and meaning of words, and in this way the power of a more independent rhythmical configuration is damped down" (L, 1022).

This uncharacteristic rash of historical nostalgia cannot, however, triumph over the many more interesting things that Hegel has to say on the matter. As is well known, the *Lectures* propose the emergence of rhyme as compensation for any modern dereliction of rhythm.[29] Yet Hegel finally turns out to be divided over the question of whether the caesura truly is lost. It is curious, for a start, that he insists that syllabic languages such as French and Italian "lack meter and rhythm in the classical sense altogether" (L, 1027) given the importance of the medial pause for the alexandrine. Indeed, Hegel comes to acknowledge that rhythmical variation does endure for modernity, albeit in an altered guise. "We are accustomed," he writes, speaking of German iambics, "to scan more in accordance with a beat than is the case with the rhymeless iambics of classical antiquity. Nevertheless, halting at caesuras, the emphasis on single words to be markedly pronounced according to their sense, and stopping on them, may produce once more a counter-thrust to abstract sameness and therefore an enlivening variety" (L, 1033).

Moreover, when Hegel breaks off his general treatment of versification to consider the lyric mode, this supposedly most romantic, abstract, and homogenizing of genres permits nothing less than—variation. His enumeration of modern prosody repeats this central claim with near-obsessive frequency: lyric is characterized by "(i) a rather variegated ranging of longs and shorts in a broken inequality of rhythmic feet, (ii) the varied kinds of caesura, and (iii) the rounding-off into strophes which in themselves and their succession may have a wealth of variation both in the length and shortness of single lines and in their rhythmical variation" (L, 1136). So much for the fateful modern loss of syncopation. "If," Hegel says elsewhere in the *Lectures*, "we are to take *begreifen* in a spiritual sense, then it does not occur to us at all to think of a perceptible grasping by the hand" (L, 404). This may be. But however much lyric indexes the increasing spiritualization of art, we continue to feel the body of its rhythmical variations; continue to feel the grasp [*begreifen*] within the abstract concept [*Begriff*]. It is to the specifically poetic nature of this body that I now turn, in another figure who would come to serve as an avatar for abstraction: Coventry Patmore. For the idealist appropriation of rhythm did not only consistently rely upon the structure and experience of verse; so too did it enable a new form of poetic expression in the English vernacular.

Patmore's Body

Coventry Patmore might well appear an unlikely candidate to demonstrate how idealism, with its constitutive focus upon negation and caesura, can supply rhythmical embodiment. In the pure theater that is Robert Buchanan's Fleshly School, this eminent Victorian does not merit so much as a walk-on part. Matthew Arnold plays Horatio to Tennyson's Hamlet; Swinburne and Morris are Rosencrantz and Guildenstern; even Robert Bulwer-Lytton gets to be "a Gentleman."[30] That Patmore is nowhere to be seen perhaps hardly counts as a great surprise, given that his general reputation, by the time of Buchanan's review of 1871, was about as far from fleshliness as it was possible to get. For the representative mid-Victorian reader, Patmore was above all the Patmore of *The Angel of the House* (1854–62), his extended verse apotheosis of sober matrimonial bliss. The association has, more or less, stuck, with the caveats that where the Victorian public reveled in Patmore's epithalamion, more contemporary readers tend to find it disconcertingly patriarchal; and that where the Victorian public devoured it in droves, today's readers rarely give it the time of day.

Those areas of the academy that have recently reconsidered Patmore's work generally confirm that here stands the most unfleshly of poets. In the past years, Patmore has become a placeholder for precisely the "abstract," "idealizing," or "immaterial" conceptions of verse and life with which Hegel came to be synonymous. Meredith Martin's *The Rise and Fall of Meter* asserts that "his metrical grid was abstract";[31] Yopie Prins similarly holds that Patmore's *Essay on Metrical Law* aimed to "formalize temporal relations between abstract quantities, mentally perceived in the act of counting and not necessarily audible";[32] Joshua King goes yet further, arguing that such a prosody was fated to be "never realized in a human voice";[33] a section heading from Jason Rudy's recent *Electric Meters,* meanwhile, tells its own story, with an uppercase subheading reading simply "BODILESS PATMORE."[34]

Yet Patmore did treat the body: did so, indeed, with an obsessiveness and excessiveness that shocked (even appalled) many of his contemporaries. The dominant view of Patmore as poet of disembodiment can only maintain itself through four willful oversights: (1) a disproportionate focus upon the morally and metrically orthodox *The Angel in the House,* to the detriment of more experimental verse; (2) the exclusion of aphoristic and epigrammatic prose writings; (3) the deracination of Patmore's writing from European currents of thought that it both borrowed from (G. W. F. Hegel) and itself influenced (Paul Claudel); and (4) the extirpation of one element within the "Essay on Metrical Law" ("abstraction") from its context.[35] The upshot of these exclusions is that Patmore appears to us today as the most English of authors, reactionary, provincial, and fastidious—when in reality he proved one of the first and finest readers of Hegel, in addition to producing some of the most technically experimental verse in the English vernacular. Even John Maynard, who for several years has been waging a lonely, impassioned, and to-date unsuccessful defense of Patmore's "eroticism," glosses over all but (1).[36]

We associate embodied rhythm far more readily with a poet like Gerard Manley Hopkins: as King contends, "Unlike Patmore, Hopkins identifies poetry's affective meaning with the spoken sound of lines."[37] Yet over the pair's voluminous correspondence, Hopkins is repeatedly disconcerted by what he takes to be Patmore's profane conception of the sacred body, which forms a far greater bone of contention than the respective merits of sprung rhythm or isochronous prosody.[38] Patmore famously cast to the flames the unfinished manuscript of his would-be magnum opus "Sponsa Dei," in response to Hopkins's strictures. Yet more than enough remains in Patmore's published writings to suggest what might have outraged his correspondent: in "Homo," for instance, one of several collections of aphorisms and epigrams collected as *The Rod, the Root and the Flower*, Patmore instructs us that the "only sin [that the Virgin Mary] is chargeable with is a little vanity in the consciousness of being the Bride and Mother of God. O felix culpa, without which she would not have been a woman! If we must think of the Infinite, the most profitable way is to think of God as having made Himself infinitely small, a mere babe sucking a woman's breast, to suit Himself to the smallness of our capacities."[39]

The striking image of God made over into a suckling infant proves anything but an exceptional lapse. For the body is the single dominant theme in Patmore's aphoristic writing, as it collapses erotic and divine poles: the pious individual "knows nothing of God on whom it feeds other than by touch and taste" (R, 81). For all that *The Angel in the House* establishes hard-and-fast gender separations, Patmore's aphoristic writings frequently muddy the divide. Sometimes God (as above) is feminized, as the "Mistress" in whose body the lover's spirit endures (R, 53). On other occasions worship feminizes the devout male: "The divine manhood, indeed, may be discerned in man through the cloud of that womanhood of which he is a participator" (R, 111). (Even the *Angel in the House* makes the arresting claim that "Female and male God made the man; / His image is the whole, not half" [P, 107]).

Hegel's influence first declares itself in this androgynous context, where Patmore pays a fine tribute to what we have observed as the sensuousness of Hegel's philosophy:

> Who, except perhaps, Hegel, has ever noted, except by way of poetical metaphor, the surprising fact, simply natural and of general experience, of the double and reciprocal consciousness of love; that marvellous state in which each of two persons in distinct bodies perceives sensibly all that the other feels in regard to him or herself, although their feelings are of the most opposite characters; and this so completely, each discerning and enjoying the distinct desire and felicity of the other, that you might say that in each was the fullness of both sexes. To note one such human fact as this is to exalt life to fuller consciousness, and to do more for true science than to discover a thousand new suns. (R, 108)

Surely it does not take a dialectical system in order to recognize "the double and reciprocal consciousness of love." Nonetheless, Patmore's flushed passage does an excellent job at rendering Hegel's absolute idealism in concrete human terms. To perceive this process in more depth, we need to turn from Patmore's scattered aphoristic writings to his *Essay on English Metrical Law* (1857), which has long been viewed as a crypto-Hegelian exercise in the "abstraction" or "mentalization" of meter. In reality, it proves nothing of the sort. Rather, it develops Hegel's general conception of rhythm as self-variation, in which the pause or caesura occupies an essential role.

Here Patmore once again wears his influences on his sleeve:

> The nature of the relation between the poet's peculiar mode of expression and the matter expressed has engaged the curiosity of many philosophic minds. Hegel, whose chapters on music and metre contain by far the most satisfactory piece of writing I know of on the subject, admirably observes, that versification affords a necessary counterpoise to the great spiritualisation of language in poetry. "It is false," he adds, "that versification offers any obstacle to the free outpouring of poetic thought. True genius disposes with ease of sensible materials, and moves therein as in a native element, which, instead of depressing or hindering, exalts and supports its flight." Art, indeed, must have a body as well as a soul; and the higher and purer the spiritual, the

more powerful and unmistakable should be the corporeal element;—in other words, the more vigorous and various the life, the more stringent and elaborate must be the law by obedience to which life expresses it.[40]

Jason Rudy cites this emphatic declaration as proof of Patmore's "utter disdain for rhythm": "Patmore's overall project throughout the 1850s," he concludes, "is to abstract poetry from corporeal experience."[41] But even if there is indeed something rather stentorian in Patmore's specification of a "stringent" and "elaborate" law (whose corporeality is nevertheless "the more powerful and unmistakable"!), the *Essay* as a whole could not be less "disdainful" of rhythm. Far from the body being simply subsumed to an unvarying higher order, law and life interrelate just as dynamically as they did for Hegel. "In the finest specimens of versification," Patmore continues, "there seems to be a perpetual conflict between the law of the verse and the freedom of the language, and each is incessantly, though insignificantly, violated for the purpose of giving effect to the other."[42] A "cultivated ear . . . rather delights in, than objects to [rhythmical variation] when there is an emotional motive, as indicating an additional degree of that artistic consciousness, to the expression of which, Hegel traces the very life of meter."[43]

Even when Patmore makes his central claim, that the ictus "for the most part . . . *has no material and external existence at all* [italics in the original]"—a claim that is often extracted from its context to serve alone as a convenient summary of the *Essay*—things are less clear-cut than they appear.[44] As Joseph Phelan notes, Patmore is specifically arguing against a physiological account of prosody that would be so reductively "material" as to identify accent with a particular region of the tongue or palate.[45] You don't have to be a card-carrying Hegelian to believe that this conception of the "material" cannot ever prove adequate to the actuality of experience (though it certainly helps). And indeed, for all that Patmore's prosody does involve a necessary operation of mind, this mental process is shown to be irreducibly affective and corporeal throughout. "The musical and metrical expression of emotion is an instinct, and not an artifice," he states, "Were the vulgar and infantine delight in rhythm insufficient to justify that conviction, history itself would prove it."[46]

Vulgar and infantine are not meant here as pejorative qualifications.

For, as with Schelling's blacksmith, the embodied subject instinctively insinuates difference within simple repetition. "If Grétry," writes Patmore, referring to the French neoclassical composer, "when a child, danced to the pulsations of a waterfall, it was because his fancy abolished their monotony. The ticking of a clock is truly monotonous; but when we listen to it, we hear, or rather seem to hear, two, or even four, distinct tones, upon the imaginary distinction of which, and the equally imaginary emphasis of one or two, depends what we call its rhythm."[47] This subjective investment of meter could not be less "in one's own head," less a merely regulative "internal metronome":[48] far from amounting to objective, suprapersonal quantity, abstraction secures for the subject phenomenological variety! Even when Patmore does seem to approach what Eric Griffiths called the printed voice of Victorian poetry, arguing that the *"ideal"* reader of Shakespeare will render the text in a more complex manner than most contemporary real persons are able, his argument hinges less upon an absolute distinction than upon the historical shift to "an age of unnatural divorce of sound and sense."[49] "Verse itself," despite Armstrong's claim for the displacement of aurality by visibility, remains "only verse on the condition of right reading."[50] Even rhyme, the distinctively "romantic" phenomenon that was supposed to have superseded rhythmical prosody, in fact only deepens the expressive possibilities for the caesura, which as we have seen even Hegel could not fully deny: "Rhyme . . . is the great means, in modern languages, of marking essential metrical pauses."[51] When even the *Essay on English Metrical Law* reveals that abstraction and law are involved in a complex dialectic with vocal performance and corporeal experience, we have to wonder what proof of Patmore's disembodiment is left standing. His ode sequence *The Unknown Eros* drastically extends and complicates this pattern of rhythmical capacity and constraint.

Mega-Catalexis

Patmore's aphoristic writing and Hegelianized prosody offer the finest British commentary on the sustained idealist conceptualization of rhythmical embodiment. The two-book ode sequence *The Unknown Eros* actuates this thinking; in the process, it both exceeds and challenges even the more dynamic and fluid specifications of the *Essay*. For where Patmore's prosodic theory would indeed reserve "high and stately lyrical feeling" for the uniform pause, *The Unknown Eros* achieves something far more interesting and variable.[52] Its actualization (or non-actualization) of the protracted pause stores and discharges several conflicting energies: most obviously, the drive for immediate consummation, along with the countervailing yet equally pronounced need for deferral. This tension constitutes the varieties of religious and erotic experience. Patmore's odes develop what remained a conundrum for Hegel's aesthetics: the rhythmical potential that the caesura could offer for a modern vernacular poetry deracinated from classical quantity. Rhythmical "law" does not simply transcend metrical strictures, which paradoxically live on at the very moment at which the subject truncates the caesura and ruptures the silence. This paradox applies to all nominally "free verse": there are only more or less pleasant ways of being unfree. Yet it operates particularly acutely in Patmore's verse, given what he took to be the devotional, political, and prosodic dividends of lawfulness.

The Unknown Eros takes some time to realize this constitutive tension. The first of the sequence's two books remains comparatively conventional, in its adherence both to the irregular English ode and to a stable speaking voice. Yet even here it stands in a dynamic relation to Patmore's prosodic theory—not least in the way in which it manipulates sustained catalexis so as to render even the silent or paused voice palpable. An early poem entitled "The Day after Tomorrow" utilizes a lexicon of pauses and beats so frequently that we are hard pressed not to read it in lockstep with the *Essay*:

> But shall I not, with ne'er a sign, perceive,
> Whilst her sweet hands I hold,
> The myriad threads and meshes manifold
> Which Love shall round her weave:
> The pulse in that vein making alien pause
> And varying beats from this;
> Down each long finger felt, a differing strand
> Of silvery welcome bland;
> And in her breezy palm

And silken wrist,
Beneath the touch of my like numerous bliss
Complexly kiss'd,
A diverse and distinguishable calm?[53]

If ever proof were needed that internal variation constituted the life of meter, it is here, where Patmore's handling of the line discharges a frank eroticism. This passage begins in a manner broadly comparable to the structured variations of a poet such as Henry Vaughan, whose *Silex Scintillans* moves liberally between iambic dimeter, trimeter, tetrameter, and pentameter. The early odd lines (19, 21, 23) are recognizable pentameters; the even lines that intersperse them (20, 22, 24) are, with the aid of elision, clearly trimeters. Yet this oscillation between metrical extension and contraction becomes more extreme and less predictable: just as the verse speaks, fittingly, of "alien pause" and "varying beats," the latest trimeter (26) brings no return to the extended norm, but rather a further, fuller contraction, with lines of five and four syllables. Number crunching alone tells little of the real drama, which concerns the manner in which Patmore fills syllabic contraction and deferred rhyme ("this" and "palm" now must wait to be fulfilled) with erotic yearning. The unrealized beat, in short, so far from being merely "imagined" or "abstract," resounds with the abeyant love object.

Catalexis, it may be objected, presumes a norm from which we depart: why, in the above lines, should we take pentameter as the yardstick from which other lines fall short, rather than a trimeter or tetrameter, beyond whose constraints verse elsewhere swells? Patmore himself declared in the *Essay* that *"there is properly no such thing as hypercatalexis."*[54] Yet we do not require his stentorian declarations of catalexis as the essential condition of English poetry, to see that the whole drama of this piece turns on metrical contraction. We might well be tempted to desecrate the poem's "calm," to hurry through its demonstrative pauses in the increasingly breathless elaboration of the lover's body ("And silken wrist"), were it not for Patmore having already deployed extreme end-stopped catalexis as a declarative statement of certainty, to enforce pause: "Tell her I come;" (8); "We know." (11).

"The Day after Tomorrow" thus names and experiences a deferred temporality, in whose pockets the pleasure in waiting battles against the pleasure to make the awaited one come. Patmore's vocal address comes increasingly to evoke not only the generic passage of time, but also a singular (if still vague) real erotic presence, a "she" who stands behind the "heaving Sea" (6), "blazing photosphere of central night" (42), and the rest. The poem struggles between a mastery of absence through a stated law of eternal return ("It all has been before" [33]), and a present-tense longing that would disrupt all such ordered procession, as the speaker beseeches "Life" to "Perturb my golden patience not with joy" (50).

Perhaps it is for this reason that "The Day after Tomorrow" ends by taking refuge in a host of personifications ("O Life, Death, Terror, Love!" [57]); and that the following series of odes, while redirecting Patmore's invocations to a consistent female subject, also redirects them into a prior temporality of controlled regret. "Tristitia," "The Azalea," "Departure," "Eurydice," "The Toys," and "Tired Memory" are all, as several of the titles directly or indirectly suggest, poems of backward turning, to a lover or other since departed. "The Azalea"—the poem from which Patmore quoted in his defense to Hopkins of womanly "vanity"—recounts a dream in which the subject's beloved was dead; the subject awakens to his relief, "Perfectly bless'd in the delicious sphere / By which I knew that she was near" (12–13), yet then awakens again from what he had only taken to be waking reality, "and she *was* dead!" (17). There is an overbearing pathos to this tale, given that the speaker had gone to bed clutching a letter bearing the now-familiar claim, "Sweet to myself that am so sweet to you!" (25). Yet so too does this letter insinuate a perhaps more disturbing state of affairs: that even in absence (the absence of mediated desire, the absence intrinsic to the act of letter writing, the absence even of death), the beloved can be recalled or called up in a manner more tangible than what passes for immediate presence.

The very title of "Eurydice" represents an acknowledgment of this predicament. But it is "Tired Memory" that provides the first book's most sustained treatment of desire in abeyance. Once again, Patmore's megacatalexis serves at first to underscore a temporal order, the finality of death:

> At last, then, thou wast dead.
> Yet would I not despair,
> But wrought my daily task, and daily said

> Many and many a fond, unfeeling prayer,
> To keep my vows of faith to thee from harm.
> In vain. (10–15)

There is a perversity of feeling here that underlies what might pass for somewhat mawkish simplicity ("Yet would I not despair"). For the subject counters bereavement not through cathartic mourning, but rather with prayers that manage to be "fond" yet "unfeeling"; the following line then suggests that it is not the departed beloved, so much as the "vows of faith," that constitutes the speaker's principal concern. The catalectic "In vain." brutally unmasks such an endeavor, abruptly disappointing the rhyme pattern that had appeared to win hope from suffering ("dead" becoming "said," "despair" finding "prayer"), its subsequent, extended silence both representing and enforcing the time that cannot be undone. (It is worth remarking here, that where Patmore's *Essay* considers rhyme as a privileged means of enforcing pause, this enforced silence also disrupts the alternating rhyme scheme that had established itself.) The "vanity" that Patmore's poetic and aphoristic writing had celebrated in woman, much to Hopkins's unease, here resounds in altered form, transformed by the vulgar pun into futility.

Yet there is a world of difference between this definitive, end-stopped pause and Patmore's ensuing use of his signature device. The bereaved speaker, having come to see that the merely dutiful act of remembrance holds no succor ("The wilful faith, which has no joy or pain" [17]), undergoes a remarkable change in his patterns of worship. Kneeling in a church at Easter,

> It came to me to say:
> "Though there is no intelligible rest,
> In Earth or Heaven,
> For me, but on her breast,
> I yield her up, again to have her given,
> Or not, as, Lord, Thou wilt, and that for aye."
> And the same night, in slumber lying,
> I, who had dream'd of thee as sad and sick and dying,
> And only so, nightly for all one year,
> Did thee, my own most Dear,

> Possess,
> In gay celestial beauty nothing coy,
> And felt thy soft caress
> With heretofore unknown reality of joy. (23–36)

It is surely a contentious bargain, to agree to "yield" a wife already departed, in the hope that the Lord who receives her might in turn return her—however much the enjambed "Or not, as, Lord, Thou wilt" confesses His authority. Once again Patmore's spiritual and erotic dynamics intersect in a manner that at least risks sacrilege: this act of relinquishment, which might just about conceivably be a self-abasement before God's domain, also has at least a tint of the erotic yielding that is pleasurable either for itself or for the deferred and therefore intensified boon to which it gives rise. Patmore's dialectic of abandonment moves from the tangible ("on her breast"), to the immaterial ("I yield her up"), back to the tangible ("soft caress"). Where the previous end-stopped catalexis ("In vain.") enforced definitive finality, the dangling "Possess" makes silence palpably vibrate, in much the same way as does the departed lover's absent body. Empty space both goads and frustrates the body that would take possession. Taking it as a complete sense unit (the unitary line forms an essential component of Patmore's prosody), we forget the past tense of the qualifying clause, bestowing upon it the priority of the present.

It is perhaps the disturbing charge of such visions that causes Patmore abruptly to change course for the remainder of book 1, and seek refuge in a series of more public odes whose reactionary politics—whether inveighing against the 1867 reform act, Disraeli's marriage of "false English Nobles and their Jew," or the settlement of the Alabama claims—remains shocking. It could well be that in these poems Patmore continues to manipulate the varied verse line in a virtuosic fashion, though I cannot hear much beneath the abruptly rabid tone. Yet the eroticism that book 1 attempts to exorcise only returns in still bolder form, in the first ode of the second volume, the eponymous "To the Unknown Eros."

Patmore's verse technique now pushes rhythmical law and variation further and harder than anything previously seen:

> What rumour'd heavens are these
> Which not a poet sings,
> O, Unknown Eros? What this breeze
> Of sudden wings
> Speeding at far returns of time from interstellar space
> To fan my very face,
> And gone as fleet,
> Through delicatest ether feathering soft their solitary beat,
> With ne'er a light plume dropp'd, nor any trace
> To speak of whence they came or whither they depart? (1–10)

There is a newfound propulsion to Patmore's non-catalectic lines, which resembles Hopkins in its interfusion of polysyllables and monosyllables ("Through delicatest ether feathering soft their solitary beat"). The extension of lines 5, 8, and 10 runs up against an element that is, however, seldom to be found in Hopkins's output, the catalexis to which we have become attuned, but which now discharges unprecedented tension and release. Complete lines such as "Of sudden wings" or "And gone as fleet" burst into being, before flying from view and voice; the arrest of sound is all the stronger given that both complete rhymes.

The speaker of book 1 fought the temptation to linger in a departed past. Now, by contrast, recollected desire reawakens present longing, through a daring rescripting of Wordsworth's own "Ode (Intimations of Immortality from Recollections of Early Childhood)":

> And why this palpitating heart,
> This blind and unrelated joy,
> This meaningless desire,
> That moves me like the Child
> Who in the flushing darkness troubled lies,
> Inventing lonely prophecies,
> Which even to his Mother mild
> He dares not tell:
> To which himself is infidel;
> His heart not less on fire

> With dreams impossible as wildest Arab Tale,
> (So thinks the boy,)
> With dreams that turn him red and pale,
> Yet less impossible and wild
> Than those which bashful Love, in his own way and hour,
> Shall duly bring to flower? (11–27)

If Love is indeed "bashful," it has a funny way of showing it, in this most vocally and declaratively sensuous of passages. That sensuousness exists not only at the level of imagery and metrical pause, but also through a series of rhymes with which Patmore takes far greater liberties than anything on offer in book 1. Those prior poems naturally varied acoustic patterns, in a manner perfectly permissible for the irregular ode; but here, "unrelated joy" stands as an appropriately unanswered singular. We might think a similar fate has befallen "meaningless desire," where once again no immediate rhyme is forthcoming, whose vocal trace has faded once we reach to "less on fire," a full seven lines later: another proof of gratification deferred. "To the Unknown Eros" pushes rhyme's capacity for (erotic) invitation and completion further still: tempting us to draw "wild" away from its true rhyme ("Mother mild") into the verbal ambit of the more proximate "fire"; and later fusing together the "fire" rhyme that had been staggered ("Thou art not Amor; or if so, yon pyre, / That waits the willing victim flames with vestal fire" [53–54]), in a quickening cycle of amorous conflagration.

Patmore thus both singularizes and eroticizes Wordsworth's Neoplatonism. The child's intimation proves a true "prophes[y]," not because it anticipates the erotic life to come in any detail, but through being overmastered by desire. But if book 2 can finally bring itself to (re-)admit the longing that constituted those prior poems, so does it raise disconcerting questions for both proper devotional practice and rhythmical measure. Why should the inflamed heart submit to law?

The question as to how we should read the odes in light of Patmore's *Essay* has, despite its obviousness, seldom been satisfactorily or thoroughly answered. Despite spending nearly 130 pages on the ode sequence in *Victorian Discourses in Sexuality and Religion*, John Maynard says nothing about how its erotic content relates to prosodic innovation. Joseph Phelan, by contrast, does attend to the metrical character of the sequence, which he reads in perfect conformity with Patmore's verse theory. "Perhaps because of its metrical idiosyncrasy," Phelan contends, "*The Unknown Eros* has not achieved the recognition it deserves, as one of the most majestic poetic collections issued during the second half of the nineteenth century. Read in line with Patmore's theories, the poems are often excruciatingly slow to read, but do unquestioningly possess what Patmore calls 'high and stately lyrical feeling.'"[55] It is difficult to know how stateliness (whatever the word really signifies) can ever be safeguarded from excruciating declamation. We might here recall Patmore's own admission, in the *Essay*, that the excessive pause renders both vocal expedients (ignoring or realizing it) equally "absurd." I myself have tried the experiment that Phelan recommends on several occasions in classroom settings: the embarrassment proved revealingly fatal to high lyric seriousness.

Yet the protracted pause achieves more than the dissolution of lyric aspiration into bathos. To grasp this value, we have to look more closely at Patmore's rhythmical variety. Phelan clinches his claim for the appropriateness of catalexis by reading a single poem from book 1 that I have previously mentioned only in passing, "Departure." Here again we find the familiar mega-catalexis:

> It was not like your great and gracious ways!
> Do you that have nought other to lament,
> Never, my love, repent
> Of how, that July afternoon,
> You went,
> With sudden unintelligible phrase,
> And frightened eye. (1–7)

"In the case of the momentous line 'You went,'" Phelan continues, "there is a pause of the full fourteen syllables allowed for in Patmore's theory; the mimetic appropriateness of this painfully distended pause for the speaker's speechless and disbelieving guilt is self-evident."[56] I fully agree that we should read the catalectic line as Phelan suggests, and that its protracted pause is appropriate to the domestic drama of the poem more generally. (I do not much care whether we can make the exact specification of "fourteen syllables"—it is enough that we can speak in the approximate language of the short, long, and very long.)

Yet other instances differently compel our voice. Indeed, as the ode sequence progresses, catalexis produces a growing range of rhythmical effects, which do not refute Patmore's theory so much as test its limits. The example from "Departure" is forcefully mimetic: as such, it takes its place among other pauses that we have seen ("In vain."), or the dangling "Possess," albeit that this syntactical groping already tempts us to abolish the pause.

But "To the Unknown Eros" troubles the voice yet further. While the early catelectic pauses ("Of sudden wings," "And gone as fleet") communicate abrupt departure, the still-more truncated lines of the poem's middle section achieve a strikingly different effect:

> What in its ruddy orbit lifts the blood,
> Like a perturbed moon of Uranus,
> Reaching to some great world in ungauged darkness hid;
> And whence
> This rapture of the sense
> Which, by thy whisper bid,
> Reveres with obscure rite and sacramental sign
> A bond I know not of nor dimly can divine. (33–40)

No mimetic justification can explain away "And whence," whose truncation delivers precisely the opposite vocal effect to "You went." Where that prior line enforced separation, "And whence" seeks continuance: through its directional preposition; through being the prelude to one of the poem's countless unanswerable rhetorical questions; through the absence of punctuation; and through being the invitation and not the response to rhyme, when Patmore's *Essay* acknowledges that the latter most effectively marks the "uniform" pause.[57] All these factors conspire to trap voice between an acquired need to pause appropriately (as if in obedience to external law), and the countermanding desire to prematurely consummate sense and body alike.

Book 2 develops Patmore's incarnate cognition in ways that its titles ("Sponsa Dei," "To the Body," "Eros and Psyche") suggest. Yet to analyze their contents would only belabor the broader point. I wish rather to conclude this section in a more eccentric manner, in the form of an obscure document that sheds a somewhat different light upon embodied rhythmical capacity and constraint. It takes the form of a 1933 letter from Richard de Bary, a prolific Catholic author and acquaintance of Patmore, to Julian Huxley, the evolutionary biologist and brother of Aldous Huxley.[58] Having recently attended the latter's talk entitled "Tissue Culture and Human Habits," de Bary writes on 5 June with news of a past "discovery" made by Coventry Patmore, strikingly described as "a pioneer student of sex," who "was worried with nerve trouble." De Bary continues, in a handwriting that at times approaches illegibility: "He discovered that if there were an absolutely perfect closure (by silk-thread if you will) of the sex-organ, and coitus attempted; the entire output of spermatozoa ["broke"?] into the nerve system of the emitter and effect *entire* 'nerve-regeneration.' The reason why this has not otherwise been discovered is because it requires one particular rather vehement act to bring it about; and what C. P. described as the act of a 'severing sword.'" It is striking that de Bary could bring himself to be this frank, even despite the mysterious euphemism of the "severing sword." Yet the subsequent reference to "'injaculation' instead of 'ejaculation,'" along with the quintessentially Victorian desire to shun "waste," strongly suggest something like the common Taoist practice of deferred ejaculation, which hopes (misguidedly) to "reintroduce" semen into the bloodstream.

De Bary claims to have learned of this "discovery" from "one who knew Coventry Patmore perfectly"; needless to say, we cannot assess the veracity of the claim, although it would seem a far-fetched thing to fabricate. He attributes Patmore's reticence on the subject to a Victorian culture whose unforgiving tendencies were apparently already clear at the point of writing. De Bary tantalizingly suggests that "he buried his discovery," the unnamed friend having assured him that Patmore's "meanings were not 'mystical' but 'physiological.'" (Among other things, this chapter has attempted to resist the accepted distinction.) In his second letter on 13 June, de Bary continues that "after the discovery referred to he wrote *To the Unknown Eros* & 5 or 6 Odes including *The Open Secret*." While Patmore is alleged to refer specifically to "coitus," de Bary freely admits having attempted the same "act" during masturbation, and to have achieved "amazing . . . brain regeneration"!

This curious set of letters consolidates the argument that this chapter has advanced: that a broadly idealist persuasion does not preclude a sustained engagement with embodied experience. This does not mean that we can "unmask" what passes for devotion, to expose what de Bary encourages us to think of as the physiological that underpins the mystical. For both orders exceed the present and palpable phenomenon, or what Hegel disparaged as false immediacy: rather, they unfold in a complex temporal process to which corporeal and vocal absence proves necessary. Rhythm proves essential to this phenomenon, through the retention and prehension of what is not immediately at hand, but which proves part of the sequence. The more Patmore's verse engages the real, human, profane, embarrassed body, the more it intuits man's relationship to an unknowable yet un-disembodied beyond. This hazardous worship distinguishes Patmore as one of the most idiosyncratic and overlooked poets of the nineteenth century, as well as one of the most significant contributors to the emergent concept of rhythm.

Muscular Consciousness

Patmore's mega-catalexis inherits and actuates the caesura that proved so foundational to the idealist appropriation of rhythm. His pause is not abstract and regulative, just as it never was for Schelling or Hegel: it rather represents a form of negativity that grounds the apprehension of embodied life. This historical connection further corroborates W. J. Mander's persuasive claim for the deep permeation of idealism within nineteenth-century British thought. His *British Idealism: A History* demonstrates the extent to which early twentieth-century analytic philosophy sought to consolidate its newfound supremacy by systematically downplaying or dismissing such historical precursors.[59] Patmore inflects this account in two ways: firstly, he demonstrates that Hegel's influence predated the 1860s, which Mander takes to mark the beginning of British idealism proper; secondly, his poetry demonstrates the extent to which other discursive forms than systematic philosophy could engage significantly with such material.[60]

By the 1860s, the concept of rhythm was firmly established in anglophone discourse. Translators and proselytizers of German idealism frequently availed themselves of the term, so as to express the complex processes of self-differentiating selfhood or dialectical change in general. When

J. H. Stirling writes in his famously gnomic *The Secret of Hegel* (1865) that "the Notion itself in its own development must submit to the law of its own rhythm and could not appear on the scene in any Minerva-like completeness," he summarizes with uncharacteristic lucidity an interruptive "non-Being" that stretches back to Novalis.[61] William Wallace's "Prolegomena" to his translation of Hegel's *Logic* (1874) similarly parses "rhythmic movement" as "the ebb and flow of the world, always recurring with the same burden but with richer variety of tones, and fuller sense of itself.... To this rhythmical movement Hegel has appropriated the name of Dialectic."[62]

For the time being, however, I want to continue to focus upon the earlier and lesser-known reception of idealist thinking, along with its close ties to poetry. To the extent that they professed a philosophical orientation, the reformist prosodists-cum-speech therapists of my first chapter were generally materialists: John Thelwall represents a case in point. Materialism might be seen to have good reason to develop an understanding of rhythm, periodic process being such a prevalent feature of the organic world. It is significant, however, that the first significant British philosophical definition of the concept comes from a very different source, namely, William Whewell, whose eclectic philosophy sought to reconcile the empirical commitment to induction with a variety of broadly idealist positions. References to Kant and Schelling litter his erudite and synoptic work. While some scholars have questioned just how substantive such influence finally proves, we cannot understand Whewell's explicit conceptualization of rhythm absent the German tradition that the earlier sections of this chapter explored.[63]

Rhythm poses afresh a question that had long been familiar to any reader of Kant: the relation between ideational concepts and sensuous particulars. In his *Philosophy of the Inductive Sciences* (1840), Whewell frequently comes very close indeed to Kant's own position: the claim that "Ideas are not *transformed* but *informed* Sensations; for without ideas, sensations have no form" cannot but recall the famous dictum that concepts without percepts are blind, percepts without concepts are empty.[64] Yet Whewell also pushed the relationship of "Idea" and "Sensation" further, in a manner comparable to Hegel. Sensation is contentless, without ideas to guide it; but where do these ideas come from? Are they simply hard-wired within human cognition? Or do human subjects or cultures need to acquire them in particular ways?[65]

Whewell attempts to address such question with a category of regulatory principles that he terms "Fundamental Ideas." These can take the form of permanent, unchanging, and subject-independent truths, of which geometry and mathematics offer ready instances. But so too can they be discovered through empirical investigation or historical process: as such they are *a posteriori*, though none the less binding for all that. Whewell offers astronomy, biological taxonomy, and statics as instances of discovered-yet-absolute truth. What Whewell calls the scientific "colligation" and "consilience" of knowledge thereby involve a more open-ended process with empirical reality than either Kant's concepts (which regulate only sensuous intuition) or his categories (a finite list of what we can know of a given object). It is entirely possible that humans will continue to discover Fundamental Ideas, which can then readily be exported across scientific fields (*PIS*, xxix). Where Kant considers the transcendental subject, therefore, Whewell focuses rather on the ways in which increasingly specialized scientific communities discover and share truth. His own compositional method sets to work this dynamic relation between empirical data and regulative principles, with the *Philosophy of the Inductive Sciences* following on from the *History of the Sciences from the Earliest to the Present* (1837). Sensuous particulars precede theoretical reflection, yet are also intelligible without it: Whewell required his readers to consult both works, and in the process become inductive scientists in their own right.

Two further subtle departures from Kant's understanding of the interaction of the faculties prepare the ground for Whewell's conceptualization of rhythm. The first concerns language, which, as several readers have observed, remains largely absent from the three Critiques. It is a matter of indifference, for Kant, what we call a concept; for Whewell, by contrast, names count. They should on the one hand be "perfectly exact and purely intellectual," yet on the other not depart from generally understood terminology so much as to be unrecognizable (*PIS*, xlvii). Whewell is at pains to point out that apparently abstract geometrical terms ("*sphere*," "*cone*," "*cylinder*") arose from tangible and manipulable objects: "a boy's spinning top, or the crest of a helmet" (*PIS*, xlix). Abstraction never fully cancels the sensuous experience from which it arises. This point segues into Whewell's second divagation from the Kantian script, through the stress that he affords to corporeality. "Colligation" is physiological activity quite as much as mental operation. If it is impossible to imagine the sensuous manifold without the idea of space, this is not because space is a pure, *a priori* form of intuition, but rather through "the muscular consciousness which reveals to us the position of objects and parts of objects when we feel them out by means of the hand" (*PIS*, 115). Elsewhere, Whewell follows the anatomist and natural theologian Charles Bell's example in calling such "muscular exertion . . . a sixth sense" (*PIS*, 116).

These two emphases—the act of nomination and the motor conduct of the body—shape Whewell's definition of rhythm. Just as the conception of space depends upon prehensile groping, so does temporal successiveness require corporeal activity. "As figure is a conception solely appropriate to space," he writes, "there is also a conception which peculiarly belongs to time, namely, the conception of recurrence of times similarly marked; or, *as it may be termed,* rhythm, using this word in a general sense"; shortly thereafter, he refers back to the "particular modification of time, *which we have called* rhythm" (*PIS*, 126, 135; emphases mine). We should note Whewell's repeated explicit reference to the act of designation.

Rhythm, then, imputes sequence into repetition. Such a phrasing might seem to imply mentation alone: indeed, Whewell writes that rhythmical apprehension involves a "sense of successiveness [that], like the muscular sense with which we have compared it, implies activity of the mind itself." Yet not the mind alone: for even "automatic" acts of mental arithmetic, Whewell continues immediately, ultimately derive from the tactile, manual experience, however much we subsequently forget the etiology (*PIS*, 133).[66] The parallelism between number and embodied rhythm remains operative throughout *The Philosophy of the Inductive Sciences*:

> But if the apprehension of number be accompanied by an act of the mind, the apprehension of rhythm is so still more clearly. All the forms of versification and the measures of melodies are the creations of man, who thus realises in words and sounds the forms of recurrence which rise within his own mind. When we hear in a quiet scene any rapidly-repeated sound, as those made by the hammer of the Smith or the saw of the carpenter, every one knows how insensibly we throw these noises into a rhythmical form in our own ap-

prehension. We do this even without any suggestion from the sounds themselves. For instance, if the beats of a clock or watch be ever so exactly alike, we still reckon them alternately tick-tack, tick-tack. (*PIS*, 263)

Whewell's rhythmical scene proves uncannily like the "unconscious counting" of Schelling's own blacksmith. We can gloss "realises in words and sounds the forms of recurrence which rise within his own mind" in three subtly contrasting ways. The first takes "realise" as an act of comprehension: through attending to the external world we learn something about our own mental processes, which precede and exist independently of such external stimuli. This is absolute idealism. The second takes "realise" in the sense of actuation, rather than comprehension: our mental processes logically precede recurrent external stimuli, but are actively expressed within them. This is process-based idealism. The third exploits the grammatical ambiguity of Whewell's clause to take "his own mind" not as subject but as object: recurrent external stimulus actuates our mental processes. This is inductive realism. This syntactical undecidability appears significant. Human subjects naturally impose measure upon periodic stimuli (the falls of the hammer); so too do they just as naturally derive difference from repetition. Mental processes and recurrent stimuli share a common property of rhythm: yet this force does not only organize subject and object according to a structural parallel. It rather requires specific activity: we carve up the world into related difference, through which we come to recognize ourselves. The subject lives on, like the ticking and tacking of a clock. The gaps that space its self-iterations are constrained not only by cognitive limit but also by corporeal finitude: finite digits. Rather than idealize rhythm, Whewell rhythmizes mathematics.

It is no accident that Whewell explicitly links this "general sense" for rhythm to versification. The alternation of strong and weak, short and long, syllables provides another example of the human need to insinuate difference (*PIS*, xxii).[67] Even here, however, the modulation of subject and object endures. The move from simple repetition to more complex temporal succession only increases the need for the subject to recognize itself, in attempting to bind the acoustic manifold: "In melodies, also, and in verses in which the rhythm is complex, obscure, and difficult, we perceive something is required on our part" (*PIS*, 134). In a series of contributions to the hexameter debate in *Blackwood's* and the *North British Review*, in the later 1840s and 1850s, Whewell developed such ideas in the specific context of versification.[68] (*The North British Review* thus featured significant articles upon rhythm by Patmore and Whewell, within three years of each other; the journal also often featured discussions of German idealism.) His retention of Greek feet, employed so as to express accent rather than quantity, proved very far indeed from Patmore's isochrony. Adherence to a particular prosodic system, however, means less in this case than does the common subscription to a form of German idealism that facilitated an understanding of the intermittences of embodied life. Is rhythm thus finally a Fundamental Idea? *The Philosophy of the Inductive Sciences* never explicitly classes it as such; yet it is hard to see how it cannot be one of those regulative principles that, once discovered, we cannot do without.

Meynell's Deceptive Compliance

Over the following decades, Whewell's link between rhythm as a capacity peculiar to human cognition, and as a demonstrable structure in the external world, would become a commonplace. From the 1880s and 1890s, we begin to see the formulation of such collocations as "the rhythm of life," an expression that is forever on the verge of collapsing into truism. (A quick Google search for the phrase yields jazz, choral, and electrofunk songs, a homeless charity in London, and a self-help book that pledges to help its readers to "live everyday with passion and purpose.") Specific treatments of versification, in this period, often employ an amorphous and undiscriminating notion of rhythm, which enables little other than a contemporary refitting of Augustine's harmonious universe governed by precise *numerus*. Such cosmologies tend to draw sharp distinctions (as between the human and the nonhuman) and to exclude mutability and variation.

Theodore Watts-Duncan's entry for "Poetry" in the ninth edition of the *Encyclopedia Britannica* (1885) offers a case in point. Watts-Duncan, today primarily remembered for his rescue of Swinburne from alcoholism, defines "absolute poetry" as "the concrete and artistic expression of the human mind in emotional and rhythmical language"; verse reflects a broader "rhythm of nature," which is, in turn, "the rhythm of life itself."[69] This numinous phrasing serves notice of a stark distinction between thinking and experience. Watts-Duncan establishes a binary between poets, such as Lucretius or Wordsworth, who deal primarily with "the distinct and logical enunciation of ideas'" while Sappho, Pindar, and Shelley generate "the suggestive richness of passion or symbol latent in rhythm." (Elizabeth Barrett Browning figures intriguingly as the supreme contemporary instance of rhythmical "energy.") This distinction requires a similarly stratified conception of metrical repertoires: Watts-Duncan opposes "weighty iambic movements whose primary function is to state" to more metrically heterodox productions such as Shelley's "Sensitive Plant," which rather dance or sing.[70] Yet Watts-Duncan never analyzes the nature of this "absolute" expression, preferring to fall back upon a notion of rhythm that recalls nothing so much as Samuel Johnson's old dictionary entry from over a hundred years before: "rhythm . . . can never be formulated but only expressed . . . in the harmony of the entire bird-chorus of a thicket."[71]

Singing and dancing are not, however, contentless forms. Patmore's pauses demonstrated how even the empty break can conduct a philosophical enquiry into embodied experience that rivals anything that academic phenomenology can offer. Like Watts-Duncan, Alice Meynell came to rely upon the phrase "rhythm of life," which offered a title both to one of her most influential essays, and to the wider collection in which it was printed. In her hands, however, the phrase means much more than a numinous truism: she extends the idealist focus upon caesura so as to give a specifically gendered account of embodied experience. Following in while also deviating from the footsteps of Patmore, her deceptively compliant verse actuates corporeal affordance and constraint.

"Periodicity rules over the mental experience of man," "The Rhythm of Life" commences: lunar tides, spherical orbits, the passage from cradle to grave offer cases in point; "disease is metrical, closing in at shorter and shorter periods."[72] Yet Meynell departs from Watts-Duncan's cosmology through her consistent emphasis upon the lived experiences of such processes, which, however regular they may prove, often come to be experienced as disjunction. Even should we be able to plot our alternations between happiness and melancholy on a waveform chart, we could never adopt a transcendental attitude to it: "[g]aiety takes us by a dear surprise," however much we anticipate its periods.[73]

Of all the parts of "metrical" life that we suffer, Meynell focuses upon one in particular: the caesura that had proven so central to idealism. "The Rhythm of Life" charts various such interruptions: the devotional ecstasy of Thomas à Kempis; the periodic departures of a Muse that Percy Bysshe Shelley cannot know will return; and finally, the "rhythmic pangs of maternity."[74] Meynell's closing four words are stunning for their abrupt concision and unconcern with elaboration: a learned discussion of interruption turns out also to have been marking the gendered body all along. Meynell's "pangs" develop the tension between two understandings of periodic break: the rational knowledge that pause regulates and guarantees sequence, on the one hand, and the lived fear that in this singular case it does not precede return (the Muse stays away, the child fails to be born). We know, or think we know, that the catalectic line will finally enjamb into the object of its desire and the completion of its sense, because that is what we have seen and known poems to do, yet within us develops the apprehension, as the pause extends, that the voice will not resume. We can retrospectively incorporate this break within a scansion that, we tell ourselves, we always knew would come about, but that does not cancel the fear that we felt. Here, at last, do we find something like a working definition of Hölderlin's "counter-rhythmical interruption," restored to its original context (poetic meter), whose force does not simply cancel the rhythmical passage of time, as Benjamin suggested, but requires the latter, in order to be felt *as* disjunction. Meynell's own verse practice keenly intuited this fact: her poetry, seemingly more "orthodox" than Patmore's wild catalexes in its broad adherence to foot-based prosody, repeatedly marks how breaks require the patterns from which they break.

This differing attitude towards metrical convention facilitates Meynell's treatment of gendered experience. Patmore's heterodox erotic worship belied his reputation for abstraction; yet we should remember that the fantasy of androgyny is in practice frequently the privilege of the established male poet. In her reading of Meynell's later poem "The Laws of Verse," Yopie Prins explores the conjunction between (apparent) metrical compliance and gendered expression. The final quatrain beseeches regularity itself:

> Dear laws, come to my breast!
> Take all my frame, and make your close arms meet
> Around me; and so ruled, so warmed, so pressed,
> I breathe, aware; I feel my wild heart beat. (1–4)

"The rhythm of the woman's wild heartbeat," Prins summarizes, "has been transformed into the metrical form of her poem, intensifying its effect (and its affect) through a formalization rather than personalization of passion."[75] I find this connection of affect and formalization suggestive, yet elusive. Does it mean that instinctive feeling intensifies itself through the emphatic patterning of iambs? Or does such affect emerge *despite* what remains a traditional metrical structure, just as the necessity for eighteenth-century poetesses to dress up singular suffering in allegorical guises generates a distinctive pathos of its own? In the related claim that we are "able to 'feel' a wild heart that beats within the regularity of its iambic pentameter lines,"[76] the "within" thus remains ambiguous. But perhaps we should question whether the lines in question truly *are* perfectly regular in the first instance. The final line certainly does conform to the general pattern: its ten syllables arrange pronouns and possessive pronouns in weak positions so as to underscore the duple rhythm. Yet this iambic patterning only attunes us to a minor yet significant variation (significant because minor), which touches precisely the point under discussion. "Wild" does indeed receive appropriate stress; yet we would typically also accentuate the monosyllabic substantive "heart"—all the more so when Meynell chooses to write "heart beat" rather than "heartbeat." The supernumerary beat of the heart thus produces arrhythmia. That this constitutes an artistic choice rather than a metrical lapse is confirmed by Meynell's use of the same effect two lines previously, where an emphatic iambic rhythm gives way to the ambiguous stress of the hoped-for "arms."

The purchase of Meynell's verse inheres in these undemonstrative microadjustments. Patmore frequently damned her performance with faint praise: Prins recalls an unpleasant passage in his occasional verse, where "I read her praise while, sweet / She gazed in contemplation / Of her fame and her small feet."⁷⁷ Yet perhaps Meynell communicated more with her "small feet" than Patmore supposed. Another essay collected in *The Rhythm of Life* suggests as much: "Unstable Equilibrium" rather eccentrically praises the male leg and the female foot, both of which grant motility to their respective owners. "A lifeless structure," writes Meynell, "is in stable equilibrium; the body, springing, poised, upon its fine ankles and narrow feet, never stands without implying and expressing life." The slender and supple foot does not ground so much as provide a platform for flight.⁷⁸

The unstable equilibrium of the female foot offers a good summary of similar micro-adjustments, two further instances of which I will consider more fully. The first occurs within one of her finest sonnets, "Renouncement":

> I must not think of thee; and, tired yet strong,
>   I shun the thought that lurks in all delight—
>   The thought of thee—and in the blue heaven's height,
> And in the sweetest passage of a song.
>
> Oh, just beyond the fairest thoughts that throng
>   This breast, the thought of thee waits hidden yet bright;
>   But it must never, never come in sight;
> I must stop short of thee the whole day long.
>
> But when sleep comes to close each difficult day,
>   When night gives pause to the long watch I keep,
>   And all my bonds I needs must loose apart,
>
> Must doff my will as raiment laid away,—
>   With the first dream that comes with the first sleep
>   I run, I run, I am gathered to thy heart.⁷⁹

This Petrarchan sonnet again conducts a struggle with duple meter that is all the deeper for being unobtrusive. The first line imposes an appropriate medial caesura at the end of the sixth syllable, only to follow it immediately with a far less conventional punctuated pause that follows the seventh, as if this "tired" verse panted for breath. What remains of the octet recovers itself into an iambic pentameter whose composure is only briefly ruffled: punctuated caesuras now balance rather than imperil the verse's progress, with the emphatically duple rhythm practically compelling us to stress even small particles such as the "in" of lines 3 and 4, the "it" of line 7, whose unexpected accent nonetheless accrues a slight frisson of erotic mystery. "I must stop short of thee the whole day long" represents the acme of this process of self-denial. Its painfully accented monosyllabicity (we might stress six stresses) offers one of the most gloriously boring lines in English verse. Seldom has willed monotony more perfectly captured the drudgery of moral restraint.

Yet the sestet tests these self-imposed bounds by degrees. The typographic layout of the poem cues us for this transformation, as the ebb and flow of the quatrains gives rise to the ebb and ebb of the closing tercets. These do not only act as visual counterparts to the shifting rhyme scheme, but also signal a self-abandonment that proceeds by small degrees, and not without resistance. Small tremors presage the end: the iambic pattern has to work a little harder to promote the conjunction "when" and to relegate the substantive "sleep" into metrical compliance; the polysyllabic "difficult" throws a further little spanner in the works. The following line proves still more disruptive, without ever quite rising to the status of dissonance or syncopation: "night gives pause" offers another example of where we might press out three successive stresses, whose force contrasts with the succeeding stop words ("to the"), in turn succeeded by two more heavily stressed long vowels ("long watch"). The iambic pattern, then, is increasingly caught between flurries of successive stress or unstress. The accumulated force that culminates in "pause" forces us, appropriately, to pause, before rushing on.

The successive lines in this closing sestet communicate scant information: they offer nearly tautological variations upon the same theme ("when I prepare myself for sleep"), which only stoke anticipation for whichever "it" has been (a little too declaratively) renounced. We can only surmise the referent for that indeterminate pronoun-cum-noun; our surmise might tell us more than we want to know. By the penultimate line, it has become impossible to uphold the iambic pattern to which affect once voluntarily submitted, with the voice caught unambiguously between unstressed and stressed parallelisms (respectively: "with the," "with the"; "first dream," "first dream"). Nothing more than slight stress promotions and demotions prepare the way for a release that, when it comes, discharges itself powerfully: "I run, I run" still forces its stated energy into the confines of the iambic foot; yet the long-deferred subsequent release loses itself in a triple measure that the verse finally fully embraces. Few subtler turns exist in the English sonnet tradition.

"Renouncement" counts as a deeply embodied poem, because of and not despite its concealment of the object of desire; its minor checks and releases, fluxes and refluxes, constitute a superfine attentiveness to the temporal apprehension of longing. Its self-imposed and therefore never total restraint contrasts strongly with Patmore's more flamboyant professions. Yet it does not directly engage what I took to be the decisive closing shift of "The Rhythm of Life": the specific rhythmical experience of the gendered body. To this end, I turn finally to one more instance of Meynell's positively minor lyric, "Cradle Song at Twilight." Where "Renouncement" only figured pause as theme or as rhythmical hitch within syllabically regular lines, this strange lullaby offers one of the comparatively rare modifications of Patmore's catalexis:

> The child not yet is lulled to rest.
>   Too young a nurse, the slender Night
> So laxly holds him to her breast
>   That throbs with flight.
>
> He plays with her, and will not sleep.
>   For other playfellows she sighs;
> An unmaternal fondness keep
>   Her alien eyes.[80]

Each quatrain's terminal line features a catalexis that Meynell regulates more regularly and modestly than Patmore's drastic truncations. But the slightest undulations in stress again make all the difference. Meynell sets up another consistently iambic pattern, the better to trouble it, lightly: the singsong quality of the first two lines, contrived rather than naïve, causes us to relegate the "him" and "her" that follows, downplaying the presence of both infant and nurse. We seek a way to discharge the four stresses to which we have become accustomed into the final catalectic line, whose force is the greater for being self-contained: the desire for "flight" both knows and relinquishes itself through the end-stop against which it comes up short.

The second quatrain starts in similar fashion, with more perfect iambs underscoring the activity of the sleepless child ("plays," "will," "sleep") and the objecthood that his nurse ("her") thereby assumes. Yet the metrical ambiguity of what ensues drastically shifts the poem's seat of agency. To say that we move from the subject position of the truculent child to that of his caregiver would be to overstate things, so little do we learn of the latter. Yet her very obliquity now predominates: the unprovoked metrical clumsiness of "playfellows" shakes us awake from the placid rhythms of singsong. The final two lines are the strangest portions of this strange quiet poem: as with the first quatrain, enjambment issues in an end-stopped catalectic unit. We might first read the awkward verb "keep" in a subjunctive mood, as if "unmaternal fondness" were the grammatical actor, before the enjambed clause reveals the syntactical inversion. "'Her alien eyes" belatedly supplies a subject that had perhaps been watching us all the while; its inscrutability resists the desire for knowledge that child and reader, both of whom have nearly been rocked to sleep, share. "The rhythmic pangs of maternity" thereby exceeds the contractions of actual labor, so as to register the aftershocks and vicissitudes of postpartum affect. The "rhythm of life" once meant something beyond a platitude of plenitude: Meynell made it so, by submitting to its disjunctions. The idealist caesura stitches up its separate iterations, to discover that it has a body.

After-contractions

It is instructive to consider how this conceptualization and practice of rhythm survived (or failed to survive) into modernism and beyond. We continue in this respect to be hobbled by some of the more grandiloquent claims regarding the putative liberation of free verse from metrical shackles: Ezra Pound's "absolute rhythm" offers a case in point. Yet Meynell's example proves that rhythmical variability depends upon a periodic variance for its effect; this periodic variation can be much more than a prison from which we ceaselessly break. The very modernists who most enthusiastically celebrated their escape from past strictures often inadvertently retained them. Virginia Woolf famously declared herself to have discovered a new form of writing "to a rhythm and not a plot": the former term implied impressionistic description rather than analytical precision. Alice Meynell, indeed, represented precisely the sort of artist from which Woolf sought to distance herself: as Talia Schaffer puts it, she "saw Meynell as a larger-than-life figure who embodied every gender idea Woolf was resisting."[81]

It is therefore all the more striking how Meynell's female caesurae surface again in even Woolf's most experimental passages. Take the moment in *Orlando,* where the eponymous protagonist, having become a woman, buckles under the piles of longwinded nineteenth-century books. The narrative voice launches into one of its characteristic digressions, apostrophizing everything in the world "that interrupts and confounds the tapping of typewriters": hymns about death, the red lips of shop girls. A barrel-organ grinds beneath Woolf's prose, which now abruptly turns in an untoward direction: "For dark flows the stream—would it were true, as the rhyme hints 'like a dream'—but duller and worser than that is our usual lot; without dreams, but alive, smug, fluent, habitual, under trees whose shade of an olive green drowns the blue of the wing of the vanishing bird when he darts of a sudden from bank to bank."[82]

"Kew will do" toys with rhyme as infantile pastiche. Yet a less obviously parodic engagement with verse convention tradition unfolds with Woolf's subsequent triple rhythm:

— ′ — — ′ — — ′ — — ′ — — ′ — —

the blue of the wing of the vanishing bird when he darts of a

′ — — ′ — — ′

sudden from bank to bank

This unusually emphatic prose rhythm no sooner gets established than it is interrupted by a premonition of dread that arrives through disjointed syntax: "Hail, happiness, then, and after happiness, hail not those dreams which bloat the sharp image as spotted mirrors do the face in a country-inn parlour; dreams which splinter the whole and tear us asunder and wound us and split us apart in the night when we would sleep; but sleep, sleep, so deep that all shapes are ground to dust of infinite softness, water of dimness inscrutable, and there, folded, shrouded, like a mummy, like a moth, prone let us lie on the sand at the bottom of sleep." This tearing interruption transfigures the anapests to which we finally return, in what amounts to one of the most remarkable extended passages of English prose rhythm. Following the punctuation-laden paratactic pile-up, we again hit another clear stretch of triple measure. Yet where Woolf's short vowels had previously emulated flight, the drawn-out vowels of "prone let us lie on the sand at the bottom of sleep" rather bear us down to the underworld.

The parallels are uncanny: like Meynell, Woolf manipulates the little feet of metrical regularity to let us take flight; like Meynell, Woolf interrupts a lullaby that then re-intrudes in more disturbed (and disturbing) form; like Meynell, the body knows itself only after the event of rhythmical disjunction. What might have seemed a philosopher's private dark night of the soul turns out to mean also something else altogether: "Orlando was safely delivered of a son on Thursday, March the 20th, at three o'clock in the morning." The text undergoes (and thereby knows) violent contractions that surface only with necessary belatedness as rational apprehension. The pangs of maternity.

How willfully did Woolf train her anapests? This interesting question misses the point. At the very moment that it attacks the legacy of the nineteenth century, modernist prose recalls the cultural memory of meter. With it survives, in trace form, the idealist thinking of rhythmical disjunction. We sometimes like to think an appeal to the primordial body necessarily suggests simpler rhythmical modes: heartbeats and pulses produce iambs and polkas, all so that more sophisticated forms such as free jazz, serialism, and streams of consciousness can then dismember standard time signatures. But perhaps we have not thought about what the heartbeat means in the first place. For a start—from *the* start—it never is single. The fetus hears its own cardiac rhythm in relay with that of its mother: "We know that the fetus is capable of responding both to pressure and to sound, and that the beating of its own heart at about 140 beats per minute and the beating of its mother's heart, with a frequency of 70, provides it with something of a syncopated world of sound."[83] Two precedes one: syncopation precedes straight meter. Whewell was the first to formulate rhythm as a distinctive human capacity, by which we impose measure upon the multiform, disparity upon repetition. We do not only constitute the world in this manner; we are also the difference that gets made.

3

Entraining Rhythms

Mollusks and Other Oscillators

In a series of unfinished reflections composed in 1868, but only published in 1963 under the title "Notes on Form in Art," George Eliot ventures a striking analogy:

> Poetic Form was not begotten by thinking it out or framing it as a shell which should hold emotional expression, any more than the shell of an animal arises before the living creature; but emotion, by its tendency to repetition, i.e., rhythmic persistence in proportion as diversifying thought is absent, creates a form by the recurrence of its elements in adjustment with certain given conditions of sound, language, action, or environment. Just as the beautiful expanding curves of a bivalve shell are not first made for the reception of the unstable inhabitant, but grow and are limited by the simple rhythmic conditions of its growing life.[1]

Eliot was following a distinguished lineage of mollusk eulogy: in categorically refuting any suggestion that it had "been made by an intelligent being," Darwin nonetheless joined William Paley in noting "the beautiful hinge of the bivalve shell."[2] A characteristically Victorian craze for marine exploration had by this stage already manifested itself in Samuel Peckworth Woodward's *A Manual of the Mollusca* (1851), Charles Kingsley's *Glaucus; or, The Wonders of the Shore* (1855), and George Henry Lewes's *Sea-Side Studies at Ilfracombe, Tenby, the Scilly Isles, and Jersey* (1858).[3] Figure 8 reproduces one of the lavish plates that Lewes appended to his work, showcasing the

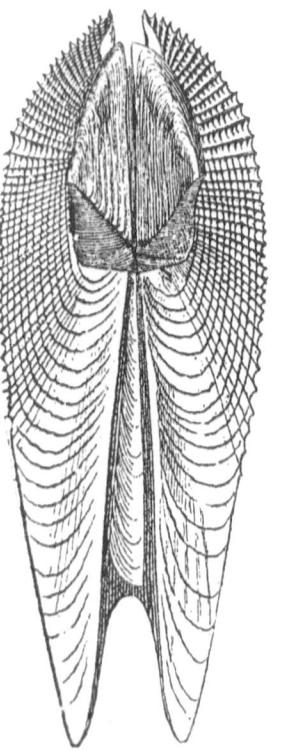

FIGURE 8. George Henry Lewes, *Sea-Side Studies at Ilfracombe, Tenby, the Scilly Isles, and Jersey* (1860), 429

shell of the *Pholas dactylus,* or common paddock, a bioluminescent clam-like mollusk.

On the heels of considering idealist philosophy and the human apprehension of temporality, this chapter's abrupt swerve to simple invertebrates might seem something of a letdown in the grand scheme of things. Yet Eliot's "simple rhythmic conditions" themselves confute this hierarchy: across the 1850s and 1860s, variations on this concept enabled thinkers across a variety of established and emergent sciences to pose anew the relationship between "civilized" and "primitive" cultures, and between human and non-human life. We previously witnessed how the nascent concept of rhythm enabled idealism to bring together nonidentical entities into a differential relation. The hard sciences did not supersede so much as transfigure this pattern of thinking. Lewes himself illustrates this complex intellectual development perhaps more clearly than any other individual: while he liked to describe a *volte-face* from card-carrying young Hegelian to rugged British empiricist, his attempted development of "discontinuous" evolution (in explicit opposition to Darwin's more seamless materialism) betrays clear residues of idealism.[4]

Lewes vacillates over his partner's speculative elision of human and invertebrate. "I have no doubt the mollusc is a moral individual," he sardonically allows toward the beginning of *Sea-Side Studies*, "but you cannot consider him to be greatly impassioned; an oyster, or a limpet, may have his theory of life: but you cannot appeal to his finer sensibilities through the medium of music, poetry, or painting."[5] Yet protracted cohabitation with marine life serves to change Lewes's tune: returning from Ilfracombe to London, where a mess of proofs and business meetings await him, he observes that "the iodine of the sea-breezes had entered me. I felt that I had 'suffered a sea change' into something zoological and strange. Men began to appear like molluscs; and their ways the ways of creatures in a larger rock-pool."[6] Elsewhere, Lewes has fun pointing out to a "a large white-waistcoated" philosopher that the human eye is "nothing more than a tactile organ" comparable, in this respect, to the Pleurohranchus and Aplysia mollusks.[7] Finally, and rather more grandly, *Sea-Side Studies* likens human habitations to a "parasitic animal living on a grander creature—an epizöon nestling in the skin of this planetary organism, which rolls through space like a ciliated ovum rolling through a drop of water."[8]

The concept of rhythm facilitates this uncertainty over the relations between invertebrates, nonhuman mammals, and *homo sapiens*. The vivisection of a sea gooseberry ("the compassionate reader ... will probably feel some repulsion at the quiet way in which he is recommended to snip off the Cydippe's tentacles," Lewes concedes) produces what he takes to be mere reflex contractions.[9] Yet in *The Physiology of Common Life*, published a year before *Sea-Side Studies*, the same dissecting knife troubles the distinction between human and nonhuman vertebrates: "Remove [the heart] from the body, and you will see its rhythmic pulsations continuing almost as if it were within a living breast. . . . This is one of the spectacles that assail the mind of the anatomist with somewhat of a tremulous awe. The beating of the heart, which from his childhood he has learned to associate in some mysterious manner with life and emotion, he here sees occurring under circumstances removed from all possible suggestions of emotion or life. What mean those throbbings?"[10] These "throbbings" presumably denote the frog's anatomized heart, rather than the "tremulous awe" of the anatomist. Yet even by suggesting a relation between them, Lewes postulates a law of rhythmical sympathy that cuts across species distinctions. (*The Physiology of Common Life* later similarly likens "the rhythmic contractions in the hearts of birds and mammals two days after death" to the continuing cardiac movements of a woman, three days after her being guillotined.)[11]

My previous chapter focused upon the ways in which philosophical idealism postulated a specific human aptitude for rhythmical apprehension. This capacity was "fitted" to periodic stimuli: yet the subject that was to be reconciled to its object in this manner remained significantly single. Lewes's rhythmical "pulsations," by contrast, radiate out beyond the human; they intimate a pattern of contagious transmission between both subjects and species. This chapter will explore how the biological appropriation of the concept of rhythm enabled a consideration not only of the individual but also of the composite whole: the nonhuman groups upon whom this analysis so often functioned in turn permitted a new conception of specifically human society.

Perhaps the clearest indication of this tendency arrives in the guise of Herbert Spencer, the close friend and constant interlocutor of Eliot and Lewes who will play a significant role across the final two chapters of this book. Lewes's physiological writings serve notice of the distinct ways in which rhythm begins to operate, following its establishment in anglophone discourse: it decomposes the unitary organism into a series of smaller organs or distributed nervous centers, whose "pulsations" or "contractions" can outlive their hosts; it further connects these distributed nervous systems to other distributed nervous systems (as when the amputated frog's heart produces cardiac response in the anatomist); and it finally assembles separate entities into composite socialities that resist standard distinctions between "individual" and "community."

Spencer's 1860 essay "The Social Organism" develops each of these interlocking claims. The work relies extensively upon Thomas Henry Huxley's *The Oceanic Hydrozoan*, published the previous year, in which Huxley offered an account of his marine observation during a stint as assistant surgeon on the survey vessel HMS *Rattlesnake* from 1846 to 1850. Like Lewes before and Eliot after him, Spencer would derive an unexpected significance from these simple invertebrates, although at first it appears that they offer little more than a negative contrast to modern society. "In complexity," he declares early in the essay, "our large civilised nations as much exceed primitive savage tribes, as a mammal does a zoophyte."[12]

Yet Spencer never makes the leap that would take him all the way from polyps and sea squirts to vertebrates. Instead, his attention is magnetically drawn back to organisms such as "the Hydra," the "*Polyzoa* or *Molluscoida*," and "The Ascidian Mollusks," all of whom exhibit "various degrees of union among the component individuals." These composite entities form and move in distinctive ways: "In the *Calycophoridæ* some of the polypes growing from the common germ, become developed and modified into large, long, sack-like bodies, which, by their rhythmical contractions, move through the water, dragging the community of polypes after them." This law of rhythmical development finally enables the creation of a distributed nervous system, which in turn permits Spencer's speculative metaphor for human society: "In the *Physophoridæ* a variety of organs similarly arise by transformation of the budding polypes; so that in creatures like the *Physalia*, commonly known as the 'Portuguese Man-of-war,' instead of that tree-like group of similar individuals forming the original type, we have a complex mass of unlike parts fulfilling unlike duties. . . . This differentiation upon differentiation is just what takes place during the evolution of a civilized society."[13] Spencer's evolutionary sociology (here as elsewhere) frequently underwrites class distinctions; nevertheless, these speculative invertebrate analogies prove radically decentralizing. As James Elwick has demonstrated, Spencer's adherence to the disputed biological concept of "composite individuality" (where entities such as salp swim in synchronized chains yet always reproduce as individual organisms) contrasts starkly with Huxley's own top-down and Hobbesian zoo-sociology.[14] Leviathan, in the latter's "Administrative Nihilism," becomes the centralized processing system, ruling all other constituent parts with a rod of iron: "The brain, like other despots whom we have known, calls out at once for sharp steel."[15]

Spencer, by contrast, increasingly retains the "lower organic existence" that he has seemed about to slough off, in his promise to offer a progressive account of the transition from invertebrate to vertebrate, from "primitive" to "civilized" society. In the end, he concludes, complexly interdependent human communities frequently resemble those "lowest animals, characterized by the absence of a nervous system [where] such sensitiveness as exists is possessed by all parts."[16] The nascent concept of rhythm provides an indispensable means of describing the interactions between these distributed agents. Take this concluding passage from "The Social Organism":

> Only animals of tolerably complete organizations, like advanced communities, are permeated by constant currents that are definitely directed. In living bodies, the local and variable currents disappear when there grow up great centres of circulation, generating more powerful currents by a rhythm which ends in a quick, regular pulsation. And when in social bodies there arise great centres of commercial activity, producing and exchanging large quantities of commodities, the rapid and continuous streams drawn in and emitted by these centres subdue all minor and local circulations: the slow rhythm of fairs merges into the faster one of weekly markets, and in the chief centres of distribution, weekly markets merge into daily markets; while in place of the languid transfer from place to place, taking place at first weekly, then twice or thrice a week, we by-and-by get daily transfer, and finally transfer many times a day— the original sluggish, irregular rhythm, becomes a rapid, equable pulse.[17]

This form of thinking suggestively anticipates Georg Simmel's own efforts to describe and measure the rhythms of capitalist accumulation.[18] Despite the interest that Marxists such as Bukharin took in Spencer's biological materialism, it would be a mistake to overstate any challenge to the accelerating rhythms of industrial capitalism: Spencer presumably prefers the "rapid, equable pulse" to the "sluggish, irregular rhythm." Yet when we bear in mind his contention with Huxley over the centralized (or distributed) biological body politic, I do not think it is a stretch to read a tinge of regret into the verb "subdue." Perhaps Spencer's sympathies remained with the mollusk.

Odd Sympathy

In order to clarify the scope and stakes of this zoological recruitment of rhythm, I wish to introduce a concept that has recently accrued significance in the otherwise disparate fields of biology and ethnomusicology: entrainment. Entrainment designates the tendency for individual oscillators to synchronize (or "entrain") endogenous rhythms to an external period or phase. "Individual oscillators" might denote human beings such as you or me, tapping our toes in a Swedish cinema; or the separate organs of which such organisms are composed (the hearts that Lewes cut from his frogs). Where Lewes devoted countless hours to the minute study of mollusks, polyps, and amoebae, biological studies of entrainment consider the phase locking of still smaller organisms such as cyanobacteria (to which we owe a great deal, given their contribution to the oxidization of the world). Sleep and menstrual cycles, the firing of neurons in the brain, all offer ready instances of entrainment, as do certain forms of non-Western music whose tempo responds to external conditions. The "rhythm method" of speech therapy, which my first chapter explores, offers another concrete example. A recent study has shown that when parents read nursery rhymes to their children, while continuing to make eye contact, the brain waves of adult and infant entrain.[19]

Entrainment helps us to orient the pattern of thinking that I have begun to sketch in Eliot, Lewes, and Spencer, where the burgeoning concept of rhythm designates not merely an objective property (of an organism, say, or metrical poem), nor a means of subjective apprehension (as Whewell had it), but also the porous and reciprocal interaction of separate entities. In their excellent summary of current literature on the subject, Martin Clayton, Rebecca Sager, and Udo Will demonstrate a means of conceiving the social order that is uncannily akin to Spencer's rhythmized economy: "The multiple independent cycles of activity of the members of a social system become coordinated with one another into a temporally patterned system of activity that is characterized by a dynamic equilibrium rather than by a fixed homeostatic pattern."[20] (We recall Spencer's definition of rhythm as conflictual disequilibrium.) In its early adoption of a concept that was yet to be formulated, the nineteenth century did more than simply "anticipate" or "dramatize" entrainment; it also tested its ethical consequences in ways that hold enduring relevance.

We can begin to glimpse this contemporary relevance by adverting to the first recorded instance of phase locking. In 1665 the Dutch horologist Chris-

FIGURE 9. Christiaan Huygens's 1665 drawing of his synchronizing pendula, from volume 17 of *Oeuvres completes de Christiaan Huygens*

tiaan Huygens lay ill in bed, surrounded by a number of pendula that he had assembled in order to measure the longitude coordinate at sea. Huygens's convalescent attention was caught by two clocks whose initially distinct oscillations appeared gradually to synchronize (fig. 9): having recovered his health and confirmed his impression, Huygens dashed off an excited letter to the Royal Society, where he named the uncanny phenomenon "odd sympathy." (We now know that pendulums entrain when a communicative medium—such as the wooden beam from which Huygens's clocks were suspended—enables a transfer of energy small enough to generate a negative feedback loop.)

Clayton, Sager, and Will establish a cardinal distinction between such phenomena and other forms of material-sonorous communication: "Resonance, for example, is not to be considered entrainment: if a tuning fork producing sound waves in a resonance box is removed, the oscillations in the box also cease. This is an important point, because it alerts us to the possibility that the mere observation of synchronized behaviour or synchronous variation in two variables does not necessarily imply entrainment."[21] This technical distinction allows us to disarticulate Huygens's "odd sympathy" from the sympathetic resonance with which it might otherwise be confused. This latter phenomenon was already well known in antiquity: the Chinese and Greco-Roman world established that harmonic resonance at the level of the octave or the unison could cause an instrument's untouched strings to vibrate.[22] Such sonorous coincidence inspired several "musical" cosmologies, in which the human body would take its place within a balanced musical order, figured as lute or harp (the Greek *neuron* and the Latin *nervus* similarly mean both "tendon" and "string"). "We resemble instruments, whose strings are our passions," writes Diderot, in a note to his translation of Shaftesbury's *Principles of Moral Philosophy*. "The madman is too highly-strung, the instrument screeches; they are too low for the fool, the instrument is deaf. . . . If, when an instrument is tuned, you pluck a string, the resultant sound produces tremors [*des frémissements*], and in nearby instruments if their strings are harmonically taut in proportion to the plucked string."[23]

I recount this familiar intellectual history partly to show that we require finer-grained precision than the generic claims that sympathy is "embodied" or "musical." My introduction observed with some surprise Samuel Johnson's definition of "rhythmical" and "harmonious" as synonyms. Entrainment permits their historical and analytical separation. For Diderot's harmonious concord relates subject and world quite differently than does Eliot's "rhythmic persistence." With the figuration of human-as-lute, the resonant subject either receives external stimulus in an attitude of total passivity (think the divine "intellectual breeze" that in Coleridge's "Aeolian Harp" sweeps over the inert speaker) or—as in the "taut" madman—actively transposes all qualia into their own dominant pitch.

The figuration of human-as-oscillator, by contrast, postulates a less asymmetrical, more porous relationship between subject and external world. The individual oscillator possesses an endogenous rhythm before it comes into contact with an external phase: having done so, the conjunction produces a further periodicity that proves irreducible to its constituents. Related differences flow from this distinction. While subject-as-lute routinely describes a singular event of concordance within the organism, or between it and its environment, subject-as-oscillator treats rhythms that become established over long periods of time, or which degrade (Huygens's oscillators phase-lock only then to fall once more out of step). If this conceptual disarticulation risks making sympathetic entrainment sound like dialectical free jazz, in contrast to sympathetic resonance's staid subject-object oppositions, I should clarify that I mean the former in a descriptive rather than an evaluative sense. As we shall see, indeed, sympathetic entrainment often generates specific and fraught ethical problems.

A distinction between "harmonious" and rhythmical "sympathy" arises across the eighteenth century. Adam Smith's *Theory of Moral Sentiments* exemplifies the tendency in its evocation of a suffering individual who

> longs for that relief which nothing can afford him but the entire concord of the affections of the spectators with his own. To see the emotions of their hearts, in every respect, beat time to his own, in the violent and disagreeable passions, constitutes his sole consolation. But he can only hope to obtain this by lowering his passion to that pitch, in which the spectators are capable of going along with him. He must flatten, if I may be allowed to say so, the sharpness of its natural tone, in order to reduce it to harmony and concord with the emotions of those who are about him.[24]

On a first read, Smith's supplementation of pitch ("concord") with tempo ("beat time") might seem no more than elegant variation; *The Theory of Moral Sentiments* does indeed sometimes treat synchrony and harmony as interchangeable figurations of "correct" sympathetic response.[25] Yet we can also read the above passage in sequential rather than logical terms: here "beat time" denotes an automatic corporeal response to "disagreeable passions," which can only be meliorated through a volitional "flattening" into proper "pitch."

Indeed, whether by accident or design, *The Theory of Moral Sentiments* employs variations on "beating time" to connote what Teresa Brennan termed the transmission of affect: a form of sympathy that is immediate, somatic, and contagious.[26] As with the above passage, this automatic response (communicated through the metaphor of synchronization) often stands in need of immediate correction. "Our heart," writes Smith with regard to the observation of suffering in another, "as it adopts and beats time to his grief, so is it likewise animated with that spirit by which he endeavors to drive away or destroy the cause of it."[27] An "indolent and passive fellow-feeling" that is rooted in the body needs once again to "give way" to what Smith calls a more "vigorous and active" response.

This contagious embodiment induces palpable discomfort, even when Smith appears to endorse the automatic response in question: we read that there is "some degree of sympathy, even with hunger.... The disposition of body which is habitual to a man in health, makes his stomach easily keep time, if I may be allowed so coarse an expression, with the one, and not with the other."[28] Yet the synchronization of hearts or stomachs does not always produce what Smith repeatedly calls "social harmony": for "persons of delicate fibres and a weak constitution of body," beholding "the sores and ulcers which are exposed by beggars in the streets" can produce "an itching or uneasy sensation in the corresponding part of their own bodies." Such responses are often significantly communal: "The mob, when they are gazing at a dancer on the slack rope, naturally writhe and twist and balance their own bodies as they see him do."[29]

The nineteenth century only amplifies Adam Smith's unease regarding emotional contagion, along with the rhythmical vehicles through which it is expressed. This despite Mary Fairclough's concluding assertion, in her study of romantic-era communal sympathy, that

> the increasingly sophisticated understanding of nervous communication in nineteenth-century medicine ensures that the quasi-occult language of sympathetic association disappears from such accounts. Winter notes that the association between sympathy and instinctive physiological phenomena such as coughing and blinking was "supplanted" in the 1830s by new physiological research on reflex action; if sympathy enters medical discourse, it tends to be understood as an emotional quality. . . . Sympathy thus becomes an individualised and privatised phenomenon even when it operates in a social context.[30]

I find this broad sketch questionable. As we have seen, the eighteenth-century conception of sympathy (to say nothing of its forbears) already thoroughly integrates the embodied nervous system. Conversely, the later nineteenth century does not break the link between physiology and sympathy; rather, it radicalizes it. The stark (and ultra-Smithian) distinction between sympathy as "an individualized and privatised phenomenon," and contagious yet content-less phenomena "such as coughing and blinking," proves untenable. The nineteenth century increasingly develops Smith's budding concept of a sympathetic response that would be somatic, reflexive, and above all, rhythmical.

Charles Dickens's *A Tale of Two Cities* serves as a striking and peculiar case in point. When George Eliot appealed to prose realism to provide "the extension of our sympathies," we often understand this perceived virtue

The sea rises

FIGURE 10. "Phiz," "The Sea Rises," *All the Year Round* (September 1859); issued 23 July 1859

broadly in keeping with Smith's positive, harmonious notion: as a volitional, rational projection of self into the other. Yet Dickens's revolutionary period piece discharges a barrage of "instinctive physiological phenomena," nearly as reflexive as "coughing and blinking," yet which tell us far more about the human condition. Phiz's illustrations, which accompanied the novel's serial publication in *All the Year Round*, luridly depict such contagion (fig. 10). Where eighteenth-century moral philosophy prefers to figure human bodies as stringed or wind instruments, "The Sea Rises" foregrounds percussion, where the revolutionary matron brandishes a bloodied cleaver in one hand, a drum mallet in the other.

A series of shrill narrative interjections render explicit Dickens's own repulsion at such scenes. Yet they also generate something ultimately more interesting than the stark opposition between cleaver-and-mallet-wielding revolutionary, on the one hand, and bland paragons of virtue such as Charles and Lucie Darnay, on the other. This sympathetic tension frequently emerges because of, and not despite, the oft-noticed flatness of characterization in *A Tale of Two Cities,* which communicates what a parlor-room full of depth studies cannot. Like no other of Dickens's novels, *A Tale of Two Cities* charts the periodic moments of crisis at which individuated human beings, with proper names and the rest, begin to break down under the force of external pressures, until they find their endogenous rhythms entraining to external stimuli. "The Sea Also Rises" contains very little of this ambiguity, in part because of its visual medium, which permits detached spectatorship and judgment of the baying mob. Dickens's inimitable prose, by contrast, entrains its readers long before they realize the end to which its rhythmical periods inevitably tend.

This process is strange and subtle enough to render finally unanswerable the question of whether Dickens knew what on earth he was doing. One of the first of a series of seismic spikes and seizures in the narrator's habitual equanimity arrives in his at-first quite reasonable moral disapproval of Stryver: the barrister, in order to assuage his disappointment at having been rejected by the morally pristine Lucie, alleges that he in fact spurned her advances. Stryver's legal colleagues show a judicial restraint that the narrator does not share: "Some of his King's Bench familiars, who were occasionally parties to the full-bodied wine and the lie, excused him for the latter by saying that he had told it so often, that he believed it himself—which is surely such an incorrigible aggravation of an originally bad offence, as to justify any such offender's being carried off to some suitably retired spot, and there hanged out of the way."[31]

How ironically should we read this plea for summary justice? Surely the narrator does not really mean that the stock type of the lying, philandering male, however disagreeable, should be lynched. Yet dim echoes sound of the novel's famous opening peroration, whose best and worst of times includes "the hangman, ever busy and ever worse than useless," unable as he is to distinguish between murders and "pilferers."[32] Might we commit a similar fault? Might such revolutionary excesses then be harder to surmount than we at first imagine? Certainly, these narrative outbursts turn out to be far from isolated occurrences. Perhaps the most striking such instance arrives with Dickens's prose counterpart to Phiz's roiling sea. I have to quote at length in order to do justice both to its sustained intensity, and to the contrastive abruptness of the subsequent moral edict:

> As these ruffians turned and turned, their matted locks now flung forward over their eyes, now flung backward over their necks, some women held wine

to their mouths that they might drink; and what with dropping blood, and what with dropping wine, and what with the stream of sparks struck out of the stone, all their wicked atmosphere seemed gore and fire. The eye could not detect one creature in the group free from the smear of blood. Shouldering one another to get next at the sharpening-stone, were men stripped to the waist, with the stain all over their limbs and bodies; men in all sorts of rags, with the stain upon those rags; men devilishly set off with spoils of women's lace and silk and ribbon, with the stain dyeing those trifles through and through. Hatchets, knives, bayonets, swords, all brought to be sharpened, were all red with it. Some of the hacked swords were tied to the wrists of those who carried them, with strips of linen and fragments of dress: ligatures various in kind, but all deep of the one colour. And as the frantic wielders of these weapons snatched them from the stream of sparks and tore away into the streets, the same red hue was red in their frenzied eyes;—eyes which any unbrutalised beholder would have given twenty years of life, to petrify with a well-directed gun.[33]

If the earlier call for the hanging of Stryver seemed in part ironic, here the narrative voice is harder to gauge, with its repetition of the very violence from which it recoils in disgust. John Gross sums things up succinctly: "Dickens dances the carmagnole, and howls for blood with the mob. Frightened by the forces he has unleashed, he views the revolution with hatred and disgust."[34]

Yet by concentrating exclusively upon the moral vantage of the author, Gross underplays the reader's own implication, which prohibits such cleancut distinctions between revolutionary enthusiasm and reactionary recoil. What could an "unbrutalised beholder" possibility be? Not we, who come to this dark fantasy of retribution having been forced to entrain to a revolutionary violence that communicates itself through the breathless sweep of Dicken's parallelism-laden and alliteration-saturated periods. Even the "twenty years of life" that we would surrender so as to commit vigilante retribution, and which seems to possess the abstract arbitrariness of a judicial sentence, transpires to be no innocent number. For it corresponds nearly exactly to the actual incarceration in the Bastille of Doctor Manette, whose methodical pacing and crafting of imaginary shoes continues to resound, provided that our bodies prove sufficiently resonant.

Several other moments demonstrate that contagious entrainment spills across violence and the revulsion to violence. We find it in the chapter mordantly titled "Triumph," as Charles Darnay is spared the guillotine through the intercession of Doctor Manette, and with us carried aloft on the shoulders of a dancing multitude that a moment earlier was preparing to execute him; we find, once again too late, that this reprieve is false, with Darnay rearrested the following day.[35] While we dance the Carmagnole in joy at Darnay's supposed release, five unnamed men are summarily sentenced to death: Dickens again manipulates rhythmical contagion so as to probe the limits of compassion. So far from the nineteenth century having severed sympathy from physiology, *A Tale of Two Cities* proves their inseparability.

Old Men Live Backward in Their Dancing Prime

Dickens's coercive entrainment poses an obvious moral conundrum: the contagiousness of embodied sympathy threatens to convert fellow feeling into involuntary reflex, as if humans were no more "moral individuals" than mollusks. Bloodshed and the Carmagnole result. In order to find a means of acknowledging the irreducibly physiological nature of sympathy, without dissolving agency altogether, I want to revert to the quote with which this chapter began. Eliot, we recall, likened humans to bivalves, through a common "rhythmic persistence" that, for the former, assumed the specific guise of "Poetic Form." We might wonder whether the term is meant loosely, as a general designation of imaginative art. Eliot's many prose fictions, after all, frequently treat rhythmical contagion: in *Romola*, to take but one of sundry examples, the eponymous heroine begins to "feel herself vibrating with the great peal of the bells," marking the dangerous access of religious enthusiasm; when the escaped prisoner Baldassare similarly "vibrated like a harp of which all the strings had been wrenched away except one," his frame marks the transition from the harmonic to the rhythmical register.[36]

Yet there is strong reason to think that Eliot did mean the adjective "Poetic" in a more specific manner. During the period in which "Notes on Form in Art" was composed, she was intensely alert to such questions, which she put most fully into practice in *The Spanish Gypsy,* also published in 1868, after four years of painstaking research and composition. Verse entrainment, she came to understand, can surpass even Dickens's compulsive prose, given two of its constituent features. The first concerns poetry's rhythmical variability: although we saw in the previous chapter how anapests insinuated themselves into *Orlando,* prose fiction struggles to keep up such patterning for any length of time, much less counterpose it with other metrical forms. The second concerns the long historical consolidation of those variable rhythms: metrical patterns do not only exist in the mind or on the fingers of single readers, but indicate broader communities of cultural production and reception. Poetry's intrinsic and acquired capacity to incorporate historically mediated polyrhythm produces something very like the compositely individual body that fascinated Spencer.

Set in the rich denominational admixture of fifteenth-century Granada, *The Spanish Gypsy* exhibits a greater degree of formal hybridity than any of Eliot's works in verse or prose. This long poem has nevertheless generally been damned with faint praise when it has not languished in obscurity. Herbert Tucker reads the work as no more (and no less) than consistently accomplished amateurship.[37] I agree that several flaws undermine Eliot's poem, yet find it a much more uneven production: when it is good it is very good, and when it is bad it is revealingly so. The work stands on its own, as a signal instance of how poetry engages with the nature and ethical difficulties of entrainment; in so doing it exemplifies the growing zoological and ethnological recruitment of poetry in order to conceptualize rhythm.

Critics who agree on the badness of Eliot's production often do so in mutually exclusive ways. For readers such as John Morley, writing in *Macmillan's Magazine,* the poem's schematic form and undeveloped characters served merely as couriers for a preestablished intellectual design.[38] The anonymous reviewer for the *Atlantic Reviewer,* by contrast, agreed with several contemporaries regarding a thoroughgoing "inequality of the versification [that] infects the expression of ideas."[39] Is *The Spanish Gypsy* all-too-transparent, then, or distortingly irregular? Eliot herself engaged in lengthy justifications of the poem's metrical compliance, sometimes with an appeal to the temporal poetics that the previous chapter explored.[40] Yet she might have issued another defense, or, better still, no defense at all: for the very prosodic inequality for which critics reproached *The Spanish Gypsy* represents an unparalleled means of both expressing and testing the limits of liberal pluralism.

Eliot's rhythmical hybridity first comes to the fore in the extended set-piece in the Plaça Santiago (1:1040–97), which showcases the finest sustained verse writing of her career. Citizens of various classes and occupations congregate to a composite Andalusian music of buskers and evening bells, with Eliot's blank verse punctuated with interludes sung by Juan, a licensed poet, and Pablo, a lame young street musician. The latter puts aside his viol to sing a lyric (1:1263–74), whose pentameter-tetrameter alternation and *abba* rhyme scheme is pretty enough, yet exerts more significant effect within Eliot's framed narration than upon our ears:

> The long notes linger on the trembling air,
> With subtle penetration enter all
> The myriad corridors of the passionate soul,
> Message-like spread, and answering action rouse.
> Not angular jigs that warm the chilly limbs
> In hoary northern mists, but action curved
> To soft andante strains pitched plaintively.
> Vibrations sympathetic stir all limbs:
> Old men live backward in their dancing prime,
> And move in memory; small legs and arms
> With pleasant agitation purposeless
> Go up and down like pretty fruits in gales.
> All long in common for the expressive act
> Yet wait for it; as in the olden time
> Men waited for the bard to tell their thought. (1:1275–1302)

Eliot's prosody here actuates the "vibrations sympathetic" that her prose writing can for the most part only depict. Blank verse, like the attentive bodies whose movements it traces, proves a porous membrane: it contracts the lyric impulse that had preceded it, and which lingers on through a series of assonances ("hoary northern"), alliterations ("pitched plaintively"), and crypto-rhymes ("limbs ... limbs"). I call them crypto-rhymes insofar that, were we to slice a random block of long prose into decasyllabic clumps, there is a statistically high probability that repetitions and rhymes would appear. Yet the texture of Eliot's verse conditions us to hear motivation in what may well be inadvertent repetition.[41] In this we are like the old man dancing in his mind, for whom rhythm is at once an act of prehension and retention: to "live backward," or "move in memory," counts as bodily privation only for as long as we do not consider the mind to be itself an embodied organ. Like the crowd in which they are subsumed, these elderly dancers (whose movements Eliot so touchingly evokes) also longingly anticipate "the expressive act." Here again blank verse powerfully entrains us in a manner that prose cannot approximate: our own rhythmic apprehension meets the end of the line, only to be stalled and therefore further induced by the enjambed qualifying clause ("Yet wait for it"). Eliot is particularly fond of these rhythmical teasers throughout the opening sections of her poem: "marble-limbed. / Yet breathing" (1:98–99), "Thus he pleads in vain; / Yet faints not utterly, but pleads anew" (1:126–27); "Spirits seem buried and their epitaph / Is writ in Latin by severest pens, / Yet still they flit above the trodden grave" (1:318–20). In all these cases, the initial and heavily stressed "Yet" disinters and resuscitates what the previous line had seemed to have buried: this rhythmical undulation depends upon the capacity for acceleration and arrest that is peculiarly the preserve of blank verse enjambment.

Such porosity between blank verse and lyric characterizes the early part of *The Spanish Gypsy* more broadly. This is not to say that the songs are particularly distinguished, certainly by the often-high standards of the unrhyming poetry in which they are embedded. Eliot might well have claimed, in a prefatory note, "to imitate the trochaic measure and assonance of the Spanish Ballad,"[42] yet the works in question more readily come over as studied exercises in the Tennysonian strain: Pablo's "Spring comes hither" (1:1237–56) echoes "Blow bugle blow"; Juan's answering "Day is dying!" (1:1396–1410) closely resembles "The splendour falls on castle walls." Yet it is precisely this contrast in quality—I mean the word in both senses—that allows Eliot's prosodic hybridity to do its work. The typical function of lyric has been inverted: here its end-stopped regularity provides periodic limits to affect or expression (Eliot's most consistent emendation of her manuscript draft consists of the addition of punctuation to line ends); freely enjambing blank verse, meanwhile, so far from being a surrogate for prose narration, describes and effects the entrainment between bodies that music by itself is peculiarly unable to accomplish.

This alternating rhythm compels the poem's heroine, Fedalma, into her first appearance, as she too picks up the existing crypto-rhyme ("The spirit in her gravely flowing face / With sweet community informs her limbs" [1:1336–37]). Pablo responds to her dance with a song, to whose fixed oscillation the blank verse again differentially entrains:

> *Day is dying! Float, O swan,*
>   *Down the ruby river;*
> *Follow, song, in requiem*
>   *To the mighty Giver.*

> The exquisite hour, the ardor of the crowd,
> The strains more plenteous, and the gathering might
> Of action passionate where no effort is.
> But self's poor gates open to rushing power
> That blends the inward ebb and outward vast,—
> All gathering influences culminate
> And urge Fedalma. Earth and heaven seem one,
> Life a glad trembling on the outer edge
> Of unknown rapture. Swifter now she moves,
> Filling the measure with a double beat
> And widening circle; now she seems to glow
> With more declared presence, glorified.
> Circling, she lightly bends and lifts on high
> The multitudinous-sounding tambourine,
> And makes it ring and boom, then lifts it higher
> Stretching her left arm beauteous; now the crowd
> Exultant shouts, forgetting poverty
> In the rich moment of possessing her. (1:1407–29)

Whereas Eliot's sundry prose depictions of self-abnegation are focalized through an individual character (think Maggie Tulliver in the grip of religious enthusiasm, or gliding downstream with Stephen Guest), here no free indirect discourse grants us privileged access to interiority. We see no further than Fedalma's body, gripped as it is by an external phase to which we too are exposed. Yet it is precisely this attention to surfaces (to selves as oscillators) that enables Eliot to conduct a depth study in social rhythm. Differing prosodic modes, individual bodies, social classes, and religious customs have been shown to coexist in Eliot's imagined fifteenth-century Andalucía; yet the sudden arrival of the "Gypsy prisoners" (1:1429) abruptly arrests Fedalma's dance and the blank verse line, with the tolling bell that restores the Christian faith (1:1443) similarly felt as an emphatic caesura that cleaves the previously undivided blank verse line into hemistichs. For as long as we regard this scene from a critical distance, its narrative clumsiness (fancy these captives turning up just now!) is apparent. When we follow it with our bodies, by contrast, we form part of a more revealing study of how social beings successively lock phases and fall out of step.

These colliding rhythms foreshadow the central drama of *The Spanish Gypsy*, where Fedalma leaves her Spanish upbringing for the Zincali tribe led by the man she discovers to be her father. Eliot's distinctive handling of this theme comes into clearer focus when we set it within the broader nineteenth-century vogue for "Gitáno" culture.[43] Eliot drew extensively upon one of the works that did much to foment this interest, George Borrow's *The Zincali: An Account of the Gypsies of Spain*, which extended through numerous editions following its first publication in 1841. Borrow's extended discussion of Zincali verse, with which the second volume of that work commences, begins in uncompromising fashion: "This poetry, for poetry we will call it, is such as might be expected to originate among people of their class; a set of Thugs, subsisting by cheating and villainy of every description."[44] An accompanying image that purports to show a Zincali woman, overcome by song, hurling her infant in the air, illustrates what Borrow has in mind (fig. 11). Despite such absurd cultural representations, Borrow goes on to allow that even "Thugs and Gitános have their moments of gentleness"; accordingly, he presents transcriptions and translations of several songs, noted down "in the midst of a circle of these singular people, dancing and singing to their wild music."[45] His concluding explication of these songs is a marvel

FIGURE 11. A Zincali woman overcome by song, hurling her infant in the air, from George Borrow, *The Zincali* (1841)

of cake-having-and-cake-eating: "We have uniformly placed the original by the side of the translation; for though unwilling to make the Gitános speak in any other manner than they are accustomed, we are equally averse to have it supposed that many of the thoughts and expressions which occur in these songs, and which are highly objectionable, originated with ourselves."[46] Heaven forfend!

Zincali verse exemplifies Borrow's ambivalence toward a culture that is held to be uncouth yet intriguingly extempore. His rendering of these poems into undeviating ballad quatrains both tames their unruly force and suggests that English poetry might recover a rugged primitivism.[47] In Borrow's hands, Zincali poetry resembles a scrubbed-up Ossian: "Unto a refuge me they led, / To save from dungeon drear; / Then sighing to my wife I said, / I leave my baby dear."[48] For all that she relied upon *The Zincali* for anthropological details, Eliot shares neither Borrow's disgust at "primitive" culture, nor the fetishizing appreciation that constitutes its dialectical corollary. Fedalma's spontaneous dance suggests an essentializing corporeal inheritance, which the remainder of *The Spanish Gypsy* severely complicates.

These large cultural questions again emerge through prosodic technique. Where Borrow's conventional English renderings purport to allow "Gypsy" culture to "speak for itself," Eliot consistently stresses the extent to which rhythm comes to us in mediated form. Her Zincali, with a single exception that I will describe below, do not sing their own songs: the ballads and lyrics that intersperse *The Spanish Gypsy*, and which prove far more metrically various than Borrow's rigid tetrameter-trimeter alterations, sediment cultural appropriation and transmission. The poet Juan accompanies Fedalma in defecting to the Zincali tribe: it is he who teaches them even their most stirring anthem ("*We Zincali!*"), to which the assembled boys and girls "dance wildly" (3:178). In what may prove a subtle critique of Borrow's putatively disinterested fieldwork, Eliot makes clear the extent to which bodily instinct can be trained: "Why, the minxes there," sings Juan, "Have rhythm in their toes, and music rings / As readily from them as from little bells / Swung by the breeze" (3:124–27). While the Zincali do spend a lot of their time dancing and whooping, in keeping with the stock caricatures of the time, Eliot emphatically disallows the possibility that bodily immediacy should prove the preserve of any one culture or race. Juan sings successive lyrics to the Spanish girl Pepita (1:2415–84) and the young Zincali Hinda (3:179–214), both of whom entrain so fully as to take his song for literal truth.

The salient distinction in Eliot's poem lies therefore not between Zincali and non-Zincali, but rather between those individuals (from whatever culture) who inhabit their bodies without grasping the root of its impulses, and those whose historical reflexivity by contrast impedes their embodiment. The rift emerges through Eliot's shifting prosodic repertoire: while fluid blank verse had earlier performed a mediating function between lyric and narration, plural liberalism increasingly shatters into song and prose, emerging first in the narrative interlude of 2:1022–145. Juan manipulates Hinda's credulous belief in the efficacious power of song, so as to compel her to return to him the ornaments and trinkets that she had stolen. "That fable of mine about the tunes was excellently devised," he concludes in frank and disabused prose. "I feel like an ancient sage instructing our lisping ancestors. My memory will descend as the Orpheus of Gypsies. But I must prepare a rod for those rascals. I'll bastinado them with prickly pears. It seems to me these needles will have a sound moral teaching in them" (3:219–25).

It is hard, in light of Juan's calculating stratagems, to credit Ruth Abbot's claim that "as if anticipating reviewers who would accuse her of stooping to something silly by writing in verse, Eliot put such opinions in the mouths of her most dubious or changeable characters, and made all the minor heroes of the piece poets and singers."[49] Song is for *The Spanish Gypsy* a rather more ambiguous cultural product, precisely because of its constitutive tension between embodiment and historicity. Juan's songs invoke a *"Memory"* (1:2415) that his auditors cannot grasp; he by contrast does not inhabit the lyric present (on several occasions he disclaims possessing feelings or a soul), living rather in a historical time that has already by the fifteenth century threatened to make poets obsolete (1:316–17), and which stirs a compensatory yet self-consciously chimerical desire for future fame. "A poet, too, may prosper past belief," he declares vaingloriously. "I shall grow epic, like the Florentine, / And sing the founding of our infant state, / Sing the new Gypsy Carthage" (3:391–94).

While never partaking in such manipulative sport, Fedalma herself suffers from the same split between embodiment and history that condemns Juan to the periphery of his adopted community. Like her licensed poet, she recounts a story that Hinda mistakes for literal truth (1:686–749); she later attempts to share Juan's projections for Africa, whose wishful vagueness ("Africa / Would we were there!") convinces nobody (3:394–412). In a phrasing that once again substitutes the rhythmical for the harmonic register, her father urges Fedalma to entrain fully to a wider community: "'T is a vile life that . . . has no ear save for the tickling lute / Set to small measures,—deaf to all the beats / Of that large music rolling o'er the world" (3:615–19). Yet her inability to forget past suffering (here the abandonment of her fiancé, Don Silva) prevents her from crediting a viable future state for the Zincali, who, as their own leader acknowledges, remain ignorant of any "Whence or Whither." Despite conforming to his parental authority, Fedalma remains clear: her past sufferings, she replies, "hide the goal / Which to your undimmed sight is fixed and clear" (3:645–46).

The same split that separates her from Hinda or Pepita also occurs more significantly within Fedalma herself. For despite being unable to entrain as her father would like, it is hardly as if she does not possess a body. Rather, her tragic fate is to be unable to reconcile its instincts and impulses with a history that remains obscure. Her initial instinctive dance knows no sequel. She is unable to grasp a prehistory so anterior that it survives only in dim impulses. The earliness of her abduction paradoxically makes her belong only all the more to the community from which she has been abducted. She may not dance in perfect forgetfulness like Hinda, but Fedalma *is* a true Zincali, insofar as that people are, as Eliot put in in a manuscript line that she curiously omitted from the final edition (perhaps because it confirmed matters too explicitly), "a people with no home even in memory."[50] *The Spanish Gypsy* is sometimes criticized for its thinness of cultural detail, which stands in obvious and stark contrast to the thick description of Judaic tradition that we find within *Daniel Deronda*. Yet it is precisely this thinness, precisely Eliot's invention of "Africa" as a more-or-less arbitrary (because unrealizable) placeholder for home, which enables her work to communicate something very distinct from any of her novels. These Zincali matter not as convincing anthropological case studies, but insofar as they are thrown into a history that cannot be known, yet which presses upon the generic body.

By the closing sections of Eliot's verse tragedy, a cordon sanitaire arises between those prosodic forms that had been liberally admixed, mimicking and enforcing the separation between persons. The Zincali finally sing music of their own, in the form of the bellicose dirge with which they threaten Don Silva in the case of desertion (*"Turn false Zincalo!"* [4:277–357]); the latter hears this repetitive din, which offers an unwitting pastiche of the Christian's own martial hymn (2:1063–67) as "hellish rhythm" (4:362). From here the denouement unfolds with alacrity: Zarca launches a successful offensive upon the garrison that Don Silva had previously commanded, killing several of the latter's former attendants. At the very point at which the Zincali are about to put to death the Catholic priest Father Isidor, Don Silva breaks loose and deals Zarca a fatal wound. The mutiny disintegrates; Fedalma proves unable to hold together the band that she now commands; she and Don Silva, having wed in a Zincali ceremony, declare that they must part forever.

I rattle off these concluding details in part so as to demonstrate Eliot's compliance with tragic convention. If this were all there were to it, *The Span-*

ish Gypsy would offer little more than the lurid exercises in compulsive entrainment that we find in *A Tale of Two Cities,* or Eliot's own "The Lifted Veil." But this is not all there is—a fact that we can tell, once again, on our bodies. In her "Notes on The Spanish Gypsy and Tragedy," Eliot envisages two distinct forms of tragedy: "The collision of Greek tragedy is often that between hereditary, entailed Nemesis, and the peculiar individual lot, awakening our sympathy, of that particular man or woman whom the Nemesis is shown to grasp with terrific force." Yet a second, more Hegelian strain also exists: "Sometimes, as in the 'Oresteia,' there is the clashing of two irreconcilable requirements—two duties, as we should say in those times."[51] She does not specify into which of the two molds she casts *The Spanish Gypsy.* Viewed in the abstract, we could well understand Fedalma and Don Silva's defections as a sacrifice of "individual" goods (security, love) to extrinsic Nemesis. Yet I believe Eliot's embodied thinking goes further than this: *The Spanish Gypsy* understands that no such "individual lot" exists separate from or prior to a collective body; its author would have concurred with Hegel that three is the minimal unit with which society begins. The poem thus more strongly conforms to Eliot's second model, according to which "two irreconcilable requirements—two duties" compete. With one qualification: these duties are not bloodless legal prescriptions, but rather embodied impulses. Eliot's physiological tragedy differs from its more purely theological precursor, in that the sentence of doom is pronounced from within our own being. Yet this variation upon tragic convention offers the very means by which *The Spanish Gypsy* recuperates a more positive use for entrainment than compulsive force.

We can begin to glimpse this recuperative potential with the aid of the one figure who does constitute a "minor hero" in *The Spanish Gypsy:* not Juan or any other actual or aspirant poet, but the Jewish astrologer Sephardo, whom Eliot modeled loosely upon the twelfth-century philosophers Jehuda Halevi and Abraham ben Meir ibn Ezra. Sephardo it is who most eloquently and passionately seeks to reconcile the historical and the embodied, and in so doing reveals that such rifts extend well beyond the human organism. His own tribute to memory proves a humbler yet wiser performance than Juan's vatic apostrophe: it means, simply, learning how to be able to walk (2:994–95). Prior to his own defection, Don Silva has enlisted the young boy

Pablo and his dancing monkey Annibal in a madcap scheme to gather information about his departed betrothed. This troupe of jugglers, singers, and mime artists already suggests a composite rhythm that extends across forms and organisms. Sephardo welcomes each creature with hospitality, remarking, in one of Eliot's few significant additions to her manuscript text, "Yea, am not I too a small animal?" (506).

He then continues, in a dignified speech that equally indicts colonialism and animal cruelty:

> Man thinks
> Brutes have no wisdom, since they know not his;
> Can we divine their world?—the hidden life
> That mirrors us as hideous shapeless power,
> Cruel supremacy of sharp-edged death.
> Or fate that leaves a bleeding mother robbed?
> O, they have long tradition and swift speech,
> Can tell with touches and sharp darting cries
> Whole histories of timid races taught
> To breathe in terror by red-handed man. (2:530–39)

Sephardo's speech demonstrates that the putative distinction between "primitive" and "civilized" cultures (which *The Spanish Gypsy* in any case voids) comes to seem like small beer in comparison to the porous membrane between human and nonhuman life. The conception of a history that lives on in "touch" or in "cries" uncannily anticipates what we have come to call intergenerational epigenetic transmission.[52] Those "timid races taught / To breathe in terror" are at once monkeys, Zincali, and mankind in general. As Walter Benjamin rather wonderfully put it in "Of Toys and Play," "Eating, sleeping, getting dressed, washing have to be instilled into the struggling little brat in a playful way, following the rhythm of nursery rhymes.... Habits are the forms of our first happiness and our first horror that have congealed and become deformed to the point of being unrecognizable."[53]

Sephardo's eloquence seems to offer the fullest and darkest confirmation of what I have termed Eliot's physiological tragedy: at the end of the poem, while Juan is still singing his songs, the Jewish astrologer is called upon to bury the many dead. Yet if distributed cognition raises the specter of a "hideous shapeless power," so too does it offer perhaps the only form of refuge. We experience as much in the very final stretches of *The Spanish Gypsy*, which belatedly deviate from tragic convention. Fedalma and Don Silva take their definitive leave of one another, in a principled separation that also provides a surrogate union.

For the intrinsic resources and accumulated expectations of Eliot's verse transfigure its dénouement. *The Spanish Gypsy* does not merely dramatize the tragic dilemma between memory and embodiment; it is itself a simple (if also emergent) organism, whose habituations condition the reader's own body. Fedalma attempts to take her leave:

> My lord, farewell!
>   He did not say "Farewell."
> But neither knew that he was silent. She,
> For one long moment, moved not. They knew naught
> Save that they parted; for their mutual gaze
> As with their soul's full speech forbade their hands
> To seek each other—those oft-clasping hands
> Which had a memory of their own, and went
> Widowed of one dear touch forevermore.
> At last she turned and with swift movement went,
> Beckoning to Hinda, who was bending low
> And hungered still to wash her shells, but soon
> Leaping and scampering followed, while her Queen
> Mounted the steps again and took her place,
> Which Juan rendered silently. (5:346–59)

For once Juan keeps his mouth shut, knowing, perhaps, that silence speaks more articulately. Any song would only travesty a blank verse that has recovered much of the grandness and verbal parallelisms that characterized its early life. This recovery comes at the cost of painful recollection. The attentive reader might note that the pair's hemistichomythic "farewell" echoes several other false leaves that they have taken of one another: as when Don Silva declares "farewell" only to steal "one last kiss" (1:2254–56); or when Fedalma reverses the expression to offer "one kiss—farewell!" to her marriage ring (1:3200); or on the successive occasions where, Don Silva having tracked down the Zincali band, she declares that he cannot remain with her (3:1043, 1065); or even on the sole occasion that Zarca expresses remorse for the Spaniards whom he has slain (4:510). The accumulation of these occurrences leads us to suspect that the word does not mean what it says. Yet the matter is not merely semantic. All of these instances happen to occur in terminal positions within their respective blank verse lines, transfiguring what would otherwise be mere lexical repetition into something felt on the flesh. Of sixteen total uses of the word, ten occur at line ends (not counting the first instance above, which by occurring at the end of the hemistich also calls attention to itself).

By "attentive reader," I mean something quite different from a brain and a pair of spectacles. I rather intend an embodied being that has forgotten itself sufficiently as to be involuntarily receptive to patterns that it might well not be able to verbalize, much less quantify. When just now I listed the proportion of farewells that occurred as terminal crypto-rhymes, I was not that responsive being; but I only reached for my calculator in order to test what had begun as a nagging corporeal sensation. The sensation nagged in large part because "farewell" is but one instance of a verse that has become habituated and habituating. The caesura that attempts to enforce the separation between Fedalma and Don Silva gives rise to an extended run of enjambed blank verse, whose syntactic groping tracks their extended bodies. The "hands" / "hands" crypto-rhyme that occurs across successive lines, and whose repetition briefly checks the momentum of the verse, beautifully mimics an act of physical searching so keen that it imagines into being that for which it gropes.

This parallelism taps into another memory bank that the poem has grown during its gestation: for this crypto-rhyme occurs too frequently for it to be inadvertent. We frequently observe the distributed cognition that Sephardo eloquently invoked: following Fedalma's first departure, Silva suffers from "the sweet habit of caressing hands / That seek the memory of another hand" (2:85–86). Eliot means the expression quite literally: hands have memories (as do prosodic feet).[54] Embodied terms frequently occur as patterned line endings in the same manner as does "farewell": "limbs," whose significance for the early dancing scene we observed above, occurs 20 times,

14 of which arrive in terminal positions; 33 of the 73 usages of "heart" occur at line ends; 46 out of 124 occurrences of "soul" do the same; as do 11 out of 25 iterations of "gaze."

When, then, in the passage above, our eyes and ears approach "mutual gaze" at the end of the line, we reach forward desperately for the continuation of the clause as for a human figure that we know to be retreating into obscurity; yet we also recall in nondiscursive and inexact ways prior bodily patterns whose endurance cancels the possibility of total departure. *The Spanish Gypsy* does not succeed in taking its leave from us, and thereby hangs back from unmitigated tragedy. We do not look down upon Fedalma and Don Silva as we do upon Maggie and Tom in *The Mill on the Floss*, carried as we are from the latter duo by the ravages and reparations of suddenly accelerating time. Unlike their deathly embrace, the Andalusian couple lives on in or at our own hands. The poem is old, and we have all grown into elders living backward in memory. Each heavily stressed terminal crypto-rhyme returns memory to us, returns us to memory, while at the same compelling us forward, through the onrushing force of Eliot's blank verse, in rhythmical expectation. Don Silva is not so gone as all that. In remaining silent, Juan finally learned how to sing. Fedalma makes a fine art of radical breaks from the past: that she can fully accomplish none of them first constituted the poem's tragedy, before becoming its belated recompense. Eliot's verse rhythm shows that entrainment need not mean automatic compulsion. It can also register the obscure yet palpable historicity that inheres in all bodies; it can incorporate social plurality, or interruption, while remaining itself.

Natura facit saltus

By both marking and being embodied memory, *The Spanish Gypsy* demonstrates why Eliot should have isolated specifically "Poetic Form." Her "rhythmical persistence" seems at first simply to suggest an intrinsic cross-species capacity, much as Daniel Dennett would liken human storytelling to a spider spinning its web.[55] Yet the provisional conclusion to her unfinished essay supplements this innatism with an extrinsic and dynamic historical process:

> A Form being once started must by and by cease to be purely spontaneous: the form itself becomes the object and material of emotion, and is sought after, amplified and elaborated by discrimination of its elements till at last by the abuse of its refinement it preoccupies the room of emotional thinking; and poetry, from being the fullest expression of the human soul, is starved into an ingenious pattern-work, in which tricks with vocables take the place of living words fed with the blood of relevant meaning, and made musical by the continual intercommunication of sensibility and thought.
>
> The old phrases should not give way to scientific explanation, for speech is to a great extent like sculpture, expressing observed phenomena and remaining true in spite of Harvey and Bichat.[56]

If Harvey and Bichat represent a leveling materialism, Eliot's suppler scientific knowledge incorporates the historical vicissitudes that insinuate qualitative difference into otherwise comparable entities. Human beings differ from animals not to the extent that they have magical capacities for moral conduct or aesthetic appreciation, but insofar as the homes that they fashion for themselves periodically cease to provide shelter. The same may well be true for nonhuman animals, only the vaster time span of evolutionary adaptation renders it hard to pinpoint where the shell no longer serves its mollusk. Accelerated human culture, by contrast, offers readier instances of habitations that no longer suffice: where formerly reassuring patterns calcify into unease or disdain; where the adult cannot bear to hear the infant's endless repetition of the same word or joke; where a culture more broadly starts to dismiss as mere jingle the rhymes or refrains that once characterized its poetry.

This is a form of truly dialectical thinking to which Lewes's own physiological aesthetics could for the most part only aspire.[57] His mammoth *Problems of Life and Mind* (1879), which Eliot edited and published posthumously, struggles to articulate a "Law of Discontinuity" that would diverge from what Lewes took to be Darwin's more seamless materialism, which postulates a difference of degree but not kind between complex phenomena (consciousness) and simpler entities (unicellular organisms). Lewes's arguments against reductionism are themselves ironically reductive: books are not composed of their print, larger numbers do not "contain" the number ten, and so on. "By [Darwin's] line of argument," he summarizes tartly, "one might maintain that not only were there 'sermons in stones', but that these stones were conscious of their eloquences. Pebbles are philosophers of infinitesimal energy."[58]

For all his claims to have surmounted his youthful idealism, Lewes's antireductive arguments share a great deal with Hegel's own argument against *natura non facit saltus*: the *Science of Logic* appends the boiling point of water as an instance of where a change in quantity produces a change in quality.[59] Lewes could not have declared that "beside the unity of Force we must accept the diversity of opposing forces," without a thorough grounding in dialectics.[60] Yet despite arguing that his "Law of Discontinuity" is an "empirical" rather than a "speculative" truth (as opposed to a Darwinism that leads invariably to "panpsychism"), Lewis strips Hegelianism of its actuality: gone is the attentiveness to historical unfolding that we find in the *Phenomenology*, gone is the realization of this process in cultural artifacts that we find in the *Lectures on Fine Art*. In contrast Eliot, by thinking the aesthetic and the historical concurrently, within and without *The Spanish Gypsy*, engages an emergent scientific culture that increasingly employed rhythm to explicate the complex workings not only of organisms, but also of human societies. To that related field I now turn.

Consenting Societies

Rhythmical synchronization occurs throughout the organic world—yet science is divided as to whether entrainment proper is a specifically human capacity. "Periodicity and entrainment seem to be among the most basic features of living things," notes the biologist Tecumseh Fitch, "yet the human ability (and proclivity) to entrain our motor output to auditory stimuli appears to be very rare."[61] Hence his question: "Why don't dogs dance"? While a rooster recently gained celebrity for crowing enthusiastically to a track by the Backstreet Boys, its musical "accompaniment" appeared an automatic stimulus-response. (The rooster's reaction to other boy bands is not noted.) Studies have shown great apes to be capable of anticipatory synchronization but not tempo flexibility.[62] Aniruddh D. Patel posits a neurological link between musical beat processing and language competence: on this view, only vocal learners such as seals and walruses entrain.[63]

Once again, the nineteenth century both prefigures and illuminates such contemporary concerns. The opening section of this chapter explored how the concept of rhythm became pivotal to the amateur zoology of Lewes and Spencer in the 1850s and 1860s. In the closing two decades of the century, such concerns would increasingly inform the nascent fields of sociology and anthropology, which probed the question of how and whether human societies at various stages of "development" could be modeled upon nonhuman impulse. Dogs may not dance, yet their instinctively rhythmical conduct grounds more complex forms of linguistic interaction, at least so far as Spencer's "On the Origin and Function of Music" (1857) is concerned. This remarkably influential essay opens in the following manner:

> When Carlo, standing, chained to his kennel, sees his master in the distance, a slight motion of the tail indicates his but faint hope that he is about to be let out. A much more decided wagging of the tail, passing by-and-by into lateral undulations of the body, follows his master's nearer approach. When hands are laid on his collar, and he knows that he is really to have an outing, his jumping and wriggling are such that it is by no means easy to loose his fastenings. And when he finds himself actually free, his joy expends itself in bounds, in pirouettes, and in scourings hither and thither at the top of his speed.[64]

Carlo's wagging tail expresses a common impulse. "Why the actions excited by strong feeling should tend to become rhythmical, is not very obvious," observes Spencer, "but that they do so there are divers evidences. There is the swaying of the body to and fro under pain or grief, of the leg under impatience or agitation. Dancing, too, is a rhythmical action natural to elevated emotion."[65]

Such passages would seem to refute Fitch's claim for the specifically human (or at least linguistic) nature of entrainment. Yet Spencer does take language to elevate corporeal impulse to a new power: "In poetry," he continues, "which is a form of speech used for the better expression of emotional ideas, we have this rhythmical tendency developed."[66] This formulation distinguishes Spencer's position from that of Rousseau's *Essay on the Origin of Languages,* with which it otherwise shares much common ground. Both trace developed language back to the primal cry: yet where for Rousseau, civilization progressively muffles emotion, Spencer takes linguistic and social organization to intensify affect. Hence his somewhat idiosyncratic aesthetic preferences (he prefers Meyerbeer over Mozart, and declares the Spasmodist Alexander Smith "unquestionably *the* poet of the age"), on the grounds of passionate expression.[67]

Charles Darwin's *Descent of Man* would offer a very different account of rhythmical etiology, which subsequently gave rise to a decade-long dispute between the pair over the origin of music. In keeping with the continuousness that so discomfited Lewes, Darwin argues much more confidently for a common and unchanging rhythmical impulse across species. "The perception, if not the enjoyment, of musical cadences and of rhythm is probably common to all animals, and no doubt depends on the common physiological nature of their nervous systems"; the vibratory "auditory hairs" of crustaceans serves as evidence.[68] His self-professed "ignorance" of music[69] does not prevent Darwin from confidently concluding that "musical notes and rhythm were first acquired by the male or female progenitors of mankind for the sake of charming the opposite sex."[70]

Spencer has tended to come off worse in this quarrel, in both his immediate and longer-term reception. In addition to being vague (he never possesses enough of a grasp of the rudiments of artistic craft to express the symbiosis of form and feeling), Spencer's organized emotivism can seem both anthropocentric and elitist. Yet I nonetheless feel there are reasons to prefer it to Darwin's more leveling, capacious, and reductive notion of rhythm. Sexual selection struggles to account for how and why the organized forms by which subjects express desire (birdsong, verse) change over time; or how these organized forms inflect (rather than simply communicate) such desire.

Yet if Spencer's model enables a more dynamic treatment of the relation between form and feeling, along with a broader sense of how this interrelationship figures in historical change, we must be honest in saying that he himself does not deliver upon its promise. In returning repeatedly to the development of recitative and poetry, his views are often both inconsistent and exclusionary. A lengthy 1890 postscript to his essay that addressed Darwin directly (his interlocutor having died eight years previously, he could at least be sure of having the last word) supplies a crude evolutionary contrast between "the monotonous chants of savages" and "the musical compositions familiar to us."[71] Yet Spencer's growing reliance upon the concept of rhythm also enabled a subtler form of thinking to emerge, in the margins. "Surely it is manifest that the utterances of passion," he observes, speaking of premodern societies in a manner that directly contradicts his more dismissive views, "far from being monotonous, are characterized by rapidly-recurring ascents and descents of tone and by rapidly-recurring emphases: there is rhythm, though it is an irregular rhythm."[72]

We recall that "The Social Organism" similarly understood premodern societies in terms of "irregular rhythm": just as Spencer had struggled to abandon the humble polyp for more vaunted forms of civilization, so do the many revisions and additions to his theory of musical development mark a growing interest in "savage" expression that in fact demonstrates surprising complexity. Perhaps he learned something from Eliot's example in this respect: for in the paragraph following his dismissal of "savage chants," he approvingly cites the testimonies of two proto-anthropologists who take "Hungarian gipsies" to possess a musical sensitivity unmatched by formally trained musicians.[73] Spencer's postscript employs countless such ethnological examples, so as to disprove Darwin's amatory theory: drawing upon his unfinished series of *Descriptive Sociology* (1871–), he itemizes the Bambara, a Mandé ethnic group who "lightened their labours by song"; the Sandwich Islanders, who sing their history; and the women of Loango, who do the same while tilling the fields.[74] Even nonhuman life resists reduction to sexual selection: hedge-sparrows and blackcaps sing long after the mating season has ceased; bleating sheep signal "various feelings, usually of no great intensity"; "the quacking of ducks indicates general satisfaction," and so on.[75]

The 1890s witnessed a series of counter-responses to Spencer's stubborn argument, which left him isolated against a swathe of more-or-less orthodox evolutionary thinkers. Richard Wallaschek's *Primitive Music* collated large swathes of contemporary ethnological research, so as to prove that the "rhythmical impulse" is primal, physiological, and nonlinguistic.[76] (Spencer retorted that music "becomes music only by that which distinguishes it from the other rhythmical products," i.e., a formal or informal system of organization.)⁷⁷ Edmund Gurney's *The Power of Sound* somewhat paradoxically adopted Darwin's amatory theory so as to drive a wedge between "savage" and "civilized" expression: the latter, he asserts in a direct refutation of Spencer, develops "by passing through the interlude of monotonous but rhythmical chanting, and so discarding or limiting instead of exaggerating the characteristics of emotional speech."⁷⁸ Darwinian thought thus licenses the established notion of "pure" music, liberated from signification: Gurney inveighs against Wagner for having failed to cast off language.

Spencer's isolation contributed to the general indifference or disdain with which he came to be viewed by the newly institutionalized sociologists who succeeded him, even when they shared suggestive affinities. I alluded above to Georg Simmel, whose "The Sociology of Conflict" is difficult to imagine without Spencer's example. Durkheim's *Division of Labour in Society* cites Spencer more than any other authority; despite the critical tone of many of these references, he too alights upon the polyp as a being whose collective activity he understands as "communism in every meaning of the word."⁷⁹ Karl Bücher's *Arbeit und Rhythmus* (1899), never translated into English, systematically develops the links between song and labor that we find in *Descriptive Sociology*.⁸⁰

The fullest development of Spencer's dual definition of rhythm (as both impulse and organization) arrives not in academic sociology, but through the concurrently developing field of literary criticism. The poetry that underpinned his resistance to Darwin's more reductive materialism here played a decisive role. Francis Barton Gummere's *The Beginnings of Poetry* (1901) is perhaps the clearest case in point. This work supplies the detailed account of verse that remained lacking from Spencer's speculative account. Gummere marks the moment at which a rapidly professionalizing literary criticism (he cofounded and served as president for the Modern Language Association) develops a more systematic sense of its own intentions, by comparison to the genteel connoisseurship of precursors such as Saintsbury. Rhythm offers the clearest instance of this newfound systematicity: Gummere has digested everything that aesthetics, physiology, and anthropology have to say on the subject, across several languages: he offers astute commentary upon everyone from Vossius to Hegel, in addition to the contemporary research of Wallaschek and Bücher surveyed above.

Gummere's lengthy second chapter, "Rhythm as the Essential Part of Poetry," proves obviously pertinent. "For the purposes of the book," he begins in recognizably Spencerian fashion, "poetry is rhythmic utterance, rhythmic speech, with mainly emotional origin."[81] Unlike Spencer, however, Gummere specifies the essential constituent of this "rhythmical utterance": meter. He chastises Shelley for having extended the poetic franchise to everyone from Bacon to Jesus, Coleridge for having similarly concluded that "Plato, Bishop Taylor and Burnet are bards," and Joseph Warton, whose assertion that "real poetry does not depend upon verse" explains his deafness to Alexander Pope. (Gummere approvingly cites Pope's assertion that "prose on stilts is several degrees worse than poetry fallen lame" [*BP*, 60].)

Until this point, Gummere's metrical tastes appear conventional. Yet a fierce dismissal of J. S. Mill's famous definition of lyric poetry as "something overheard" carries his thinking in a very different direction:

> Now this is sheer nonsense, although more than one critic has hailed it as an oracle; of that which comes down to us as poetry, a good part is anything but soliloquy or the fruit of solitude. "Read Homer," cried out Herder, perhaps at the other extreme, but certainly with better reason than Mill, "as if he were singing in the streets!" It will be shown how vast a proportion of poetry, too, that belongs to the higher class, was made and sung in throngs of men. Poetry is a social fact. (*BP*, 52)

Meter thus must be elastic enough to encompass both the polish of Pope and the communal singing of Homer: it must effect, that is to say, a Spencerian reconciliation of instinctive feeling and organization. The "social fact" of poetry invites material that less obviously confirms to accentual-syllabic convention. We fail to perceive the Old Testament as "metrical," Gummere contends, only because we have become "slave to the eye," forsaking our ears. In place of a rather dogmatic insistence upon meter as "*the last line of separation*" between verse and prose, a rather suppler "rhythm" now proves "the real boundary line of poetic territory" (*BP*, 62–63).

The domination of the oracular over the aural signals an increasing privatization of experience. For rhythm represents not only a distinctive property intrinsic to verse, but also a means of grasping the social order in which it is embedded. It even, in Gummere's grander moments, models something like an ideal polis, grounded upon the "social consent which is born of rhythmic motion" (BP, 89–90). Consensus is not a state so much as an act. The redescription seeks to resolve a problem that this chapter posed some time ago: how a physiological sympathetic response can avoid devolving into involuntary reflex. While Gummere's imaginative reconstructions of premodern societies can be wishful and vague, they reveal an open-minded curiosity sadly uncharacteristic of ethnographic work of the time:

> East Africans are reported to have "no metrical songs," and they sing in recitative; but at once it is added that they dance in crowds to the rhythm of their own voices, as well as to the drum, moving in cadence with the songs which they sing: and here can be no recitative. Moreover, when cleaning rice, they work to the rhythm of songs, to foot-stamping and hand-clapping of the bystanders,—in other words, choral dance, choral song, exact time, rhythm absolute: although, by culling a bit here and there, the theorist could have presented fine evidence from Bushmen and East Africans that savages in low levels of culture have no rhythm in their songs, and dance without consent or time. (BP, 91)

The Carmagnole imposed one brutal and top-down rhythm upon the individual members of a very new society. By contrast, Gummere's ethnological discussions postulate more durable communities, in which individual voice intersects with—without being wholly subordinate to—a broader rhythmical order.

Gummere is today most often remembered for his related theory of the "communal throng": a form of collective expression that runs the perpetual risk of naïve idealization or racialist essentialism. Virginia Jackson has recently offered a more sensitive appraisal, viewing *The Beginnings of Poetry* as symptomatic of an increasingly ethnocentric rhythmical discourse, and also as a salutary corrective to any wishfully "enlightened" postracialist account. Jackson agrees that modern poetry (which here overwhelmingly means lyric poetry) exists in an increasingly privatized sphere: yet rather than subscribe to Gummere's "(somewhat fanciful) chronicle of the loss of communal life and the isolation of the individual," she contends rather "that modern ideas of poetry became lyricized because stipulative verse genres (ballads, odes, elegies, epistles, epitaphs, drinking songs, psalms, hymns, riddles, etc.) collapsed into an idealized version of poetry as lyric."[82]

But just how "fanciful" is Gummere's postulation of a loss of communal life? Jackson's phrasing bestows strange agency upon genre, signaled by the active verb "collapsed": as if the spontaneous combustion of drinking songs prevented people from gathering together, rather than the other way around. If the privatized lyric came to exert an increasingly hegemonic role, this surely reflects broader social trends. Gummere's account of modern alienation may be a little rough around the edges, but his enumeration of industrialization, capitalist accumulation, the privatization of feeling, and a system of pedagogy that increasingly divorces cognition and the body (*BP*, 102) rings true to my ears.

It is also—for a communal theory of social expression—surprisingly inclusive. *The Beginnings of Poetry* offers staunch critiques of the idealizing and prohibitive primitivisms of Herder, Rousseau, and Kipling. Rhythmical "consent," Gummere insists, does not incarnate an eternal *Volk*, but rather brings into being an "imagined community." (Steve Newman points out his anticipation of Benedict Anderson's famous phrase, arguing that Gummere's "opposition between the popular-communal and the individual-artistic is more sophisticated and less reactionary than it may first appear."[83]) If it is difficult to believe in this rhythmical community, it is no less difficult not to believe in it. Jackson herself, stirred by Amanda Gorman's public recitation during Joe Biden's inauguration, declared the poet to have "summoned a communal fantasy of a public poetry that is more familiar in fiction than in fact."[84] What else can this public be than a fiction? What else can it be, once summoned, than a fact? Communal fantasy: this sounds quite a lot like an imagined community.

That being said, how can we hope to give an account of, much less participate in, a community of rhythmical consent? The widespread enthusiasm that greeted Gorman's performance quickly subsided. It is difficult for anyone following Gummere's example (including Gummere himself) not to lapse into either the fetishization of past "integral" cultures, or the melancholy recognition of a privatized modernity. (I think once again of the subject that I was in the art deco cinema in Sweden, gripping the vibrating wooden headrest, entraining to and cut off from the historical community that beheld Aretha Franklin sing "Amazing Grace.") One answer to this question emerges once again through poetry, and more specifically, through the specific mode upon which Gummere modeled his theory of social consent: the ballad. Yet this mode did not simply deliver unmediated access to the "communal throng"; rather, the scholarly excavation of its historical iterations escaped the normative schemes that even Gummere's dynamic account would impose upon it. The ballad was a composite individual whose rhythmical variations and interruptions register the fact and the pathos of historical distance.

To perceive this fact, we should turn from Gummere's critical writing to the editorial work that he undertook alongside Francis James Child, during the compilation of the latter's monumental *English and Scottish Ballads* (1882–98). Remaining true to Child's precepts throughout his career, Gummere represented a major protagonist of the so-called Ballad Wars. His criteria remained geographically exclusive: Gummere rejected Louise Pound's suggestion that Missouri folksong constituted a contemporary extension of the ballad mode. (We should note, however, the impossibility of holding a nonexclusive concept of this or any other genre. Pound may have been happy to extend the ballad franchise to Midwestern laborers, yet her notion of ballad remained predicated upon a very American individualism that directly counteracted Gummere's communal emphasis. "To derive ballads from 'aboriginal song,'" she countered, "is an absurd chronology which assumes that individuals have choral utterance before they are lyrically articulate as individuals.")[85]

Despite the stringent criteria for inclusion, the Child Ballads extend to 305 works, each of which features several variations. Scholars seldom inquire into the actual reading experience of these works, as opposed to their function as anthropological repositories. Their aesthetic force endures rather through the countless musical settings and adaptations that continue to this day. This lack of interest in the Child Ballads as verse (rather than as historical document) represents a real shortfall, given their significant difference from previous compilations whose selectiveness often imposes a misleading formal regularity. Susan Stewart has brilliantly demonstrated how the eighteenth-century collections of Percy and Ramsay discharged specific ideological work in this respect.[86] George Borrow's renderings of "Gypsy songs" offer but one ready-to-hand instance of the rendering of "primitive" feeling in ironically fixed form: here rigid common meter, whose unvarying alternations of tetrameter and trimester emulate the runaway success of Macaulay's *Lays of Ancient Rome*.[87]

The Child Ballads generate a very different experience of the cultural past. We seldom think of scholarly editions, with their variations, scholarly apparatuses, clarifying editorial introductions, and other paraphernalia, as inducing embodied response. Yet such paratexts condition a readerly experience no less than does a "unitary" text. Child and Gummere may well, as Newman insightfully suggests, have compiled the folk literature of yesterday in order to avoid descending from newly constructed ivory towers into the "streets" of real life.[88] Child's intentions were certainly no less ideological than those of Percy, Ramsay, or Motherwell.[89] Yet the excessive zeal of his antiquarianism produces an expressive pluralism that liberates singular items from the taxonomies in which they would otherwise be interred.

Rather than attempt a broad overview of the Child Ballads (a thankless task), this chapter instead concludes by reading a single piece across its successive versions. We can grasp the representativeness of rhythmical constraint and variation only through attending to the ballad's composite singularity. The piece in question is Child Ballad 69 ("Clerk Saunders"). The story is simple: The maiden Margaret and the eponymous hero are lovers; he steals into her bed before their wedding day, suggesting ingeniously that she cover her eyes, so as to claim in all honesty never to have "seen" him. Margaret's seven brothers catch them *in flagrante*, however; following lengthy deliberation, one of the seven takes matters into his own hands. Margaret wakes to find her lover slain: in separate versions, she either professes a vow of chastity, or communes with Clerk Saunders's ghost.

Like all the Child Ballads, "Clerk Saunders" begins with a lengthy editorial note explaining its successive variations. Seven alternatives are listed, taken from Robert Jamieson's *Popular Ballads and Songs* (1806), George Ritchie Kinloch's *Ancient Scottish Ballads* (1827), and Peter Buchan's *Ballads of the North of Scotland* (1828), in addition to manuscripts that had belonged to William Motherwell and David Herd.[90] Child is characteristically forceful in his suggestion of both aesthetic and moral worth: "The austerities vowed in D 13–15, E 17–20, found also in A 20–22, G 23–25, make a very satisfactory termination to the tragedy," he declares, "and supply a want that may be felt in B, and A as it stands here."[91] These "austerities" in all cases takes the form of a penitent Margaret renouncing all future love: she will no longer comb her hair, she will only wear black, and so forth.

Having provided its "very satisfactory termination," version A (which comes from Herd's manuscript copy) nonetheless continues into what Child calls "a rather unsufficing conclusion." Margaret's father entering the room, the manuscript becomes fragmentary:

> 24 In an come her father dear,
>   Stout stepping on the floor;
> . . . .
>
> 25 'Hold your toung, my doughter dear,
>   Let all your mourning a bee;
> I'le carry the dead corps to the clay,
>   And I'le come back an comfort thee.'
>
> 26 'Comfort well your seven sons,
>   For comforted will I never bee;
> For it was neither lord nor loune
>   That was in bower last night wi mee.'[92]

Child specifically regrets "Margaret's refusal to be comforted": it is perhaps for this reason that he arranges his seven variants not in chronological order, but in a manner that smooths out the heroine's noncompliance. Versions F and G (respectively taken from Jamieson's and Buchan's collections) moderate Margaret's refusal: in the first case, she tells her brothers that they could at least have slain Clerk Saunders in the open air; in the second, she declares to her lover's ghost that "we baith shall be in Paradise" (G 37). This cosmetic moral surgery proves inseparable from the later versions' increasing metrical compliance: F renders the tale within the same rigid tetrameter-trimeter alternations that would so characterize ballad form; G rarely strays from octosyllabic lines. Both uphold the *abab* rhyme scheme throughout; neither features much lexical redundancy or refrain.

By ordering the same piece into increasing metrical and moral compliance, Child's chosen sequence relays in miniature form the broader historical process that we found within Gummere's *Beginnings of Poetry*, according to which individualizing "art" intervenes within (even) the ballad mode. This process might be taken in a positive or a negative manner: as proof of a tragic loss of spontaneous utterance, or, in keeping with Child's conception of Margaret, of a taming of unruly impulse. Of more importance, however, is that this process is imperfect. We see this when, instead of jumping to the concluding version of "Clerk Saunders," we pass through Child's successive iterations. Perhaps the most interesting of these variations is version E, previously unpublished. Child found the text in the manuscript notebooks of William Motherwell, who transcribed a number of ballad performances in preparation for his own compilation; we do not know whether such pieces were sung or recited. In his *Minstrelsy: Ancient and Modern* (1827), Motherwell had published Herd's version of the ballad (A in Child's compilation), as it had been further smoothed out by Walter Scott.

Yet the version that Motherwell had recited to him by one "Widow Smith, George Street, Paisley," and which bears the title "Seven Bluidy Brothers," diverges strikingly from all these prior published versions. Whereas in versions A and B, Clerk Saunders commands Margaret (in keeping with my summary above) to blindfold *her* eyes, Widow Smith reverses the dynamic:

> 4 'O take a napkin from your pocket,
>   And with it blindfold my een,
> That I may swear, and avow richt clear,
>   That your flowery bower I have never seen.'
>
> 5 O she's taen him upon her back,
>   And carried him to her chamber-bed,
> That he might swear, and avow it clear,
>   That her flowery [bower] he did never tread.
>
> 6 O she's taen a napkin from her pocket,
>   And with it blinded both his een,
> That he might swear, and avow it clear,
>   That her flowery bower he had never seen.[93]

The comic bawdiness of this scene, in which Margaret carries the full weight of her blinded lover, proves inseparable from the poem's sonorous texture, whose erotic excitation carries the verse beyond socially ordained ballad constraints. Rhymes multiply liberally both across and within the line, with "That he might swear, and avow it clear" itself recurring, word for word, as the penultimate unit of three successive quatrains. The third of these stanzas is, strictly speaking, redundant, telling us nothing that we did not already know. Yet the refrains that the other published versions dutifully pruned return here as the repeated "flowery bower," whose voluptuous self-generation is the whole point. This sonorous ballast invariably tips the ballad well beyond the recognized tetrameter-trimeter alternation, which surfaces in both the early and the late versions within Child's sequence. Here, by contrast, the "flowery bower" channels syllabic as well as phonemic excess. The reciting voice, which may or may not be extemporizing, does not so much negate the mode as turn it against itself, through an intensification of the very phonemic patterns that constitute it.

These compulsive repetitions also facilitate a violence more conspicuous than in any other variant:

> 11 Out then spoke the seventh bluidy brither,
>   Aye and an angry man was he;
> 'Altho there was no more men alive,
>   The ensign's butcher I will be'
>
> 12 He's taen out his rusty broad-sword,
>   And ran it three times along his throat,
> And thro and thro the ensign's body
>   The tempered steel it went thro and thro.[94]

Note the remarkable narrative focalization that occurs in the transition from the eleventh stanza's past tense to the twelfth stanza's present perfect. So too does that transition involve a shift from a comparatively stable ballad form, with syllabic contractions and the simple rhyme of "he" / "be," into something less controlled. Once again, the excited refrain drives this process: in this case, "thro and thro," whose propulsive force in the penultimate line produces its own repetition in the gloriously violent "The tempered steel it went thro and thro." It could be that in performance Widow Smith dropped the "t" in "throat" (the glottal stop being a common feature of the Glaswegian accent), and as such retained the *abab* rhyme scheme. Yet it is not only for contemporary readers that "'thro'" both echoes and cuts "throat": strict and regulated rhyme gives way in this passage to a more widespread phonemic bleeding.

The concluding stanzas further test a ballad form that we only mistakenly call standard. Margaret is, once again, bewailing her departed lover:

> 20 'I will do for my love's sake
>   What other lovers they will be slack;
> Seven years shall come and go
>   Before I cast off my robes of black
>
> 21 'Go make to me a high, high tower,
>   Be sure you make it stout and strong,
> And on the top put an honour's gate
>   That my love's ghost may go out and in.'[95]

The penultimate stanza restores Child's satisfactory conclusion, undergirded by a recovered ABAB rhyme scheme, only for the concluding quatrain once more to disrupt both the medium and the message. Some readers may find themselves re-creating the gestures and phrasing that a performer might once have made, in speaking or singing of the suggestively ironical "honour gate." (Even Child's introductory notes conceded the suitability of ballad for humor.)[96] In the abruptly unrhyming "in," with which this rugged ballad concludes, sounds the resistant voice not only of Margaret but also of the Widow Smith from George Street, Paisley, about whom we know nearly nothing, but who sings through historical difference.

For Child's poem reveals no linear historical trajectory, but a series of oscillations between manuscript and the published page, between strict ballad form and its undoing. We can compare the specific entrainment effects of Child's editions with the several more recent and more immediate renderings of these old standards. When the coal miner and union activist Nimrod Workman recites Child Ballad 53 ("Lord Baseman"), he takes hold of the "original" with singular force.[97] Yet his very singularity counters the effect that I have been elaborating in the preceding paragraphs: the grain of Workman's voice, the posture of his body, so dominate the ballad that he becomes it. Child's scholarly appendages and variants, by contrast, inadvertently produce something like the experience that I described at the very beginning of this book. Just as *Amazing Grace* captured and enabled a differential rhythmical community, so do the small metrical differences that separate A, E, and G, which may seem matters of scholastic pedantry, chart an ongoing social process to which our own bodies can consent. Version E's internal rhymes and skipping triple rhythms do not entrain us with the unilateral force of Workman's declamation: they give us not the live voice of past performance, but a ghost whose very unknowability enables it to speak through us. However much Child sought to establish a definitive and teleological account of the ballad, his edition ended up capturing the difference of historical experience better than any high-resolution photograph or high-fidelity field recording.

The Child Ballads thereby inherit and transfigure the historical dialectic that this chapter has traced. Nineteenth-century zoology articulated a fore-concept of rhythmical entrainment, so as to express the patterned interactions of subjects and species. Philosophy and verse worried alike over the differences between involuntary reflex and a more rarified form of human sympathy. (Does the rhythm to which Fadalma could not but dance continue to vibrate within you?) Anthropology and sociology imported the concept of rhythm, so as to articulate the process by which modern society developed (or became disillusioned with itself). The variable ballad exemplified and ultimately exceeded the speculative social histories that figures such as Gummere and Child imagined. That such traditions never survive undamaged should not surprise us. For as Eliot intuited, the rhythmical shelters that we fashion periodically break down.

4

Thermodynamic Rhythms

Out of Sorts

Toward the end of 1858, Herbert Spencer was feeling out of sorts. His malaise surfaces in an undated letter written around that point to a close friend, the physicist John Tyndall, whom Spencer had recently seen. "That which was new to me in your position enunciated last June, and again on Saturday," Spencer states, "was that equilibration was death. Regarding, as I had done, equilibration as the ultimate and the *highest* state of society, I had assumed it to be not only the ultimate but also the highest state of the universe. And your assertion that when equilibrium was reached life must cease, staggered me. Indeed, not seeing my way out of the conclusion, I remember being out of spirits for some days afterwards. I still feel unsettled about the matter, and should like some day to discuss it with you."[1] It is difficult to behold Spencer's dismay without a modicum of vindication. From at least as early as Richard Hofstadter's *Social Darwinism in American Thought* (1955), which connected his evolutionary sociology to a variety of more-or-less totalitarian twentieth-century worldviews, our culture has been accustomed to regard Spencer's remarkable celebrity as one more Victorian *faute de goût*.[2] Yet where Spencer's notion of equilibrium ("the ultimate and *highest* state of society") sought to reconcile economic supply and demand, or competing class interests, the second law of thermodynamics (to whose consequences his letter refers) identifies it rather with the inexorable cooling of the universe into dispersed, entropic heterogeneity. However bleak that eventuality appears, we might at least derive consolation from the fatal compromise of Spencer's teleological optimism.

Yet Tyndall's revelation did not simply spell the end for Spencer's elaborate system, as Bruce Clarke supposes in a rather summary treatment of the above letter.[3] The previous chapter demonstrated how "On the Origin and Function of Language" established rhythm as a speculative concept that enabled Spencer to relate human and nonhuman life, the individual and the composite body. From the receipt of Tyndall's letter, Spencer would increasingly brandish the concept as a sort of talisman, as if to salvage some vestige of equilibrium for the physical and moral world. His *First Principles of a New System of Philosophy*, published in 1862, serves notice of this intensification, featuring the formal definition that my introduction cited ("It will be seen that rhythm results wherever there is a conflict of forces not in equilibrium"). In a footnote to the same passage, Spencer elaborates that "after having for some years supposed myself alone in the belief that all motion is rhythmical, I discovered that my friend Professor Tyndall also held this doctrine."[4]

Only in 1873, however, would Spencer return directly to the dispiriting second law, engaging in an exchange of letters with James Clerk Maxwell, to whose credentials Tyndall had earlier appealed. The debate hinges on the best way to account for the highly erratic kinetic motion of gases, which Maxwell was in the process of investigating at length. Spencer, who was always a popular expositor and synthesizer rather than a true experimentalist, suggested that his own philosophical concept of "the instability of the homogeneous" might usefully describe what Maxwell had termed "agitated" fluctuations.[5] Even molecules whose path diverged significantly from the overall distribution within a stationary container could, Spencer continued, be described as "rhythmical," to the extent that we could measure divergence itself.[6]

Maxwell demurred. On 17 December 1873, he responded to Spencer that "if, as I understand the word rhythmic, it implies not only alteration, but regularity and periodicity, then the words 'agitation' excludes the notion of rhythm, which was what I meant it to do. . . . A great scientific desideratum is a set of words of *little* meaning—words which mean no more than that a thing belongs to a very large class. Such words are much needed in the undulatory theory of light, in order to express fully what is proved by experiment, without conceding anything which is a mere hypothesis."[7] Maxwell's desire for linguistic hygiene is justifiable: no one wants a concept of rhythm capacious enough to include everything (and thereby nothing). Yet the language game over "agitation" or "rhythm" masks a serious question: To what extent can a given pattern tolerate variation before it ceases to count as such?

This concluding chapter will replay this thought in a metrical key. Although Gillian Beer, Michel Serres, and Bruce Clarke have traced the cultural and literary responses to the second law of thermodynamics, such work largely dwells upon the aesthetic *representation* of entropy, waste, equilibrium, and associated terms.[8] By not merely figuring but also actuating this nexus of concerns, I contend, verse qualitatively altered the anxieties attendant upon it. As such, it offers one final instance of the dialectic of rhythm that has defined this book. Chapter 1 elaborated the concept through the stuttering tongue; chapter 2 broadened it to include subjective apprehension more generally; chapter 3 called upon rhythm to resolve separate subjects and species into societies; and finally, chapter 4 extends it from the terrestrial world to the universe at large.

Rhythmical Innatism

This chapter enumerates three broad, complementary responses to the specter of entropy, each of which recurrently engages with prosody: I call these *rhythmical innatism, rhythmical transmission,* and *entropic rhythm.* Several figures (such as Tyndall, Edmund Gurney, and Spencer himself) offer theoretical impetus to each of these tendencies. As with much of the material treated in the preceding chapters, while this historical process often occurs through propositional argument and discussion, thermodynamic rhythm also establishes itself in large part through engagement with the nondiscursive experience of verse.

Many cultural responses sought to mitigate the trauma of the second law of thermodynamics with a renewed appeal to the first: Sadi Carnot's *Reflec-*

tions on the Motive Power of Heat (1824) was among the first of several simultaneous accounts to formulate the general principle that energy could be neither created nor destroyed. The law of the conservation of energy might intuitively seem to contradict the later formulation of entropy, but in fact does not: for while the quantity of energy in a given system remains constant, the amount convertible into work will diminish. It is not surprising that responses to these two complementary laws should nevertheless have differed so starkly: where the first law suggested that Nothing Ever Really Dies, the second proclaimed that Everything is Always Dying.

John Tyndall offers a textbook tribute to the conservation of energy, in his *Heat Considered as a Mode of Motion* (1863):

> The law of conservation rigidly excludes both creation and annihilation. Waves may change to ripples, and ripples to waves—magnitude may be substituted for number, and number for magnitude—asteroids may aggregate into suns, suns may invest their energy in florae and faunae, and florae and faunae may melt in air—the flux of power is eternally the same. It rolls in music through the ages, while the manifestations of physical life, as well as the display of physical phenomena, are but modulations of its rhythm.[9]

Tyndall, as we have already observed, fully understood the consequences of the second law. Yet heat death figures here as no more than a faint suggestion (the reassuringly plural "suns" that "invest their energy in florae and faunae"), within a Heraclitean eternal flux. I term such rhetoric *rhythmical innatism*: thermodynamics compels the author to acknowledge a break or dissolution, which is nevertheless recuperated into a broader homeostatic system.

This rhythmical innatism burst into sudden and splendid life during the final three decades of the nineteenth century. Tyndall's lectures on *Sound* (1867) demonstrate the extent to which this pattern of thinking both relies upon and reformulates aesthetic questions. Tyndall repeatedly approaches the problematic of dissonance just as he does the "melting" of individual flora and fauna: as a singular rupture that nonetheless forms part of a broader "rhythm." Indeed, the "ripples" and "waves" are here quite literal. For Tyndall resolves the aesthetic and physiological problem of dissonance by decomposing the acoustic phenomenon into a specifiable quantity of

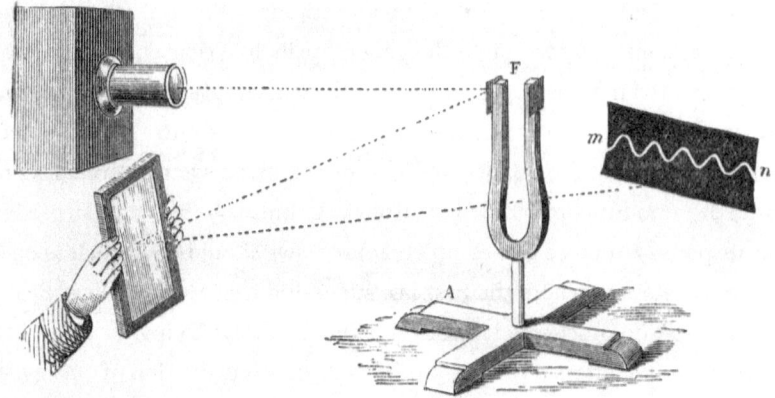

FIGURE 12. Illustration from John Tyndall, *Sound* (1867), 61. (Courtesy of the Cambridge University Library)

"beats," or "vibrations," which can in turn be converted into the visible form of the rhythmical series. Jarring aurality thus becomes gratifying visuality.

Figure 12 demonstrates how the surveying eye replaces the fatigued ear: Tyndall trains a beam of light upon a tuning fork, whose reflecting vibrations trace a series of oscillations upon a screen. "I augment the dissonance by increasing the load," he writes; "the rhythmic lengthening and shortening of the band of light is now more rapid, while the intermittent hum of the forks is very audible." Tyndall frequently struggles to express his aesthetic regard for such figures ("The rapid rippling of the scrolls from one form of beauty to another cannot be rendered"). Figure 13, which charts the changing vibrations of a progressively shortened violin string, demonstrates most clearly the recuperation of dissonance within a symmetrical order: the sudden rise following the unison at c' demonstrates a sudden increase in dissonance, whose counterpart (and resolution) arrives at the end of the series, as the dissonance vanishes at c'', one octave higher. Discord is but one plunging line within a rhythmical whole.

Friedrich Kittler is therefore too hasty when he asserts that brute "frequency," which in the nineteenth century supersedes harmonic intervals, contributes toward the abolition of "so-called man."[10] Tyndall's visualizations convert chords into waveforms, yet continue to permit a consolatory humanism that proves more robust than its detractors suppose. It also, like

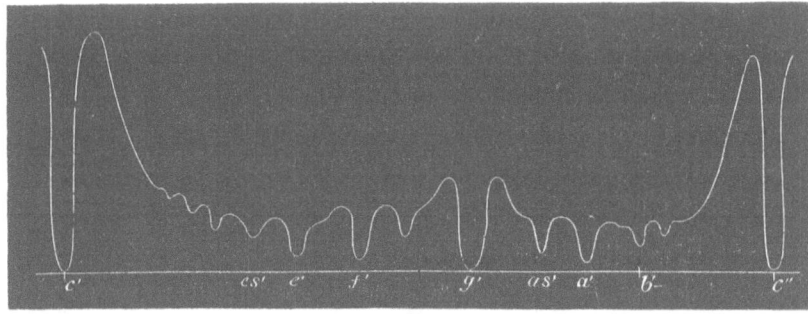

FIGURE 13. Illustration from John Tyndall, *Sound* (1867), 305. (Courtesy of the Cambridge University Library)

Tyndall's reference to the "investment" of sun in flora and fauna, suggests a model economy. As Anton Rabinbach's magisterial *The Human Motor* has shown, Helmholtz's 1847 lecture entitled "The Conservation of Force" inspired a plethora of scientists, philosophers, and engineers to reconceive of the human body as a thermodynamic system, with the entropic tendency accordingly redefined as a managerial problem of corporeal fatigue. Rabinbach summarizes: "With the discovery of fatigue as the dystopia of universal labour power, the search for a thermodynamics of society began in earnest. As entropy revealed the loss of energy involved in any transfer of force, so fatigue revealed the loss of energy in the conversion of *Kraft* to socially useful production. As energy was the transcendental, 'objective force' in nature, fatigue became the objective nemesis of a society founded on labor power."[11] When Tyndall defines consonance as "the spiritual pleasure derived from the perception of order without weariness of mind," he dutifully adopts Helmholtz's equivalence between dissonance and fatigue; the former produces a series of "shocks," which leads naturally to the latter.[12]

Helmholtz conducted a series of experiments that sought to mitigate or reverse such nervous wear-and-tear; Thaddeus Bolton's 1894 dissertation "Rhythm" demonstrates the extent to which its central concept proved essential to such developing concerns:

> It may safely be said that nervous action in general, and especially of the lower and vaso-motor centres, is rhythmical. . . . Helmholtz found that when

he stimulated a nerve going to a muscle by a submaximal stimulus and then added another stimulus at any time afterward within four seconds, he obtained a contraction. If he used a maximal stimulus in the first place and then added another stimulus during the latent period, it produced no effect upon the contraction due to the first stimulus. But if the second stimulus was added after the latent period, the effect was a greater contraction than that which followed the first stimulus alone.[13]

Bolton's summary clarifies how a Helmholtzian emphasis upon conservation and fatigue encouraged a utilitarian calculus of labor power: in place of a "maximal stimulus" that renders the nerve insensible and the laboring body unproductive, a series of lesser shocks enable a continuous discharge of function. The cardiograph, pneumograph, sphygmograph, kymograph, and ergograph, which respectively measure the heartbeat, breathing rate, pulse, blood pressure, and degree of muscular fatigue, and as such uncannily anticipate our sports watches and fitness trackers, all derive from Helmholtz's experimental example.

A rich seam of scholarly work has recently explored such technological developments, as they were taken up by Etienne-Jules Marey and Angelo Mosso, among others. Yet in this context I am particularly interested in how rhythmical innatism appealed repeatedly to the sanction of poetry; for Spencer's claim that he and Tyndall were "alone in the belief that all motion is rhythmical," if it had ever proven correct, soon ceased to be so. Sidney Lanier's *Science of English Verse* (1880) offers one particularly striking instance of the influence of the Spencer-Tyndall nexus: in the section entitled "Of Rhythm, throughout All Those Motions Which We Call 'Nature,'" Lanier reels off a list of periodic phenomena extensive enough to put even that duo to shame. The dance of primitive tribes and the music of Chopin and Liszt; the "spiral distribution of the remote nebulae" and the twinkling and dimming of stars; planets, satellites, sunspots, sea tides, trade winds, long grasses in running brooks, storms, earthquakes, diseases, minor fevers, lungs, the diastole and systole of the heart, and "the cilia of the animalcule": "everywhere," concludes Lanier, "we find rhythm."[14]

The inspiration for this catalogue is familiar: "Mr. Herbert Spencer claims to have observed such a prevalence of this rhythmic periodicity throughout nature as to convince him that it is universal: and states that this belief is shared by Mr. Tyndall."[15] Such borrowings help to explain Lanier's poetic positivism, where *The Science of English Verse* (the clue lies in its title) consistently attempts to fuse together popular versions of physics and biology with a dogged insistence upon the metrical foot. Lanier is at least a good enough reader of Spencer to grasp where that cosmology comes under strain:

> And there is yet a more general view of the rhythmic principle which hints that this proportion in which the worlds move and by which "things stand to be good or beautiful" is due to antagonism. Mr. Herbert Spencer has formulated the proposition that where opposing forces act, rhythm appears, and has traced the rhythmic motions of nature to the antagonistic forces there found, such as the two motions which carry the earth towards, and away from, the sun and so result in the periodicity of the earth's progress, and others.[16]

Just as Spencer was moved to redefine rhythm as "a conflict of forces not in equilibrium," so Lanier's generative antagonisms suddenly contain "the fret, the sting, the thwart, the irreconcilable me as against all other me's, the awful struggle for existence, the desperate friction of individualities, the no of death to all requests."[17] Just when he appears to be on the cusp of a more dynamic conception of cosmological rhythm or poetic meter, however, Lanier retreats from fretfulness into a more numinous realm: having appealed to Edgar Allan Poe's *Eureka* (whose vision of a universe in which atoms "aggregate into worlds, to fall into the central sun, and to be again rediffused" recuperates thermodynamic dissolution within a larger scheme),[18] Lanier concludes his discussion with an appeal to classical versification, which imparts order to "the otherwise chaotic fabric of things." "We may," Lanier concludes with vague pithiness, "be able to see dimly into that old Orphic saying of the seer, 'The father of metre is rhythm, and the father of rhythm is God.'"[19]

Lanier's rhythmical innatism, with its extension of the conservation of force into an economy of artistic expression, would prove powerfully representative. The late nineteenth-century vogue for Delsartism developed techniques for dance, gymnastics, and kinesthetic gesture, which were underpinned by Helmholtzian principles.[20] Henrietta Russell offers a colorful illustration, in her article for *The Delsarte Series* entitled "Yawning," which recovers the apparently involuntary reflex as a viable form of rhythmical exercise: "Gymnastic," she writes, "becomes necessary when civilization has made it possible for a group of people to exist without work."[21] Russell concludes that "when a man is tired, he has, either by inactivity or over-activity, committed a chemical, physiological, and psychological violation of the laws of economy. Nature, instead of leaving him in a condition approaching stagnation, immediately sets to work to restore him to a pleasurable state by a light stimulative gymnastic called a yawn."[22]

Russell's ongoing collaboration with her second husband, Richard Hovey (who despite the esteem of Ezra Pound has long since fallen from favor), reveals more clearly how such notions depend upon and enable poetry. In a series of articles published in the 1890s (to which Russell may well have contributed), Hovey connects Delsartism—via Spencer and Lanier's theory of rhythm—to an essentialized account of metrical feet: "Delsarte and Poetry" claims that "feet like the trochee, which are accented on the first syllable, are emotional in expression, and feet like the English pseudo-anapest, which are accented on the final syllable, are physical."[23]

The nadir of such rhythmical innatism arrives with the Canadian poet Bliss Carman, who fermented Hovey's ideas into a reactionary brew. Carman had heard Herbert Spencer himself lecture in New York, in 1882, on the thoroughly Helmholtzian topic of "The Gospel of Relaxation": "We have heard too much of the gospel of work," Spencer declared; "perhaps we need to hear about the gospel of relaxation."[24] Such a contention became, in Carman's hands, a call to arms for virile labor and proper repose, as against a vitiating, effeminizing modernity. The essay "Personal Rhythm," which appeared in *The Friendship of Art*, proves emblematic: "It is one of the great evils of modern life," Carman writes, "that it tends to throw us out of rhythm. We are nearly all hurried to a point of hysteria. It is not so much that we have more than we can do, as that we allow the haste to get on our nerves."[25] Despite the wasting pressures of civilization, each individual is naturally fitted in a certain manner, modeled explicitly upon metrical feet. "Dons and dowagers and policemen are always iambic in their rhythm" given their "ponderous" temperament. Scholars or policemen should take note, though such persons at least have the consolation of not being "undecided people" who are condemned to move in "dactylic measure." Amorous men (is it needless to say?) converse in trochees.[26] Inadvertent slapstick cannot disguise profound illiberalism.

Rhythmical Transmission

While Carman's prosodic essentialism represents a low point for what I have called rhythmical innatism, that loose tradition of thought at least contains attempted solutions to a real problem. Those solutions differ substantially from a parallel response that sought to extend the concept of rhythm in a contrasting manner. Where the first response sought to manage fatigue, this second approach more ambitiously questioned whether entropic dissolution need even emerge. Where previously rhythm had been taken to inhere in organisms, or musical tones, or the universe, this second mode of thought considered rather the active processes by which those separate bodies communicated or metabolized apparent waste products. In place of rhythmical innatism, we find rhythmical transmission.

Perhaps the clearest demonstration of this divergence from the conservation of force arrives with *The Unseen Universe, or Physical Speculations on a Future State*, the 1875 theologico-scientific polemic coauthored by the physicists Balfour Stewart and P. G. Tait. (Maxwell corresponded with the latter during his contention with Spencer over agitated molecules.) In a characteristic passage that grapples with the second law of thermodynamics, Stewart and Tait seek not to minimize waste but to deny its very existence:

> Just as no single action of the body takes place without the waste of some muscular tissue, so, it is believed, no thought takes place without some waste of the brain. Nay, physiologists go even further, and assert that each specific thought denotes some specific waste of brain-tissue, so that there is some mysterious and obscure connection between the nature of the thought and the nature of the waste which it occasions. In like manner memory is looked upon as dependent upon traces, left behind in the brain, of that state in which it was when the sensation remembered took place.[27]

In a spiritualized Lockeanism, waste is productively recycled into those memory traces that constitute our very identity. From here it is a short leap to Stewart and Tait's bolder speculative claim for the survival of personal identity beyond bodily death, in a form subtle enough to elude conventional scientific forms of measurement.

Tyndall's *Sound* lectures similarly contain a form of rhythmical transmission that cannot but invite superstition, for all that he proved a far more uncompromising materialist than Stewart and Tait. We saw how Tyndall encouraged rhythmical innatism by converting dissonance into a periodic visual unit, whose waveform proved metonymic of the universe at large. His sixth lecture, by contrast, opens with a barrage of rhythmical phenomena that "impress" not for their internal regularity, but through their communicative force. "Friction is always rhythmic," Tyndall commences. "When we pass a resined bow across a string, the tension of the string secures the perfect rhythm of the friction."[28] Similarly the "rifle bullet sings in its passage through the air," while when a candle is moved rapidly, "an indented band of light, declaring intermittence, is the consequence, while the almost musical sound which accompanies is the audible expression of its rhythm."[29]

These phenomena pave the way for some of Tyndall's famously crowd-pleasing experiments, conducted upon the "sensitive flame": where the screen merely registered the undulations of a vibrating tuning fork, these flames actively respond to acoustic stimuli. *Sound* contrives their sensitivity in two separate ways: firstly, "when the gas flame is simply enclosed within a metal tube, the passage of air over it is usually sufficient to produce the necessary rhythmic action, so as to cause the flame to burst spontaneously into song."[30] Secondly, in a section suggestively headed "sensitive naked flames," Tyndall simply submits his object to a current of air discharged through a blow-pipe, causing it to flutter. "And now, when the whistle is blown," he concludes triumphantly, "you see an extraordinary appearance. The flame thrusts out seven quivering tongues." Figure 14 indicates this transformation.[31]

Considered objectively, this flame does no more than the oscillating waves: it provides an index (whether visual or acoustic) of a given stimulus, in this case a whistle. Yet Tyndall's pathetic fallacy ("burst spontaneously into song") suggests that "rhythmical action" somehow enables a less circumscribed subjectivation. And this is as nothing compared to what follows:

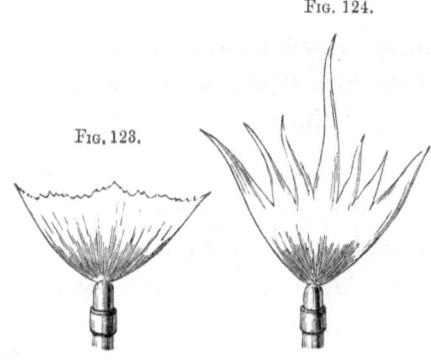

FIGURE 14. Illustration from John Tyndall, *Sound* (1867), 234. (Courtesy of the Cambridge University Library)

The most marvellous flame hitherto discovered is now before you. It issues from the single orifice of a steatite burner, and reaches a height of 24 inches. The slightest tap on a distant anvil reduces its height to 7 inches. . . . The creaking of my boots puts it in violent commotion, or tearing of a bit of paper, or the rustle of a silk dress, does the same. It is startled by the patter of a raindrop. . . . From a distance of 30 yards I have chirruped to this flame, and caused it to fall and roar. I repeat a passage from Spenser:—

> Her ivory forehead full of bounty brave,
>   Like a broad table did itself dispread;
> For love his lofty triumphs to engrave,
>   And write the battles of his great godhead.
> All truth and goodness might therein be read,
>   For there their dwelling was, and when she spake,
> Sweet words, like dropping honey she did shed;
>   And through the pearls and rubies softly brake
> A silver sound, which heavenly music seemed to make.

The flame picks out certain sounds from my utterance; it notices some by the slightest nod, to others it bows more distinctly, to some its obeisance is very profound, while to many sounds it turns an entirely deaf ear.[32]

This wavering specimen comes across as a twenty-four-inch-tall caricature of Keats, with an exquisite sensibility that starts at the rustle of silk or tread of a boot. While the content of Spenser's poem (as opposed to its exact aural frequency) has no bearing upon the flame's motion, the line "A silver sound, which heavenly music seemed to make" somehow seems to hold extra-scientific significance. Appropriately, the flame flutters most pronouncedly when Tyndall expostulates the lyric syllable "Ah!"[33]

These cumulative factors explain why, despite Tyndall's own commitment to an economical materialism of matter and motion, his natural supernaturalism could easily tip over into unabashed spiritualism in the hands of his several followers. The sensitive flame lecture makes specific reference to one such figure, paying tribute to "Mr. Barrett, late laboratory assistant in this place."[34] William Barrett, after having fallen out spectacularly with Tyndall following several years of patronage, would extend his mentor's theatrical empiricism into the more contentious realm of the occult. His *On the Threshold of the Unseen: An Examination of the Phenomena of Spiritualism and of the Evidence for Survival after Death* (1917), whose title chimes self-evidently with Stewart and Tait's more systematic undertaking, reveals both a continuity and discontinuity with Tyndall's example. The responsive medium now is no longer a sensitively fluttering gas flame, but the familiar ghostly presences of the Victorian séance:

> We found the raps grew in intensity when a merry song was struck up, or music was played; the raps in a most amusing way keeping time with the music, occasionally changing to a loud rhythmic scraping, as if the bow of a 'cello were drawn on a piece of wood. Again and again I placed my ear on the very spot whence this rough fiddling appeared to proceed and felt distinctly the rhythmic vibration going on in the table, but no tangible cause was visible either above or below the table.[35]

Barrett himself never graduated beyond the superstitious exploitation of Tyndall's work.[36] Yet other figures generated a more productive yield from this unpromising cocktail of "rhythmic vibration" and Victorian spiritualism. F. W. H. Myers and Edmund Gurney prove significant cases in point; their close intellectual and biographical circumstances require their being taken together. Both were fellows at Trinity College, Cambridge, where, with their common friend and preceptor Henry Sidgwick, they established the British Society for Psychical Research—an organization that offered a soberer and more scholarly variant on Barrett's contemporaneous investigations.

Myers's programmatic declaration that "science, while perpetually denying an unseen world, is perpetually revealing it" affiliates him explicitly to the broader pattern of thought under consideration.[37] His *Human Personality and Its Survival of Bodily Death*, as its title suggests, offers a textbook instance of the attempt to deny waste, with its author keenly aware of the consequences of entropy (as we shall later see). As with Barrett, Myers's various accounts of occult communication frequently rely upon the concept of rhythm: we read of a certain "Mme. X," who one day "felt herself lifted by force from her arm-chair and compelled to stand upright. Her feet and her whole body then executed a systematic calisthenic exercise, in which all the movements were regulated and made rhythmic with finished art"; later, at the Paris Exhibition of 1889, the same Mme. X observed a Javanese dance "consisting of rhythmic motions of the body with contortions of the arms. The occult agents caused her to repeat this dance several times with perfect execution."[38] Myers's dedicated psychical research succeeded a youthful period of poetic composition: the metrical experimentation and manic alliteration of his long poem *St. Paul* (1867) offer a practical demonstration of his belief, articulated in an essay on Virgil, in the sympathetic rhythmical inducement of poetry.[39]

It is Edmund Gurney, however, who offers what is by some distance the most suggestive theorization of rhythm as communicating principle across the boundary of the supersensible—along with the centrality of poetry to such an agenda. (His thinking in this regard represents a positive contrast to the Darwinian justification of absolute music, upon which I briefly touched in the previous chapter.) The variety and richness of Gurney's work has long been unjustly obscured: he remains primarily (and often pejoratively) identified with *Phantasms of the Living* (1886), a psychical compendium coauthored with Myers. I wish to focus rather on several of Gurney's ancillary writings, which, freed from a psychical context, inherit and extend Tyndall's notion of rhythmical transmission in distinctive ways.

In addition to his paranormal research, Gurney was a musicologist of unusual breadth and sensitivity, as evidenced by his ambitious treatise *The Power of Sound* (1880)—a work to which I will later return. So too was he an astute reader of verse; one such contribution—the essay "Poets, Critics and Class-Lists," later collected into his two-volume *Tertium Quid*—assumes particular relevance given the present discussion. The essay constitutes an appeal to the "non-reasonable" element, pleasures of sonic harmony or tension that Gurney contrasts with the "presentative" or discursive dimension of verse.[40] Yet Gurney's pitch for unreasonableness does not impel him to any doctrine of Pure Sound. Indeed, he resists the thought that poetry aspires to the condition of music (as with Sidney Lanier's "science"); a pugilistic footnote attacks the Wagnerian critic and librettist Francis Hueffer, whose attempt to prove "the identity of musical and metrical laws" preserves not much more than the uniquely sonorous Dante, and unnecessarily dispenses with "the barbarous harshness of Goethe's, Shelley's, Victor Hugo's, Lord Tennyson's and Mr. Swinburne's best verses."[41]

The "barbarous harshness" of poetic rhythm may, therefore, hold a distinctive positive effect. It is at this point that parallels begin to emerge for Gurney's pseudoscientific research:

> The off-hand notion is that, as Poetry consists of sense and sound, the pleasure which is not due to the sense must be due to the sound; but if we call the sense "oxygen" and the sound "nitrogen," the intoxicating effect is obtained, not by *mixing* the two constituents, as in air, but by *combining* them, as in laughing-gas. Our "non-reasonable element," thus regarded, is not an element proper but a *reaction*, in which the nature of the constituents, as known in separation, is quite transformed. The point is one which might well be emphasised for its scientific (as apart from its artistic) interest. For this sort of combination, this veritable *psycho-chemistry*, has not been nearly enough recognised in psychology.[42]

We cannot simply isolate the "sound" of a given poem, which has always already entered into a process of combination with "sense," that transfigures both. This composite irreducibility exposes a bad choice between two forms of listening: on the one hand, "our normal experience of language throughout our lives has taught us to regard it as simply a set of symbols whereby ideas are conveyed from one mind to another"; on the other, "when our ears are occupied with sound as such—whether in submission to the soothing influence of winds or streams or distant city-noises, or in observation of some rhythmically recurring stimulus, such as the ticking of a clock or the breaking of waves, or in attention to instrumental music," we typically neglect all ideational content.[43] Verse rhythm, in contradistinction both to ticking clocks and to music proper, brings "an unexpected gratuity," a cognitive yield. "Rhythm," Gurney continues, extending the word that had become cardinal to his argument, "perpetually not only transfigures the poetical expression of an idea, but makes the idea of that expression possible."[44]

The scientific language of Gurney's *"psycho-chemistry"* survives into a series of appeals to try this rhythmical truth through the "self-experiment" of reciting verse.[45] It is through this communication of "unreasonable" yet cognitively significant material that we glimpse consequences for Gurney's ancillary paranormal activity. However little his essay makes that connection explicit, it surfaces in the stray word "medium," inserted into a passage that channels Plato's *Ion* through latter-day spiritualism: "The poet speaks through a medium which seems to intensify the point and to extend the range of what he would tell us by some power outside his own volition. Such a power, in fact, a rhythmic order, in its fundamental appeal to human nerves, literally is."[46]

It is one of the sad ironies of intellectual life that Gurney's paranormal activities should have overshadowed his remarkably sensitive grasp of poetic rhythm, which would surely never have been formulated without the assistance of the former. We conventionally detach eccentrics such as Myers and Gurney from the main currents of intellectual history, which in so doing we distort. William James, to name just one comparatively canonical figure, warmly and frankly acknowledged Myers's influence.[47] It cannot be coincidental, meanwhile, that several of the most forceful later theorists of rhythm should have had involvement, of one kind or another, with the Society for Psychical Research: Alfred North Whitehead was close to Sidgwick and other members of the group, during his own time at Trinity in the 1880s, while Henri Bergson, meanwhile, was even elected president. (Bergson had earlier written a short paper upon the breathing rhythms of individuals under hypnosis; his presidential address, "Phantasms of the Living and Psychical Research," doffs its cap to Myers.)[48]

Such accesses of Victorian spiritualism are easy enough to ridicule from a contemporary perspective that likes to pretend that it more rigorously polices the boundaries between science and pseudoscience, although the successively discredited philosophical doctrine of panpsychism has recently undergone a surprising resurgence in the work of Steven Shaviro among others.[49] And while for my part I draw the spiritual borders of my world more narrowly than Shaviro, let alone than Gurney, I also feel that the latter's evocation of rhythm as "an abstract order of sound [that] gets wrought into the very tissue of . . . thought" resonates powerfully in my own body. I would seek to modify Gurney's postulation of a rhythmical "medium" in but one crucial manner, by suggesting that the poem, voice, or motor activity, which is thereby communicated to us, never manifests itself without remainder. The following section will explore the nature of this remainder, in the form of a waste that cannot be mitigated or denied.

The Poetics of Waste

Rhythmical innatism and rhythmical transmission alike represent genuine attempts to answer a real problem, namely the profound disquiet that the second law of thermodynamics occasioned. In their respective attempts to recuperate or deny waste, however, they finally prove less compelling than a third and final tendency, to which I now turn. This pattern of thinking accepts the entropic implications of that second law, which it tries to render livable. This rather vague designation—"livable"—spans a wide affective range. Here for example is the irrepressible John Tyndall, this time speaking not as a dutiful conservationist of force, but rather as one who has comprehended the inexorability of entropy and come out smiling:

> With terrible jolts and oscillations the religious life of the world has run down "the ringing grooves of change." A smoother route may have been undiscoverable. At all events it was undiscovered. Some years ago I found myself in discussion with a friend who entertained the notion that the general tendency of things in this world is towards equilibrium, the result of which would be peace and blessedness to the human race. My notion was that equilibrium meant not peace and blessedness, but death.[50]

It is tempting to surmise that this unnamed "friend" is no other than Spencer himself. Tyndall's pithiness lends weight to Paul Sawyer's complaint that "the Lucretian universe of Tyndall, purged of troublesome projections, seems blandly salutary; for Tyndall feared neither analysis, nor Mother Earth, nor life, nor death."[51] Yet he was also, if more infrequently, capable of profounder response, as in his "Musings on the Matterhorn, 1868":

> Did that formless fog contain potentially the *sadness* with which I regarded the Matterhorn? Did the *thought* which now ran back to it simply return to its primeval home? . . . Supposing our theologic schemes of creation, condemnation, and redemption to be dissipated; and the warmth of denial which they excite, and which, as a motive force, can match the warmth of affirmation, dissipated at the same time; would the undeflected human mind return to the meridian of absolute neutrality as regards these ultra-physical questions? Is such a position one of stable equilibrium?[52]

Such moments suggest that Bruce Clarke is a little unjust to write off Tyndall as a simple proponent of the conservation of force.[53] The allusion to Tennyson's "Locksley Hall" ("the ringing grooves of change") proves telling in this respect. For what I am marking as a third distinct response to thermodynamics engages with verse still more concertedly than its two counterparts. Examples abound: James Clerk Maxwell's "Paradoxical Ode after Shelley," composed upon the physicist's deathbed, casts doubt upon Stewart and Tait's scientific justification of the immortal soul:

> Till in that twilight of the gods
> When earth and sun are frozen clods,
> When, all its matter degraded,
> Matter in aether shall have faded,
> We, that is, all the work we've done,
> As waves in aether, shall for ever run
> In swift expanding spheres, through heavens beyond the sun.[54]

Our "work" may endure, but in what form, given an entropic world of frozen clods?

In a formal review of *The Unseen Universe* for the *Fortnightly Review*, the strident atheist W. K. Clifford responded more forthrightly to Stewart and Tait. Here again, critique leads naturally to verse:

Consider a mountain rill. It runs down in the sunshine, and its water evaporates; yet it is fed by thousands of tiny tributaries, and the stream flows on. The water may be changed again and again, yet still there is the same stream. It widens over plains, or is prisoned and fouled by towns; always the same stream; but at last

> "even the weariest river
> Winds somewhere safe to sea."

When that happens no drop of the water is lost, but the stream is dead.[55]

Like many before him, Clifford seeks to balance the death of the individual organism with the endurance of the whole; yet the grammatical structure of his final sentence lays the emphasis squarely on the latter. The preceding quotation derives from Swinburne's "Garden of Proserpine"; Clifford would make a habit of citing his verse in scientific reviews.[56] He was not alone in situating the poet within an explicitly thermodynamic context. While F. W. H. Myers clung to rhythmical transmission as a means of recovering what appeared lost, he was also able to see in Swinburne a subtly different scientific relevance. His "Modern Poets and the Meaning of Life" (1893) asks expansively, "Does the law of the conservation of energy condemn man's consciousness to extinction when the measurable energies which build up his chemical texture pass back into the organic world, or may his conscious life be a form of activity which, just because it is not included in our own cycle of mutually transformable energies, is itself in its own proper form as imperishable as they?"[57]

Myers has so stacked the second part of his grand rhetorical question (which he immediately rephrases a further four times), that we feel certain that the answer will be—no: we are not condemned to extinction! Yet Swinburne's example changes the response that he was elsewhere not slow to provide. Having approvingly quoted a "long passage in which Tristram of Lyonesse proudly avows, before the great spectacle of the universe, the inevitable nothingness of man,"[58] Myers concludes his discussion with a familiar reference, the evocative force of which would be remarkable even were it not delivered by a committed spiritualist:

And of all Swinburne's poems, perhaps the most wonderful, with melody farthest beyond the reach of any other still living man, is that "Garden of Proserpine," whose close represents in well-known words the deep life-weariness of men who have had enough of love. There is here far more than the Lucretian satisfaction in the thought that we shall sleep tranquilly through the hazardous future as we slept tranquilly through the raging past—*ad confligendum venientibus undique Poenis*—when all the perils which menaced Rome were as nothing to us yet unborn. No, there is here a profounder renouncement of life; there is the grim suspicion which has stolen into many a heart, that we do in truth feel within us, as years go by, a mortality of spirit as well as flesh; that the "bower of unimagined flower and tree" withers inevitably into a frozen barrenness from which no new life can spring.[59]

Swinburne's verse assumes a similar significance for Gurney, who referred approvingly, we recall, to the poet's "barbarous harshness," which he attributes in large part to the compulsive monorhymes that pervade the "Garden of Proserpine" ("it," "it," "it"; "him," "him," "him").[60] His sensitivity to these jarring effects contrasts starkly with what elsewhere appears a rather conventional adherence to metrical propriety, as when Gurney contends that perceived hypermetricality in Keats's "Ode to Autumn" results in "the back of the metre [being] completely broken": "The irritation produced may be quite on a par with the pleasure which has preceded it."[61]

Swinburne thus exposes a broader tension within Gurney's work, regarding the nature and acceptability of the dissonance that Tyndall had sought to redeem. At his most astute moments, Gurney intuits that the progressively "harsh" character of late nineteenth-century poetry and music productively challenges prevailing notions of aesthetic and physiological economy. In an appendix to *The Power of Sound* entitled "On Discord," Gurney takes issue with Helmholtz's theory of nervous wear and repair, as it specifically applies to the reception of audible stimuli. In discussions of "*muscular* fatigue" he claims, it is mistaken to elide the ear with the eye: there is no exact aural equivalent to the retina of a subject dazzled from staring at the sun.[62] Grant Allen and other physiological aestheticians, he continues, frequently confuse the fatiguing effects of dissonance itself with simple "*loudness*."[63]

Yet this does not mean that the problem of fatigue vanishes from acoustic science. When Gurney declares that "it may be suggested that the very mode of life of a nerve-cell is rhythmic," in that "exhaustion and nutrition, waste and repair, succeed each other in regular order," he may seem to offer but one more variation on Lanier's cosmology. Yet this "regular order," we immediately discover, does not apply to the rhythmical apperception of a human subject, which rather follows something much more like Spencer's notion of conflictual disequilibrium:

> As regards repair after exhaustion, the one condition in which the nerve substance could be in the *same* state of readiness for stimuli of all rates and strengths would be if it could arrive at a state of *complete* repair in a time shorter than the shortest interval. . . . But then, on this hypothesis, it becomes hard to imagine how a sense of rhythm could be produced at all, if we are to recognise no other objective conditions for agreeable sensation than *degrees* of stimulation and of repair—for one would naturally suppose that for a succession of stimuli to produce a sense of rhythm, each must occur before the effects of its predecessor have quite disappeared, that is, *before* the condition of complete nervous equilibrium has been re-established; and on the theory we are discussing, complete equilibrium seems unsusceptible of any other meaning than complete repair.[64]

Aesthetics is not a closed homeostatic system: rather, "Mr. Grant Allen well expresses it in regard to rhythm: 'if the opportunity for the discharge is wanting, the gathered energy has to dissipate itself by other channels, which involves a certain amount of conflict and waste.'"[65] Gurney differs from Allen here only insofar as this "conflict and waste" is not only inevitable but also aesthetically desirable. "Helmholtz says that thirds and sixths are melodically and harmonically the most attractive of intervals," he declares, yet "harmony which dealt in thirds and sixths and avoided discord would very soon pall."[66] The intuition of recurrence depends upon imperfect recovery: waste is a condition of possibility for rhythm itself.

I do not think it coincidental that so many scientists were drawn expressly to Swinburne's work. The only figure that Clifford, Myers, or Gurney cite nearly as frequently is Tennyson; literary criticism has subsequently pursued this route, most often considering the poet laureate or Gerard

Manley Hopkins for their more explicit treatment of thermodynamics.[67] Yet Swinburne's engagement with the specter of entropy is all the more powerful for existing not at the level of representation but as experience. By stressing this property, I aim to develop several evocative analogies that have been drawn between his verse and specific modes of scientific enquiry. Herbert Tucker, for example, alternately calls *Tristram of Lyonesse* "a fractal transform of the one aeonic narrative of excitation and equilibrium" and a "blaze across the thermodynamic inane."[68] In the introduction to their masterful edition of Swinburne's *Major Poems and Selected Prose*, meanwhile, Jerome McGann and Charles L. Sligh contend that "the contemporary relevance of Swinburne's work springs from its intellectual affinities with a quantum mechanical model of reality, on one hand, and postmodern autopoetical ideas on the other."[69]

Swinburne's own comments often frustrate the attempt to read such significance into his verse. His explicit references to contemporary science are unhelpfully cursory or sardonic. The essay "Under the Microscope," for instance, which ventured a polemical riposte to Robert Buchanan's notorious Fleshly School, opines with Austenesque irony that "we live in an age when not to be scientific is to be nothing"; Swinburne goes on to declare that he has done his bit, by taking an interest in comparative entomology—the critters in this case being quickly revealed, however, to be critics.[70] An August 1874 letter to Theodore Watts, in which Swinburne declares his admiration for Tyndall's infamous Belfast Address, delivered earlier in the same year, gives us a little more to work with. "Even my technical ignorance," he writes, "does not impair, I think, my power to see accurately and seize firmly the first thread of the great clue, because my habit of mind is not (I hope) unscientific, though my work lies in the field of art instead of science, and when seen and seized even that first perception gives me an indescribable sense of music and repose. It is Theism which to me seems to introduce an element—happily a factitious element—of doubt, discord and disorder."[71] Swinburne's contrast of repose and discord helps to open up the question of his relation to thermodynamics. To follow it through, however, we must depart from the discursive treatment of his work that characterized Swinburne's reception in scientific circles.

Tired Verse

Swinburne's verse engages the culture of thermodynamics not through propositional claims or distinct imagery, but rather through rhythmical experience. It is not difficult to see why W. K. Clifford appealed to "The Garden of Proserpine" when searching for an imaginative representation of heat death, given that poem's concluding image ("Only the sleep eternal / In an eternal night"). Countless literary allusions might have performed similar work, however; for the apocalyptic prophecy of a frozen futurity, we need go no further than the Book of Isaiah.

Yet Clifford did stumble upon a distinguishing mark of Swinburne's verse, however much its full significance may have eluded him. For in his specific reference to the weary river winding to sea, we begin to glimpse the centrality of Swinburne to a concept whose significance has accreted over the course of my discussion: fatigue. The word "weary" and its many cognates prove signal instances of what Edward Thomas called Swinburne's "harem of words, to which he was constant and absolutely faithful"—a rebuke that leaves suggestively open whether Swinburne sins through licentiousness, or a still more illicit fusion of licentiousness and devotion.[72] The sheer force of this devotion transfigures what would otherwise prove mere semantic repetition. When Sappho declares in "Anactoria" that "I am weary of all thy words and soft strange ways" (35), she may appear to offer no more than a tired tag. As McGann and Sligh point out, however, this line sets in motion six couplet rhymes (beginning "ways" / "days") that are no sooner finished than they repeat themselves word for word:[73]

> I am weary of all thy words and soft strange ways,
> Of all love's fiery nights and all his days,
> And all the broken kisses salt as brine
> That shuddering lips make moist with waterish wine,
> And eyes the bluer for all those hidden hours
> That pleasure fills with tears and feeds from flowers,
> Fierce at the heart with fire that half comes through,
> But all the flowerlike white stained round with blue;

The fervent underlid, and that above
Lifted with laughter or abashed with love;
Thine amorous girdle, full of thee and fair,
And leavings of the lilies in thine hair.
Yea, all sweet words of thine and all thy ways,
And all the fruit of nights and flower of days,
And stinging lips wherein the hot sweet brine
That Love was born of burns and foams like wine,
And eyes insatiable of amorous hours,
Fervent as fire and delicate as flowers. (35–52)

The rhyme scheme recurs, now shorn of Sappho's complaint ("I am weary"); the same verbal material that had indicated satiety now generates "insatiable" desire. Has Swinburne then somehow succeeded in countering the irreversibility of thermodynamics, in making the human body an engine that reconverts waste into productive energy? Not quite. For the anaphora-strewn run-ons into which this extract tumbles ("And," "And") strain against the limits of our vocal endurance, as soon as we take the trouble to articulate the words on the page. We cannot actively embody desire without finding it (positively) exhausting.

This conversion of fatigue from a burden into the very source of desire proves representative. For however much Swinburne alleged to prefer a science that brought "repose" to the "factitious . . . discord" of religion, he offered a more honest self-appraisal when he said of "Dolores" that it described one "foiled in love, and weary of love, but not yet in sight of rest."[74] If the religious life did indeed as Tyndall claimed induce "terrible jolts and oscillations," then Swinburne was, in this specific sense, a religious thinker. T. S. Eliot proved alert to this restlessness of spirit, however much he morally disapproved of it. In his essay entitled "Swinburne as Critic" in *The Sacred Wood*, he complains of Swinburne's prose writing that "one is in risk of becoming fatigued by a hubbub that does not march."[75] The corresponding "Swinburne as Poet" is more specific still: "In the verse of Swinburne," Eliot writes, "the object has ceased to exist, because the meaning is merely the hallucination of meaning, because language, uprooted, has adapted itself to an independent life of atmospheric nourishment. In Swinburne, for example, we see the word 'weary' flourishing in this way independent of the particular and actual weariness of flesh or spirit."[76] Eliot indicts a failure of linguistic reference: the word multiplies so licentiously that it no longer adequately denotes Sappho's state. Yet what if the superfluity of weariness proved (self-)performative rather than referential? Eliot aptly suggests that in Swinburne's verse "one is in risk of becoming fatigued by a hubbub that does not march"; unlike him, I number this exhaustion among his finest expressive effects. Such practice lays down an implicit challenge to any age that seeks to maximize efficiency through the elimination of fatigue.

What counts as productively tired verse? By this I do not mean the standard tropes of spleen, ennui, *Weltschmerz*, and the rest, long since established as indispensable constituents of the fin de siècle; rather, I intend the phenomenological apprehension of tiredness. The question seldom arises for the indefatigable literary critic, who (in print at least) quotes selectively, in manageable chunks, between which his energy (if not always that of the reader) is magically replenished. Yet while Nicholas Dames has explored the way in which the ever-expanding Victorian novel tested the motor endurance and nervous systems of its avid readers, poetry criticism tends by contrast to treat the "lyrical" suspension of time as its unit of (non-)measurement, adhering in its treatment of larger works to Poe's unnecessarily constricting stipulation "that what we call a long poem is, in fact, merely a succession of brief ones—that is to say, of brief poetical effects."[77] Motor endurance represents an untapped means for poetics to resist the bad choice between subjectivism and positivism. As the universal phenomenon of sleep demonstrates, human bodies (for the moment at least) still tend to break down in broadly similar ways; we might choose how to declaim a given line, but not when our voice gives out.

Here is one candidate for productively tired verse:

> And gentler the wind from the dreary
>   Sea-banks by the waves overlapped,
> Being weary, speaks peace to the weary
>   From slopes that the tide-stream has sapped;
> And sweeter than all that we call so

> The seal of their slumber shall be
> Till the graves that embosom them also
> Be sapped of the sea. (*MP*, 192)

I cull this stanza from the first section of Swinburne's "By the North Sea" (113–20), published in his *Studies in Song* (1880); it is hard to think of another passage that so compels (rather than simply indicates) languor. That whole section has maintained the same prosodic scheme: seven roughly ballad lines of tetrameter, with an occasional extension into ten syllables in the third and seventh line, followed by a concluding catalectic unit of five. Lines are consistently end-stopped; even when the ensuing line begins with a preposition, it is possible to slice the clauses so fully as not to enjamb (e.g., 59, 220).

This latter fact helps to explain the disjunctive force of the above stanza, which requires a sudden and substantial vocal effort to force an enjambment that for the first time is unavoidable, heaving itself from the feminine trailing-off of "dreary" to the spondaic "Sea-banks." And that effort prepares the way for the appropriate answering feminine rhyme, "weary," whose premature appearance in line 3 furthers the sense of a meter syncopating itself in the manner in which a machine begins to break down. "Being weary" contains appositely long, assonant vowels, just as "speaks peace" distend and coincide; both redouble the spondaic tendency of the verse. And "speaks peace" does what it says, through the manner in which it slows what had been the line's tumultuous flow, which briefly threatens to break out into a triple measure before again meeting "weary," now in its proper rhyme-place, whose repetition confirms the diagnosis and confesses its need for respite, only for the verse to push off again with another enjambed preposition. This verse denies our growing desire for a break, which subsequently propels us through lines whose triple rhythm contrasts starkly with the heavily stressed material that preceded it, before with no small relief we at last arrive at our definitively end-stopped terminus, "sapped of the sea."

Such effects litter Swinburne's verse, where weariness emerges first as theme, only then to be transfigured through experience. The remainder of this chapter focuses in detail upon a single exorbitant instance of this trend, the long poem *Tristram of Lyonesse* (1882). In part I do so simply because it is a long poem. For *Tristram* continually produces nonlinear phase transitions, where a difference in degree produces a difference in kind: it subjects our vocal and motor systems to an excess, through which they cognize in a manner that the properly rested body cannot. The poem's various tropes of entropy finally prove significant only within a broader rhythmical economy that acknowledges (indeed depends upon) the invariability and irreversibility of waste. Swinburne thereby actuates what Spencer could only rather nebulously describe: a form of conflictual disequilibrium; a rhythm that emerges through, rather than despite, variation. *Tristram of Lyonesse* engineers this variation within the traditionally closed system of the heroic couplet, which Swinburne here pushes harder and further than perhaps any other poem (a possible exception being Browning's *Sordello*).

Tristram of Lyonesse is of course more specifically a long narrative poem, which recounts a story whose familiarity justifies Swinburne's almost total unconcern for narrative exegesis, suspense, or consistency. "So many and many of old have given my twain / Love and live song and honey-hearted pain," the Prelude declares (239–40), with the strictly superfluous "many and many" suggesting that the reiteration of narrative matters more than its actual content. Apparently climactic moments (the drinking of the potion, Tristram's slaying of the monster Urgan, even the ultimate death of our hero and heroine) could be reassembled in a different order, without significant alteration to the feel of the whole.[78] The pair are already in love before they drink the love potion; always already doomed, before respective marriages render their love illegitimate.[79] What counts is not the priority of the sequence, but, like the irreversible second law, that it is a sequence. To the extent that my own reading proceeds in broadly chronological terms, it does so not to summarize plot but to preserve a sense of this linearity.

With that in mind, the Prelude already contains all that is to come, despite Swinburne's having composed it in 1870, more than a decade before the publication of the completed work. A full two hundred lines in, neither of the eponymous protagonists has been designated any more specifically than "these twain," despite a welter of proper names (Guinevere, Rosamond, Helen, Angelica). Yet the drama that their life contains (or which rather contains their life) is already present, with the narrator's inclusive premonition:

> We too shall surely pass out of the sun;
> Out of the sound and eyeless light of things,
> Wide as the stretch of life's time-wandering wings,
> Wide as the naked world and shadowless,
> And long-lived as the world's own weariness. (Prelude, 210–14)

The declaration that "we too shall surely pass out of the sun" might well be taken as a direct figuration of heat death; yet "weariness" again emerges more fully through prosodic experience than as direct reference. As with "By the North Sea," the passage oscillates between leaden stress and attempted release: note how the assonance of appropriately distended vowels ("wide . . . life's") and alliteration ("wandering wings") further weighs down the prosodic ballast of line 212. A triple rhythm having tried and failed to assert itself (with the repeated "wide as the"), the final line again collapses under the weight of consecutive stresses compounded by their already living in recent memory ("lived," "world"). Just as the feminine ending of "weary" proved pivotal to the effect of the stanza from "By the North Sea," so the Prelude positions "weariness" significantly at the line end. Its dactylic tendency (along with that of "shadowless") contrasts starkly with the surrounding monosyllabic masculine rhymes ("none" / "sun," "things" / "wings"). The effect is still more pronounced than the above citation suggests: these rhymed polysyllables arrive after eleven such monosyllables, and subsequently usher in an unbroken run of thirty-six monosyllables that carry the Prelude to its end. They thereby prove microcosmic of the rhythmical tension that animates the passage more broadly: given the dominating prosodic context, we cannot fully release "shadowless" or "weariness" into tripping dactyls; their concluding suffixes hover somewhere between compelled emphasis and an expiring sigh.

Monosyllables already dominate in the above passage; yet Swinburne can achieve still more striking shifts in tempo by using nothing else. We are familiar with Alexander Pope marking such lines as metrical contraband—just one of the stipulated laws of couplet form that Swinburne will revel in breaking. The Popean dictum is often taken to chastise a perceived fault of diction (these words are "low" because simple), yet the monosyllable also potentially upsets metrical regularity (we might accentuate as many as eight of "And ten low words oft creep in one dull line"). Adelaide Crapsey's *A Study in English Metrics* (1918) sought to apply rigorous measurement to such features, tabulating the proportion of polysyllabic words across the output of a number of poets. Swinburne, alas, can often only muster fewer than 3 percent of words with three or more syllables, a figure that is dwarfed by Pope and Milton, among others; in book 6 of *Paradise Lost*, for example, we scale the empyrean heights of 9.03 percent.[80] Crapsey's conclusions are as disappointing as her tables are illuminating: "In the analysis presented it is seen that Swinburne works within a very limited range. Unless he can be shown to have made exclusions for special technical purposes, this, if it holds for his work in general, means I think that we find in him not a highly developed but an early technique. He has not mastered all the resources of the language; he has not even divined their existence."[81]

Crapsey intends her tables to contradict Gilbert Murray's impression that Swinburne is "a poet using all the resources of language." Yet the identification of complexity with polysyllabic is crude: prolixity comes cheap to any adolescent with a dictionary. While I leave comprehensive statistical inference to Crapsey, *Tristram of Lyonesse* certainly features an unusually high proportion of those exclusively monosyllabic lines that Edmund Gurney held to be such a characteristic feature of Swinburne's verse; they cumulatively demonstrate the unit's paradoxical capacity to generate both fleetness and ponderousness. Those elementary single-cell words "life" and "death" feature prominently in such cases: "How sore a life dead love should lead her through" (1:346); "Death that bears life, and change that brings forth seed" (6:374); "His bright light heart held half a thought of death" (8:393); "And peace more strong than death round all the dead" (9:514). Such instances represent only a small sample.

The Prelude alone contains abundant examples where monosyllabic strings generate diametrically opposed effects. There we find lines leavened with prepositions and pronouns:

> Ah, and these too felt on them as God's grace. (189)

Or a time that crawls so slowly that it may stay even mortality, as in this remarkable line whose rhythmical excess culminates with seven successive stresses:

And bid the short-lived things, long dead, live long. (83)

Sometimes the effect lies somewhere between the two poles. Take the narrator's pledge to recover Tristram and Iseult's animating love, delivered in a clump of monosyllables:

> Was such not theirs, the twain I take, and give
> Out of my life to make their dead life live
> Some days of mine. (235–37)

The second line begins with lightly accented pronouns and prepositions, in which the first iteration of "life" is but an isolated beat; its latter half, by contrast, contains a series of grinding consecutive stresses ("dead life live") whose very heaviness signals the effort of the simple voice to raise the departed.

We begin to gain some sense of the attraction that "The Garden of Proserpine" exerted for W. K. Clifford, with its weary stream winding to sea. For all Helmholtz's emphasis upon the conservation of force, fatigue is an ineradicable consequence of living. That fact causes us in different moods to desire that life be brought violently to an end; or that we may survive not just despite but because of our languor, as if living it fully might recycle waste product or afford a perverse pleasure for irreparability. My settled paraphrase necessarily travesties Swinburne's inexplicit transitions between these emotional attitudes, which both acknowledge and inhabit the universal tendency for any closed system to wind down.

Once they have made their delayed entrance, Tristram and Iseult further extend this complex pattern of feeling. Their successive repetitions (rather than any substantive change in external circumstance) generate a rapid oscillation between desire for life, and its renunciation. The opening to canto 3, for example, finds Tristram quoting back to himself the words that he had pledged to Iseult three years previously, at the close of the preceding section ("'As the dawn loves the sunset I love thee'" [2:468; 3:1]). Yet that very self-quotation, across a distance of time in which he happens to have married his lover's namesake, Iseult of Brittany, exposes a world that "dies of loving." That bleak prospect unfolds through Tristram's long ensuing monologue, which from the start pushes the monosyllabic tendency still further than did the Prelude:

> In her I lived, and in me she is slain,
> Who loved me that I brought to her doom,
> Who loved her that her love might be my tomb.
> As all the streams on earth and all fresh springs (3:10–13)

The aerodynamic propulsion of this verse enjambs freely into a direct echo of "The Garden of Proserpine": these streams similarly "tend toward the sea, all born most high / Strive downward, passing all things joyous by, / Seek to it and cast their lives in it and die" (20–22). At such moments, Tristram and Iseult's love potion seems but one instance of a universal tendency that we have all already begun to taste.

Yet Tristram's premonition of mortality is never stronger than when he finds himself defying that very process. If the wheel of nature perpetually turns, he continues, then there is after all "surely no irrevocable death" (3:34), a most Tyndallian conclusion. Unlike Tyndall, however, Tristram's verse monologue suffers (rather than merely paying lip service to) the painful breaks necessary for the world to return in any guise. Feel this latest supremely weary couplet:

> Day after day night comes that day may break,
> And day comes back for night's reiterate sake. (3:35–36)

Such internal repetitions mark the strong influence of Coleridge's "Rime of the Ancient Mariner," whose parallelisms ("A weary time! A weary time!") similarly test the reader's capacity to tolerate a discrete repetition that alone can guarantee continuity.[82] Tristram's monologue labors increasingly under its awareness of this necessary periodic rupture, until it itself breaks with the sudden apostrophe, "'Would God yet dawn might see the sun and die!'" (3:53).

This plea, once more emphatically monosyllabic, seems fatally to contradict the self-quoted pledge to Iseult ("'As the dawn loves the sunlight I love thee'") with which Tristram's monologue commenced. That, at least, is the conclusion of the narrator, who tells us that his "soul, / That had seen all those sightless seasons roll / One after one, wave over weary wave, / Was in him as a corpse is in its grave" (3:58–61). Yet this summary misrepresents Tristram's waxing mood, as does the ensuing wishful consolation that "The mood was rare upon him" (64). Tristram, in fact, is almost always like this.

"This," however, means no simple despair, but rather a concession of death whose very utterance continues to assert its necromantic power. Tristram's closing plea for the dawn to die seems to demand a final dissolution of the world. Yet this culminating exclamation ("die!") also repeats once more one of his monologue's most prominent rhyme words (22, 34, 43); where earlier each serial "day" required "break," here the apostrophized rupture is but one iteration in a series of repetitions. His exclamation both abolishes and preserves: a state of affairs whose metrical counterpart is the unfinished rhyme that obliges the narrative voice to pick up Tristram's apparently definitive conclusion (54).

The "weary wave" that washes over Tristram's soul is therefore (whatever the narrator advertises) neither the terminus nor agonist of desire; it rather forms desire's essential constituent. Three years' absence has not carried him further from his love but deeper into it. For that love was from the first already aware of its mortality: its essential fatigue expresses the paradoxical desire at once to protract and abolish the passage of time. How else to explain the fact that, still fondly clinging to memory at the start of his monologue, Tristram states that he loves Iseult "as the worn-out noon / Loves twilight" (3:5)? Indeed, even before Tristram's marriage, both amorous parties had unsparingly perceived their common situation, as Iseult demonstrates in another monosyllabic surge: "Live thou and have thy day, and year by year / Be great but what shall I be? Slay me here; / Let me die not when love lies dead, but now / Strike through my heart: nay sweet, what heart hast thou?" (2:398–402).

This dialectic of weariness, expressed both as a satiety that cannot renounce itself and as the desire for violent change, explains other passages from this second canto that would otherwise seem strange paradoxes. Full in the first flush of love, Tristram's vision seems "More fair than heaven doth in some tired saint's dreams" (2:120); shortly thereafter, he compares that same love to "a rose athirst that pants for drouth / Even while it laughs for pleasure of desire" (2:149–50), where a delicious ambiguity attaches itself to "pants for." One of the biblical texts that Swinburne is fond of quoting is Isaiah 32:2 (which the King James Bible renders, "Each will be like a hiding place from the wind, a shelter from the storm, like streams of water in a dry place, like the shade of a great rock in a weary land").[83] The Hebrew

עָיֵפָה [*'ā-yê-pāh*] has been translated variously as "weary," "thirsty," "arid," and "hot."[84] When Sappho in "Anactoria" states that she is weary of love, she therefore means at once that she is weary of it, that she is sated of it, that she is empty of it, and that she is desirous of it.[85]

The passages that I have cited above are representative in the strongest sense. Yet abstracting them from their context is also fatal to their effect, not because we need a sense of a whole to which these parts belong (Tristram's concluding apostrophe contains within itself the whole drama) but rather because one needs to have cumulatively experienced many such representative passages so as to intuit (rather than abstractly cognize) the poem's complex weariness. (To do full justice to such passages would require citation of the poem in its entirety, an expedient more at home in a short story by Jorge Luis Borges than a piece of literary criticism.)

As it is, I can do no more than trace the most acute of such repetitions, as in canto 5, the shortest and most intensely distilled episode, in which Iseult conducts a night vigil for her absent lover. Once again internal repetition seeks to join two days that are separated this time not by time but by space:

> Ah love, are thy days my days, and to thee
> Are all nights like as my nights? does the sun
> Grieve thee? art thou soul-sick till day be done,
> And weary till day rises? is thine heart
> Full of dead things as mine is? (5:106–10)

Weariness once again assumes prosodic importance, as the single exception within nine otherwise exclusively monosyllabic lines (104–12). And once again it functions as a pivot, upon which Iseult's desire, which has been on the point of expiration, revives: "Ah, what years / Would I endure not," she continues, "For all these windy weary hours of earth? / One, but one hour from birth of joy to death" (239–47). This antiphonal passage sets Iseult's monologue against the sea and wind, which continually pick up her dangling rhymes, which they transform into unspeaking noise (114–15, 196–97, 248–49, 270–71, 308–9). For as long as she is set against the elements in this manner, Iseult berates a God whose contentment contrasts with man's lot: "O happy God, how men wax weary of woe" (254). Yet having asked God that she "'die / With all thy wrath upon me that most have sinned'" (307–8), the sea and wind relent enough for Iseult to admit that she has not repented of all desire. "Let not my soul and his for ever dwell / Sundered," she beseeches, succeeding for the first time at completing a concluding rhyme with her own voice (322–23). The environing elements no longer cancel her words; rather, their "sore trembling" and "heavier cheer" mirror her own state, "worn with watch long held on pain" (326–32).

This conversion (from the weariness *of* desire to the weariness that *is* desire) distinguishes such passages from a prosodic mimesis by which metrical effects represent objects or qualia that have been cognitively preprocessed: the grinding lines of Elizabeth Barrett's Browning's "Cry of the Children," for instance, "embody" the factory machinery to which the poem's weary infant subjects were doomed. Similar instances of "tired" prosody abound, as in the leaden stresses of Rudyard Kipling's "Boots" ("We're foot—slog—slog—slog—sloggin' over Africa"), which slips in an appropriate pun on "foot" for good measure.[86] Swinburne's rhythmical excess, by contrast, pushes weariness so far as to transfigure the experience thereof. Carried to the limits of our own vocal, emotional, and motor endurance, we desire both the termination and continuation of a pattern that we no longer take for granted.

Strife / Life / Wife

It is surely no coincidence that Swinburne should drastically test the limits of our motor endurance in an unprecedented fashion, at the very moment that European society, under the auspices of the conservation of force, regarded waste as both a moral and a technocratic failure. That tendency is sufficiently widespread as to encompass aesthetics: in *The Principles of Success in Literature*, George Henry Lewes compares the efficacious author to an efficient author: "The analogy of a machine is perfect. In both cases the object is to secure the maximum of disposable force, by diminishing the amount absorbed in the working . . . waste is inappreciable in writing of ordinary excellence, and on subjects not severely tasking to the attention; but if inappreciable, it is always waste; and in bad writing, especially on topics of philosophy and science, the waste is important."[87] Even those late nineteenth-century readers who set out with half a mind to praise Swinburne's proliferation could not resist a note of censure: "Swinburne is an inveterate waster," declared Oliver Elton, "but then he has more lyrical wealth to waste than almost anybody; he has as much as Shelley, more than Herrick."[88] (I rather like Elton's designation, not least because "waster" or, better still, "wastoid," survived into my adolescence as a term of abuse, despite my classmates' feigning disdain for productive activity of any kind: the work ethic proves resilient.)

I would modify Elton's claim only so far as to specify that Swinburne's "lyrical wealth" positively requires wasting. For the weariness that I have traced at appropriate length opens up a broader category of excess, just as Helmholtz's whole motivation for treating the problem of human fatigue resided in the broader thermodynamic tendency for work to degrade into waste. Swinburne by contrast imputes a seemingly paradoxical generative force in both cases: on the one hand, we witness a loving communion characteristically described as "sweet as night's dim dawn to weariness" (4:493); on the other, "The Pines" (the short lyric composed upon the work's completion in April 1882, and inserted before the Prelude) depicts "all our wide glad wastes aflower around" (2). How could wastes ever flower, or prove glad?

Alliteration drives through this substantive and causal link between weariness and waste. That sonic recurrence provides an organizational scheme that is frequently more powerful than signification itself. When pushed to its extreme, however, it tests our capacity to hear each alliterated syllable *as* the same: our developing satiety or boredom or relish insinuates a difference within repetition. Swinburne frequently pushes alliteration to just this extreme: much of the power of Iseult's monologue, which we witnessed a moment ago, inheres in its compulsive //w// phonemes, where in the space of two representative lines we have "wild," "wan" "worn," "watch." "Waste" offers a logical extension to this parade, which at the same time names the continuing extension itself. (This is already very far from a simple dictionary entry of the term.)

At times, to be sure, waste offers little more than one further item on an alliterated laundry list, as when Swinburne diffusely evokes "the wan waste weary skies" (3:350). At other moments, by contrast, "waste" and "weary" do not prove isomorphic so much as mutually generative. During Iseult's monologue, she asks Tristram rhetorically whether "thou hear to-night, / Sleeping, my wild waste speech" (3:103–4), following this self-accusation with the query "art thou weary till day rises?" (3:109). Yet the weariness that arises from perceived excess now transfigures that excess into a bounty from which Iseult no longer wishes to be delivered. Finding herself, via another squarely thermodynamic image, "in the waste ways emptied of the sun" (3:150), she asks the most rhetorical of all questions: "Look on me, and behold if I repent" (3:159).

"Waste," then, proves another of the more furtive members of Swinburne's lexical harem, whose significance once again changes across a series of rhythmical disequilibria: a series of waste effects. These emerge from the first canto, which Swinburne published separately in 1877. It is by some distance the longest of all the cantos, due in large part to Swinburne's mercifully short-lived endeavor to contextualize the larger Arthurian world to which his lovers belong. Iseult poses Tristram a series of thinly veiled questions regarding the beauty of Guinevere, and the exploits of Merlin and Lancelot, which finally serve the sole purpose of bringing the pair close. Henceforth Swinburne discovers his exclusive theme, as the spray of the sea (and by chiastic association Tristram and Iseult), "bloomed like blossoms cast by God away / To waste on the ardent water; swift the moon / Withered to westward as a face in swoon / Death-stricken by glad tidings" (1:428–31).

This remarkable first flush of desire consolidates the association between blossoms and waste, so that superfluity generates a perpetual yield:

> And as the august great blossom of the dawn
> Burst, and the full sun scarce from sea withdrawn
> Seemed on the fiery water a flower afloat,
> So as a fire the mighty morning smote
> Throughout her, and incensed with the influent hour
> Her whole soul's one great mystical red flower
> Burst, and the bud of her sweet spirit broke
> Rose-fashion and the strong spring at a stroke
> Thrilled, and was cloven, and from the full sheath came

> The whole rose of the woman red as flame:
> And all her Mayday blood as from a swoon
> Flushed, and May rose up in her and was June. (1:461–72)

Note the manner in which enjambment does not so much defeat end-stopped rhyme as delay and thus amplify its force. The first clause breaks belatedly, with an emphatic stress "Burst" that is the stronger for being deferred. The ensuing enjambed verbs are more powerful still: the second "Burst," occurring after an answering rhyme that refuses to complete the syntactical unit, terminates sense with glorious force. "Thrilled" performs similar work, while "flushed" also recuperates the consonantal energies within "flame." We customarily posit a binary opposition between end-stopped and enjambed lines: yet where Swinburne flouts the sanctity of the line, this hardly makes these enjambments free. Unlike Milton's epic enjambment, "burst," "burst," "thrilled," and "flushed" all defer the anticipated pause by but a single syllable. The smallest transgression often communicates the keenest excess. Swinburne does not dismantle the heroic couplet; rather, in keeping with the formulations of chapter 1, he syncopates it.

Such effects often emerge most fully at a scale that precludes continuous quotation. I therefore urge the reader to read in its unbroken entirety canto 1, lines 483–557, a remarkable single sentence sustained across seventy-four lines. In contrast to the citation above, the enjambment is pervasive and extended; this passage communicates *in nuce* the poem's joyful mordant conviction that death is a sentence that seems never to end. Tristram, having left off his account of Arthurian legend to draw close to Iseult, again picks up the narrative thread. But from this point on, there is barely the slightest pretense that he (or Swinburne) really endeavors to give an exact account. "There Tristram spoke of many a noble thing," the sentence begins (483), but the rapid summary lingers on no Arthurian character for long enough to give any sense of distinctness, being rather powered by the restless, compulsive anaphora of "And," with which a full twenty-three lines commence. This parataxis constitutes the real theme of Tristram's discourse: a continual shuttling from a void state to the plenitude of desire and back again, which process both mirrors and anticipates the lovers' own trajectory.

Throughout this single passage, the waste that had recently been linked to blossoming resurfaces compulsively: we move from the noble records of knights to the barren zone that fringes the Arthurian kingdom, "through whom such holds lay waste" (492); from Merlin's upbringing amid "gaunt rare gaps and hollow doors of death," to the "heavenly hands of holier Nimue," and back to "the fire that wasted afterward / The loveless eyes and bosom of Ettarde" (524–25); from the "misborn head of Mordred, sad as night / With cold waste cheeks and eyes as keen as pain" (548–49) to "Gracious Gawain, scattering words as flowers" (551)—which is to say, once again, as blossoms. Merlin's weariness ("fain to sleep; / Yet should sleep never" [513–14]) corresponds to our own, as the line end never quite amounts to an end-stop: "Should shut him in with sleep as kind as death:" (520 offers the half-closure of the colon). Yet in each case this desire for an end, "Love-wounded and world-wearied'" (523), regenerates itself into a "hungering out of life" (529), whose delicate ambiguity captures the passage's general feel. By the time we have reached a line such as "Led through much pain to one last labouring day" (544; note once again the conjunction of effort with the sole polysyllable), our vocal engines seem also to have been pushing a boulder uphill, surprised by the periodic pleasure of such Sisyphean travails.

Such enjambment (of both the restricted and the free kind) proves but one rhythmical waste-effect, by means of which Swinburne's verse exceeds a limit so as to regenerate itself. We earlier observed that Edmund Gurney, who had much praise to lavish upon Swinburne, complained of Keats's "broken" hypermetrical verse. Yet *Tristram of Lyonesse* frequently makes use of syllabic expansion, to a variety of ends. This tendency first emerges programmatically in book 2, where King Mark, enamored of his new wife Iseult, rides daily in the woods with her. The passage, like Iseult's desire, chafes at metrical limits, just as "he rode / Hard by her rein" (2:138–39). The poem's general adherence to decasyllables encourages us to elide successive polysyllables ("sovereign," "mightiest," "lordliest" [137, 138, 139]) into compliance. Yet when Swinburne's verse then swells into a triplet, the tendency becomes more pronounced still:

> Not as that white queen's of the virgin hunt
> Once, whose crown-crescent braves the night-wind's brunt,
> But with the sun for frontlet of a queenlier front. (2:140–42)

Swinburne here revives one of the most short-lived experiments in anglophone verse: the triplet with alexandrine ending. As Conrad A. Balliet has explored, the variation had no motivation to arise in the freer, frequently open couplets of the earlier seventeenth century; by the time of Pope, meanwhile, such practices were generally proscribed for being lax.[89] Between those bookends, however, John Dryden made frequent use of the triplet with Alexandrine termination; an appalled Jonathan Swift counted each instance of this "vicious way of rhyming."[90]

Where Dryden generally availed himself of this couplet variation so as to achieve epigrammatic finality, however, Swinburne stuffs the third line with willfully superfluous verbal matter, which intensifies within the line what the triplet achieves at the larger structural level. The example above serves as a case in point: "frontlet" rhymes with the last syllable of what we might, till now, have imagined was a completed couplet ("brunt"), in addition to "sun" and "front." Internal assonance and rhyme make us feel keenly how this line chafes at metrical limits still more fully than Dryden's alexandrine triplets: we can elide "queenlier," if we like, to round the clause down to a neat dozen, but Swinburne makes us feel the cost of so doing. Another triplet swiftly proves that such variations are not incidental. King Mark has reluctantly relinquished Iseult to the knight Palamede, whereupon insistent hooves are once again heard, this time belonging to Tristram:

> And the day
> Sprang: and afar along the wild waste way
> They heard the pulse and press of hurrying horse-hoofs play: (2:241–42)

Here waste not only names but also performs itself, with the alliterating "wild waste way" giving rise to another alexandrine that again strains at the limits of twelve (now we must force ourselves to elide "hurrying"). Alliterated /p/ phonemes at first underscore the iambic meter; alliterated /h/ phonemes then threaten to capsize the long ballasted line, four of whose final five syllables (if we do elide) can be stressed.

Such syllabic and accentual ballasting of the line emerges most fully in the sixth canto, "Joyous Gard," one long passage of generative rhythmical excess. The canto names "the full deep glorious tower that stands / Between the wild sea and the broad wild lands" (6:199–200), in which the two lovers shelter following their enforced separation. The lexical item "waste" once again marks and induces prosodic excess:

> For all this wild sweet waste of sweet vain breath
> Thou knowest I know thou hast given me life, not death. (6:440–41)

Such a couplet deepens the suggestion that Swinburne's rather phallic "full deep glorious tower" is in reality not isolated from "the broad wild lands," but rather as their necessary dialectical counterpart. Verbal parallelism ("Thou knowest I know") again demands that we recognize the second line's superfluity as such; and so doing enables a serious metrical joke to unfold. Swinburne's "breath" / "death" rhyme counts as only one of the most prominent instances of willfully unoriginal rhyming that he glories in pushing towards further unacceptability; *Tristram of Lyonesse* is parasitic both upon literary tradition and itself, whose accumulated tics and muscle memories it glories in reinhabiting.[91] We cannot read "breath" without being cued, automatically, for its sister; and yet Swinburne tempts us for just the slightest moment into concluding the line on its designated tenth syllable, and thus replace "life" for "death" in flagrant contravention of the rhyme scheme. And even when "death" does succeed, as succeed it must, its belatedness means that we cannot quite cancel the force of the living, alternative line-ending; rather, it needs to feed off an excess in order to exist, and in so doing insinuates a regenerative force at the very moment that Tristram declares, emphatically, "not death."

"Joyous Gard" features other such artfully disappointed rhymes, whose disappointment consists not in the failure to tie up the couplet with a pretty bow on top, but rather in the momentary yet inextinguishable desire to conclude a hypermetrical line prematurely, on the stipulated tenth syllable. This process converts heaven into earth, where the latter once again wrenches what might have been a couplet into a triplet:

> Or how, sealed thine to be, love less than heaven on earth? (6:455)

Vocal excess not only preserves heaven, but also extends it into this profane world. The specific recurrence of such prosodic blasphemy ("Than here smiles high and sweet in face of heaven and time" [8:250]) proves Swinburne's blatant intent.

Swinburne's hypermetricality is perhaps most pronounced when it crams in not ten but *twelve* "low" monosyllables into a line. Take, for instance, the unusual emergence of an alexandrine not within a triplet, but a couplet:

> We have loved thee, and for love we have shown of old. (6:37)

Or another glorious triplet Alexandrine that induces us to stress multiple syllables hard:

> As though the sun's own hand had thrilled them through with light. (8:240)

The monosyllable, whose accentual precision had done so much to regulate Swinburne's metrical system, finally generates an excess that threatens to undermine it. The parallels with thermodynamics are suggestive. For the discovery of the second law transforms the way in which society regards both waste *and* its contrary: what information theory, borrowing its vocabulary from thermodynamics, would later name redundancy. Norbert Wiener would seek to guard against entropic dissolution through redundant pockets of order (negentropy), or negative feedback. Swinburne's verse, by contrast, proves closer to Claude Shannon or Gregory Bateson, according to whom the relation between the two states proves more dynamic ("noise is the only possible source of new patterns").[92] In a lesser poet, obsessive repetition might express a cyclical conception of nature, or vatic aspiration. In Swinburne's hands, the reiteration of a word (and the word "waste" more than any other) summons the specter of entropy. Poetic redundancy is no stable state, but a temporary refuge from the forces that it itself unleashes.

Swinburne pushes the hypermetrical tendency further than before with a triplet line whose second line already attains the alexandrine, with its successor swelling still further into heptameter:

> How hard soe'er it held his life awake
> For passion, and sweet nature's unforbidden sake,
> And will that strove unwillingly with will it might not break,
> Fell silent as a wind abashed, whose breath
> Dies out of heaven, suddenly done to death. (4:219–23)

Regular couplet form recurs and reassures not because it is some Platonic idea, but rather because it offers momentary respite from its own tendency to superfluity. Periodic excess is the condition of possibility for what equilibration *Tristram of Lyonesse* attains. For want of a better term, call it the instability of the homogeneous.

The *OED*'s separate entries for "waste" illuminate such matters. We are perhaps a little too accustomed to view the term through the retrospective lens of Eliot and the other modernists, to read it as a barren hypostatization, and so to exclude the process verb that Swinburne so often employs. Entry 1a lists waste in the standard sense, as "waste or desert land"; equally familiar to us is its definition as a transitive verb, meaning "to lay waste, devastate, ravage, ruin." Yet entry 1b identifies a now largely archaic usage that would still have been operative in Swinburne's mind: "applied," reads the entry, "e.g., to the ocean or other vast expanse of water (often waste of waters, watery waste)."[93] The *OED* cites Walter Scott's *Heart of Midlothian* ("As these broad black rain-drops mingle with the waste of waters")—a citation that envisages the ocean not as barren excess but as prodigious expanse. Such watery wastes occur everywhere in Swinburne's output: they are at separate moments void spaces, processes of attrition, and unformed excess from which life springs.

Just as a moment ago I described "Joyous Gard" as springing from (rather than securing itself against) the wilds or waste lands that fringe it, so the broader narrative action of Swinburne's *Tristram* turns on no more (and no less) than the continual metabolizing of waste product into life, and back again into waste. That is why each moment of amorous plenitude between Tristram and Iseult necessarily arrives at a limit point or void zone, through the heat of its own desire. The eighth canto begins with a profession of weariness that desires terminus ("Enough of ease, O Love, enough of light, / Enough of rest before the shadow of night" [8:1–2]), while the wider section (and the love of Tristram and Iseult) labors under the serial premonition that this is "the last" (44–47). Swinburne alters the standard narrative at this point, interposing the conflict with the giant Urgan that in Walter Scott's *Sir Tristrem* occurred much earlier. This narrative sleight-of-hand appears somewhat adventitious, given that Tristram has just been dwelling upon his necessary separation from Iseult, whereupon we hear "A sound of summons in the high king's name" (58). The monstrous Urgan in fact proves less significant than the necessarily violent rupture that he enables, in which Tristram exults, while also fearing it. He rides "through the wild glad wastes of Wales" (87), this only apparently oxymoronic phrasing recalling Swinburne's prefatory lyric, "The Pines." The eventual slaying of Urgan then appears secondary to Tristram's consequent revelation that there was not "More certitude in all the waste world's range / Than the only certitude of death and change" (292–93)—a revelation that enables his soul at once "To shrink and triumph and mount up and mourn" (300). Urgan, then, represents the latest obligation for Tristram to put himself close to death (and waste), as if for the last time.

There is accordingly a real question as to how such a poem (in which each violent break is both death sentence and condition for painful rebirth) can ever truly end. Rhythmical excess again dictates the answer. We have already observed a number of prominent infringements of Pope's stipulations regarding proper couplet form—stipulations that Swinburne must have loved ardently, in order to derive such pleasure from their transgression. Those infringements have included the gratuitous use of derivative rhyme, the access of free or restricted enjambment, the outbreaks of hypermetricality, and the periodic swelling of couplets into triplets. Until now I have said almost nothing of this final case. We earlier noted briefly how Swinburne's harem-word "waste" generated a triplet, among other metrical excesses. That moment arrived immediately prior to the battle with Palamede in canto 3; their conflict generates another supernumerary rhyme:

> Back were the steeds hurled from the spear-shock, fain
> And foiled of triumph: then with tightened rein
> And stroke of spur, inveterate, either knight
> Bore in again upon his foe with might,
> Heart-hungry for the hot-mouthed feast of fight
> And all athirst of mastery: but full soon
> The jarring notes of that tempestuous tune
> Fell, and its mighty music made of hands
> Contending, clamorous through the loud waste lands,
> Broke at once off. (2:266–75)

A taut "rein" again both regulates and urges metrical surplus, as the triplet "knight" / "might" / "fight" upsets the balance of the verse. The two knights square off against one another in (and as) respective lines within a couplet, whose contention produces a further rhyming outgrowth and the "jarring" discord to which Edmund Gurney proved so attuned.

Such triplets are significantly scarce throughout *Tristram of Lyonesse*. The above example contrasts significantly with another excrescence, in canto 8. Just prior to his battle with the fifteen assailants of his namesake, the other Tristram (which after so much crying wolf really is his last), our hero summons the wife whose love he has so little reciprocated:

> Go, Ganhardine, with tiding of the vow
> That bids me turn aside for one day's strife
> Or live dishonoured all my days of life,
> And greet for me in brother's wise my wife,
> And crave her pardon for my knighthood's sake. (8:366–70)

If the effect of this triplet differs substantially from its predecessors, it is to a large part because it disrupts one of Swinburne's most prominent derivative rhymes, up there on a par with "breath" / "death," "eyes" / "skies," and the rest. "Life" and "strife" so reliably generate one another that the two come to stand in matrimonial relationship, which this interloper ("wife") then converts into an irregular ménage à trois. Or perhaps the marital metaphor is ill-suited: for the stable relation between "life" and "strife" is only stable in a peculiar sense. That single rhyme microcosmically expresses what I have taken to be the poem's contention: that life must depart from itself (to the point of discord) to continue living. "Wife," then, does not so much unsettle this already volatile relation, so much as attempt to impose a neat synthesis upon it, just as Tristram would seek to expiate the sin that constituted his only reason for living.

The remainder of the poem grapples with this dilemma, which might be distilled into the question whether we rhyme "life" with "strife" or "wife." Until now the former option has nearly always prevailed.[94] But in the absence of any more synthetizing triplets, the verse now swings between both alternatives: Tristram has barely issued his summons when he is prone to another erotic apprehension of death that cannot but recall his mistress, the other Iseult ("each glad limb became / A note of rapture in the tune of life, / Live music mild and keen as sleep and strife" [8:504–6]). The ninth and final canto, which finds Tristram laboring under his mortal wound, continues this theme of tuneful dissonance: Fate is Lord of all,

> Till joy be found a shadow and sorrow a breath
> And life no discord in the tune with death,
> But all things fain alike to die and live
> In pulse and lapse of tides alternative,
> Through silence and through sound of peace and strife,
> Till birth and death be one in sight of life. (9:16–21)

The "life" / "strife" rhyme then recurs, in a cycle of quickening repetition (9:57–58, 129–30). Yet Iseult of Brittany having returned to her husband, she overhears his instructions to bring back her namesake, Tristram's mistress—a stratagem whose success is to be measured by the famous white or black sails. From this point on, "wife" once again interposes itself into Swinburne's unstable equilibrium of a rhyme scheme, chiming successively with "'life" (9:179–80, 265–66) and "strife" (9:211–12). Throughout this extended concluding passage, Swinburne's other pet rhymes ("breath" / "death," "sinned" / "wind") recur with if anything greater intensity that usual—in which context the sundering of "life" and "strife" (comparable to that of the poem's protagonists) is felt as bereavement. This displacement of rhyme reaches a peak, as Iseult of Brittany continues to eavesdrop on her husband's expressions of love for his mistress, so comparable in their intuition of death to all those that have come before. Her response is crucial:

> "Come therefore, let us twain pass hence and try
> If it be better not to live but die,
> With love for lamp to lead us out of life."
>   And on that word his maiden wedded wife,
> Pale as the moon in star-forsaken skies
> Ere the sun fill them, rose with set strange eyes
> And gazed on him that saw not: and her heart
> Heaved as a man's death-smitten with a dart
> That smites him sleeping, warm and full of life:

So toward her lord that was not looked his wife,

His wife that was not. (9:373–83)

Iseult of Brittany forces her husband's dangling "life," full of the apprehension of death, to rhyme with her own "wife." Yet when the same rhyme recurs barely five lines later, it no sooner consolidates the link than it is definitively refuted ("His wife that was not"). Iseult of Brittany goes on, of course, to lie about the color of the sails, dooming our two protagonists to die unreconciled. Yet this mutual distance is their paradoxical triumph, just as it has proven on so many previous occasions. The poem knows it: we see it in the restoration of that most vital of rhymes, "life" and "strife" (9:491–92, 507–8). Where Pope imagined the heroic couplet as a homeostatic system, Swinburne demonstrates its decay into conflictual disequilibrium; he does this not through canceling the conventions of the form, but through measurably exceeding them. However much the closing lines claim our protagonists no longer prove subject to "sleepless languor with its weary wing" (503), they live on in our worldly exhaustion, our own continuing desire—even at this terminal stage in the poem—both to protract and to arrest a rhythmic pattern that has been carried to its very limit.

Imperfect Economies

However rechargeable are the batteries of literary criticism (as it devours the given text in digestible chunks, taking proper pauses between each act of hermeneutic virtuosity), my own body can turn from *Tristram of Lyonesse* only with a sense of positive exhaustion, which makes all immediate thought of "broader relevance" difficult to envisage. This difficulty *is* Swinburne's broader relevance. My emphasis upon rhythmical excess differs somewhat from Yopie Prins's perception of punishing metrical regularity, whose recurrent beat or foot stands in for the smack of the whip. Prins ties an "abstract" metrical pattern to poems in which Swinburne himself foregrounds beating:

> Chief the Stripling Songster's Breech invites
> The full Performance of thy frequent Rites,

> Most the Nurslings of the Muse require
> The Lash that sets their lyrick Blood on Fire
> The Lash that ever when they cry keeps Time,
> When Stroke to Stroke responds in glowing Rhyme.
> And still the humbled Bottom hails the Rod sublime,
> Till Heart & Head the rhythmic Lesson learn
> From Wounds that redden & from Stripes that burn,
> As Twig by Twig imprints the Crimson sign in turn.[95]

This extract does indeed begin regularly enough, with a couplet form that is more predominantly iambic than anything we find in *Tristram*. Yet the compulsive regularity of these lines again generates a rhythmical excess without which it cannot be truly felt: note how the pentameters swell out into the alexandrine triplet, "As Twig by Twig imprints the Crimson sign in turn." As we have seen, such generative prosodic waste is as nothing in comparison to *Tristram of Lyonesse*, which in addition to syllabic excess also generates superfluity of accent and rhyme. Were a link between metrical regularity and sadomasochism truly to obtain, Pope's far more predictable lines would represent the true specimens of erotic perversity!

Swinburne therefore sets verse to work less as a mechanism of punishing regularity than as what Edmund Gurney saw as a reservoir of energy, in which some degree of waste or "imperfect economy" is necessary for the very apprehension of rhythmical succession. No perfect recovery could enable each new lash of the whip (or accent) to feel like the last. Such factors make Swinburne's verse both an invitation and a challenge to forms of rhythmical description that attempt to move beyond standard foot-based equivalence and substitution. Richard Cureton, for instance, seeks to capture complex rhythmical gestalts that exist at a larger unit than the individual foot or line.[96] As the above analysis has shown, however, *Tristram of Lyonesse* requires for such a gestalt nothing less than the poem in its entirety, across whose wide bounds waste and weariness do their work. Such a drastically enlarged scale calls into question what constitutes rhythmical equivalence.

This successive and variegated experience of fatigue constitutes Swinburne's significance for the broader scientific and rhythmical culture that this chapter commenced by outlining. In *The Case of Wagner,* Friedrich Nietzsche declared that "Wagner is a great corrupter of music. With it, he found the means of stimulating tired nerves,—and in this way he made music ill. In the art of spurring exhausted creatures back into activity, and of recalling half-corpses to life, the inventiveness he shows is of no mean order."[97] Let us temper the sting of Nietzsche's animus; this verdict nevertheless offers a fine sense of the manner in which Swinburne's art addressed a culture in which he was similarly steeped. His expressive affinity with Wagner therefore cannot quite be summarized through the feature of harmony, as Jerome McGann attempts; it more fundamentally concerns dissonance, whose threshold, as we have repeatedly seen, proves inseparable from the limit of corporeal endurance.[98]

Unlike the lyric, with its self-withdrawing capacity for temporal suspension, the long poem conveys the temporal irreversibility that lies at the heart of the second law of thermodynamics. Where Helmholtz employed the conservation of energy as a charm to ward off the consequences of entropy, Swinburne not only demonstrates the inevitability of waste within a closed system (whether metrical or actual); he strives also to render such a predicament habitable. Where John Tyndall inspired a litany of attempts to prove that rhythmical transmission could recuperate even the unseen or departed, *Tristram of Lyonesse* demonstrates that the force that exothermically binds two bodies (or a couplet) necessarily produces excess or discord. His unwillingness to minimize the force of such strife denies Swinburne the consolation of an eternal hereafter, or the glib materialism that finds in every death a rebirth. His poetry continues to be all the stronger a consolation.

CODA

(Re-)Turn

This book has been an attempt to explain to myself the nature and consequences of that moment, in Uppsala, in 2019, when I found my body entraining to the percussive vibrations of the wooden armrests either side of me. That bodily response in turn channeled and clarified an experience that I had previously only dimly intuited over the decades that I had read nineteenth-century verse, mostly silently, in my head, mostly from the printed page, yet with the recurrent sense that something was dragging my body beyond its privatized sphere. These two impulses neatly encapsulate the tension that has constituted *The Turn of Rhythm*, which has endeavored to show how concept acquisition and nondiscursive experience cumulatively form a concrete historical dialectic that culminates in the enunciation of rhythm as a portable and sharable entity.

The contemporary (and hopefully temporary) reality of Zoom calls and mandatory self-distancing make such supra-private experience increasingly hard to come by. Yet in reality this difficulty long precedes the ongoing pandemic during which I have finished this book. In his remarkable document of the acid house movement of the 1980s, *Everybody in the Place*, Jeremy Deller shows footage of dancing ravers to a group of British high school students. The students regard this historical material, which after all happened not so very long ago, with an admixture of bewilderment and respect. Nobody, several of them say, would dance like that today, for fear of being livestreamed for eternity. I regard several of the jeremiads over digital culture as overblown: if nothing else, Twitter and Instagram certainly do show us the power of contagious sympathy that my second chapter probed. Yet the pile-ons and viral vectors of our contemporary everyday significantly exclude the body, except insofar as it hunches over the screen.

If this evacuation of corporeality holds true for rave culture, it holds all the more true for nineteenth-century poetry. Over the preceding pages, I have tried to restore to that verse its proper body, or bodies: these included the stuttering tongue; the androgynous devotional erotic subject; the maternal; the ethnic minority vibrating to a past that she could never fully know; Widow Smith, reciting a ballad at some unspecified time somewhere in Paisley; the anatomized vibrating mollusk; the tired person. To call these bodies " nonnormative" would only beg the question as to what counts as normal. Certainly not me. The first-person singular that I have often used to communicate my experience of a given poem indicates no rational and self-sufficient actor, but rather an entity onto which are imposed several suprapersonal constraints, which relate me to (even when they do not make me into) a mollusk, stutterer, or Glaswegian widow. Doubtless I have my own idiosyncrasies: the capacity to relish rather than become exasperated at the contortions of Browning and the redundancies of Swinburne, for example. Yet these personal proclivities come into dynamic contact with a large variety of generic (corporeal and historical) constraints.

My experience of *Amazing Grace*, along with the nineteenth-century verse that flowed into and from it, thereby gives one version of the future research program that, toward the end of his life, Henri Lefebvre designated as "rhythmanalysis." His neologism sought to herald a future science that would supplement more standard forms of historical materialism with an attention to the rhythms of late capitalism and the subjects that it produces. "The rhythmanalyst," Lefebvre writes, "calls on all his senses. He draws on his breathing, the circulation of his blood, the beatings of his heart and the delivery of his speech as landmarks."[1] This speculative itinerary is enticing yet incomplete. For when Lefebvre conducts a brief case-study ("Seen from the Window"), a chasm opens up between the rhythmanalyst who observes, and those pedestrians "immersed in the multiplicity of noises, murmurs, rhythms." To practice this would-be new science, we should regard dynamic flow through a window, or, more preferably still, a balcony, from which vantage "the noises distinguish themselves, the flows separate out, rhythms respond to one another."[2]

But you already have to be a certain kind of person to be able to look down upon those shoppers who throng Beaubourg, in order to abstract their rhythms into order. A truer if more risky rhythmanalysis truly would, as Lefebvre's elsewhere contends, "situate [itself] inside and outside." A true rhythmanalyst would climb down from the balcony. It would not be enough, on this account, to note that the British government's 1994 Criminal Justice Bill, which prevented more than twelve people gathering in the open to listen to "amplified music," defined as "the emission of a succession of repetitive beats," without entering into the experience of those subjects whose rhythmical sociality was thus administered. (The electronic duo Autechre offer a ready way to test this experimentally, having responded to the bill by issuing an EP whose side A, they warned, contained repetitive beats. The flip-side featured unrepetitive yet very danceable beats.) It would not be enough to note in passing interesting neuroscientific research that demonstrates that certain subjects tend to entrain far more powerfully than others, without exploring the broader ethical consequences of who leads and who follows in group dynamics.[3] It would not be enough to speculate upon the different forms of rhythmical training that all pedagogical methods involve—from Émile Jacques-Dalcroze's eurythmics to the more uniform exercises that form a part of the Chinese *Gaokao*—without seeking to put into practice new forms of embodied knowledge.

I am painfully aware, in racing through these scattered examples, of my general ignorance regarding the political management of aural spaces, or the detection of synchronized neural oscillations via electroencephalography, or of the pedagogical theorization of kinesthetic knowledge. Many academic books conclude with such gestures toward the contemporary pertinence of their topic, underscoring in the process the rift that separates detailed scholarly reconstruction and pressing social concerns. But literary critics are also involved in the world of praxis, however little their books may betray it. The first-person singular of the scholarly monograph suggests that I can lay claim to its readings as my own private property. In reality, whatever thoughts I have been able to form from the poems at hand have come about from discussions and recitations with colleagues, friends, and, above all, students. The token acknowledgment that I offer this last group, before the book proper, offers a poor tribute to the common production of knowledge. In innumerable cases, I am unable to parcel out where my views end and theirs begin.

Yet nearly every part of the contemporary humanistic education militates against the recognition of this production of communal knowledge: our students write monological essays that form the basis for examination and classification; the literary critic reads texts in the first-person singular, hoping to carve out in the process a distinctive discursive space for the forthcoming single-authored monograph. (There is here an ironic contrast to the exacter sciences, which are often accused of producing more narrowly instrumentalized knowledge, yet which in practice proceed in a far more collaborative manner.)

How might we find ways to acknowledge and practice the more communal experience that is the concealed basis of this book? How might we activate in pedagogy its central contention: that the turn of rhythm implicates singular corporeal experience in a differential relation to past historical communities? The call for a renewed attention to the relation between theoretical inquiry and pedagogical praxis is not new: the contemporary humanities, anxious and embattled for very good reasons, offer but one iteration. In his brilliant *Literary Criticism: A Short Political History*, Joseph North argues polemically against the twentieth-century tendency to elevate "scholarship" over a "criticism" that involves a more explicit consideration of the role of education and literacy within the public realm. Among the early positive signs of a pushback against this process, North enumerates a "radical pedagogy" with figures such as Jane Gallop and D. A. Miller, whose newfound affective enthusiasm for literature contrasts strikingly with the hermeneutics of suspicion in which both critics previously distinguished themselves.[4]

I agree with North's general contention regarding the centrality of pedagogy, along with the identification of Gallop and Miller as brilliant critics. Yet their brilliance does not eliminate what a moment ago I identified as the problem of the singularity of humanistic knowledge production. What makes us learn from Gallop and Miller is, simply put, the charisma and generosity of their writing. Good luck trying to emulate something like *Jane Austen, or The Secret of Style*, without Miller's wit. Perhaps, then, we should begin, as a discursive community, to imagine forms of pedagogical practice that depend less upon the charismatic individual, and which dwell rather upon portable and sharable pedagogical strategies, through which we can reflect on and develop the communal and discursive forms of knowledge production that, even in the age of Zoom, we all know to be central to the study of literature.

That is why, in tandem with the writing of this book, I have begun unsystematically to develop a series of teaching strategies that relocate authority from the pedagogue to the protocol. I call these routines "Oblique Pedagogical Strategies," in a nod to Brian Eno's efforts to shake the music groups that he produced out of their compositional habits. Each protocol seeks to acknowledge and to actuate the nondiscursive knowledge that has underpinned this monograph. They begin with a common instruction: "All numbered steps should be followed in order, except where their transgression can be justified in a specific manner." (We can relocate but never destroy pedagogical authority, particularly in the moments that we resist it.)

To describe these protocols in detail, along with the responses that they have occasioned, would be the subject of another book. A quick summary nevertheless will signal the kind of thinking that I have in mind. In "Close Listening," rather than have each student read silently on the page, I email them an MP3 recitation of a given poem. Each student listens to the unseen (unheard) text while taking a walk through a part of Cambridge that they have never previously investigated. During this time, they should attempt to notice the manner in which their experience of the artwork shapes and is shaped by (even entrains and is entrained by) the paces of their stride, the necessary stops at the red lights, the ambient sound of the shoppers, or the birds, the silence of the green field, or the deserted carpark. Having walked for thirty minutes, the student finds a place to stand and sit, and records on their smartphone a voice memo that constitutes their weekly essay, along with a map of the itinerary and a short statement of how it shaped their response. It is hard to overstate how the voice changes in the shift from written to spoken essay. In my experience, students often start with a barrage of preformulated and shrewd observations, before pausing; in the pausing, the true thinking often begins.

In another oblique pedagogical strategy, "Close Looking," each student walks the short distance from my office in Downing College to the Fitzwilliam Museum. There, they select one aesthetic object (painting, sculpture, vase, item of furniture), which they behold for twenty uninterrupted minutes. That evening they try not to think of the object. Two days later, they return and look at the same entity, trying to notice how it has changed from their first visit, and whether those changes correspond to internal or external factors (weather conditions, the quality of light, the footfall in the museum, what they had for breakfast). That evening they try again not to think of the artwork, and note the success or failure of the attempt. The following day they return to regard the same object for another twenty minutes, this time with a friend or classmate, so as to consider how the act of common beholding does or does not shape what is seen.

These little exercises are an attempt to reintroduce serious playfulness into an increasingly instrumental and mechanical institutionalized pedagogy. As a tenured associate professor at Cambridge, I benefit from privileges that make such experiments possible: small class sizes; a nonmodular curriculum that does not mandate continuous quantitative assessment; the presence of the Fitzwilliam Museum, with its remarkable collection of Chinese and Japanese ceramics, on my doorstep. Yet both of the above examples have been designed so as to be accomplished by anyone, so long as there is space to walk through, and objects to behold. My intention is to disrupt in however minimal and transitory a manner our cultural over-dependence upon vision to the detriment of tactility; to relate such individual embodied experiences to broader natural or social rhythms; and to direct attention not only to the moment of cognitive alertness, but also to the breaks, hiatuses, and moments of fatigue or distraction in which new cognition so often occurs.

My embryonic articulation of this program depends upon a historical precursor: the nondiscursive conceptuality of nineteenth-century verse. The progressive estrangement of poetry from cognition deforms past cultures in which very different relations obtained. We cannot comprehend this culture without also reanimating it, because nondiscursive embodied experience proved the condition of its operation. Unlike those who lived and spoke in 1770, we all think we know what we say when we say *rhythm*.

Yet perhaps we need to recover that moment where the word struck the mouth that spoke it as strange and yet to be fully defined. To do so involves submitting our present selves to a form of embodied cognition that drives and resists conceptuality. Rhythm might then transcend its status as a historical fact, so as to prove, in turn, a future prospect.

NOTES

Introduction

1. Curt Sachs, *Rhythm and Tempo: A Study in Musical History* (W. W. Norton, 1953).
2. These include imperfect OCR, the political priorities of digitization, and the presence of multiple editions, which means that Alexander Pope occurs more often in the 1820s than in the 1710s. See E. A. Pechenick, C. M. Danforth, and P. S. Dodds, "Characterizing the Google Books Corpus: Strong Limits to Inferences of Socio-Cultural and Linguistic Evolution," *PLoS ONE* 10.10 (2015), https://doi.org/10.1371/journal.pone.0137041.
3. "Metre" is of course also a unit of spatial measurement, yet this is unlikely to skew the results in the period to hand, the pre-metric nineteenth century.
4. In the Burney Collection, which includes texts across the seventeenth and eighteenth centuries, "rhythm" appears 12 times, and "metre" on 1,571 occasions; "rhythmical" occurs only twice, as opposed to 271 usages of "metrical."
5. Samuel Johnson, "Rhythmical," in *A Dictionary of the English Language, in Which the Words Are Deduced from Their Originals*, 2 vols. (London, 1755–56).
6. Martin Heidegger and Eugen Fink, *Heraclitus Seminar, 1966–1967*, trans. Charles H. Seibert (Evanston, IL: Northwestern University Press, 1993), 55.
7. Ibid. Heidegger is working here largely with the accounts of Greek usage that he finds in Werner Jaeger (see note below).
8. The most pertinent account of *rhuthmos* remains Werner Jaeger's *Paideia: The Ideals of Greek Culture*, 3 vols. (New York: Oxford University Press, 1944–86), 1:125–27. "We must not," writes Jaeger, "be misled . . . into thinking that Archilochus's rhythm is a *flux*—although the modern idea of rhythm is something that flows, and some derive the word itself from ῥέω, 'to flow.' The history of the word warns us against that interpretation" (1:125–26).
9. It is through Aristotle that Democritus's conceptions reach us; see his *Metaphysics*, 8.2.1.

10. See Émile Benveniste, "The Notion of Rhythm in Its Linguistic Expression," in *Problems in General Linguistics,* trans. Mary Elizabeth Meek (Coral Gables: University of Miami Press, 1971), 281–88.
11. "We said also that none of the other creatures attains a sense of order, bodily and vocal, and that this is possessed by man alone; and that the order of motion is called 'rhythm'" (Plato, *Laws,* trans. R. G. Bury [Cambridge, MA: Harvard University Press, 2014], 129).
12. Ibid., 145, 147.
13. See for instance the moment at which the Athenian stranger (who may or may not be Socrates) states that "it is absurd of the general crowd to imagine that they can understand what is fully harmonious and rhythmical, or the reverse, when they have been drilled to sing to the flute or step in time" (ibid., 149).
14. I borrow this latter designation from Lewis Rowell's excellent "Aristoxenus on Rhythm," *Journal of Music Theory* 23.1 (Spring 1979): 63–79. Particularly relevant in the context of the present discussion is Rowell's statement that "Aristoxenus' concept of musical time is atomistic, and his temporal forms—expressed as rhythmic proportions—are treated much like geometric forms. If his rhythm can be said to 'flow,' it does so within strictly defined channels and is articulated by clearly located points" (67).
15. See in particular §84, from the second book of *The Gay Science* ("*On the Origin of Poetry*"). Here Nietzsche begins by describing rhythm as an overpowering "compulsion; it engenders an unconquerable desire to yield, to join in; not only the stride of the feet but also the soul itself gives into the beat—probably also, one inferred, the souls of the gods!" So far, so excessively Dionysian; yet Nietzsche's historical clear-sightedness then emerges through the manner in which he links Greek rhythm (as "binding") *not* to Dionysus but rather to Apollo: "Apollo, who as god of rhythm can also bind the goddesses of faith." By the end of this entry, then, Nietzsche has come nearly full circle from his youthful enthusiasm: "In short: was there anything more *useful* than rhythm to the old superstitious type of human being?'" The above quotes come from *The Gay Science,* trans. Josefine Nauckoff (Cambridge: Cambridge University Press, 2001), 83–86.
16. J. W. Rankin, "Rime and Reason," *PMLA* 44. 4 (December 1929): 997–1004 (998).
17. Agamben, for example, reads the Greek conception of rhythm in a Heideggerean manner that ignores Heidegger's own specific comments on the matter. In "On the Originary Structure of the Work of Art" (in *The Man without Content,* trans. Georgia Albert [Stanford, CA: Stanford University Press, 1999], 94–103), Agamben attempts to make sense of Hölderlin's riddling (and nearly meaningless) claim that "everything is rhythm, the entire destiny of man is one heavenly rhythm, just as every work of art is one rhythm," by relating it to the broader Greek philosophical tradition. That effort involves no little hermeneutical violence. Agamben starts with Aristotle's *Physics:* "To

be sure," he concedes, "Aristotle does not directly use the word rhythm (ῥυθμός); however, he employs the privative expression τὸ ἀρρύθμιστον, meaning that which in itself lacks rhythm." The passage in question (from book 2, part 1, of the *Physics*) is in fact more frequently translated as "lacking in structure," and with good reason: Aristotle is talking about the wood from which a bedstead is fashioned. Nonetheless, this does not prevent Agamben from asserting that *rhuthmos* (despite its absence from the *Physics*) represents "the original principle" that opens and binds both matter and the work of art. "But what, then, is the essence of rhythm?" Agamben asks. His answer: "The word 'rhythm' comes from the Greek ῥέω, 'to flow'; yet temporal experience does not in reality involve an infinite succession of moments"—rather, "we perceive rhythm as something that escapes the incessant flight of instants and appears almost as the presence of an atemporal dimension in time." This disjunctive element does not accord very well with how the Greeks actually employed *rhuthmos*, so Agamben suggests that we simply replace it with another word that better suits his purposes, a conjugation of *epoché* ["suspension"]: "The verb ἐποχή . . . has a double meaning: it means both to hold back, to suspend, and to hand over, to present, to offer. If we consider what we have just said about rhythm, that it reveals a more original dimension of time and at the same time conceals it in the one-dimensional flight of instants, we can perhaps, with only apparent violence, translate ἐποχή as rhythm, and say: rhythm is ἐποχή, gift and reserve." How much this "violence" is "only apparent" I leave to the reader's judgment. There is no little irony in this location of Heideggerean *ek-stasis* within Greek conceptions of rhythm, given Agamben's enthusiastic recycling of the etymological story ("flow") that Heidegger himself so powerfully rejects.

18. Herbert Spencer, *First Principles of a New System of Philosophy* (London, 1862), 317.
19. For a comprehensive summary of this historical tendency, see Wilhelm Seidel, *Rhythmus: Eine Begriffsbestimmung* (Darmstadt: Wissenschaftliche Buchgesellschaft, 1973).
20. Catherine Dale, *Music Analysis in Britain in the Nineteenth and Twentieth Century* (Aldershot and Burlington, UK: Ashgate, 2003).
21. Jean-Jacques Rousseau and Jean-Baptiste-René Robinet, "Rhythm," in *The Encyclopedia of Diderot & d'Alembert Collaborative Translation Project*, trans. Valerie Porcello (Ann Arbor: University of Michigan Press, 2005), http://quod.lib.umich.edu/d/did/did2222.0000.491?rgn=main;view=fulltext. Rousseau's conventional diatribe against "the barbarous invention of rhyme" suggests that he has all the romance vernaculars in mind.
22. Charles Burney, *A General History of Music: From the Earliest Ages to the Present Period*, 4 vols. (London, 1782–89), 1:65.
23. Ibid., 1:63.
24. Joshua Steele, *Prosodia Rationalis: or, An Essay towards Establishing the Melody and Measure of Speech, to be Expressed and Perpetuated by Peculiar Symbols* (London, 1779).

25. Jonathan Odell, *An Essay on the Elements, Accents, and Prosody, of the English Language, etc.* (London, 1806), 146.
26. Thomas Laqueur, *Making Sex: Body and Gender from the Greeks to Freud* (Cambridge, MA: Harvard University Press, 1992), 23.
27. Hans Ulrich Gumbrecht, *Presence Effects: What Meaning Cannot Convey* (Stanford, CA: Stanford University Press, 2004).
28. For examples of a psychoanalytic account of rhythmical experience, see Nicolas Abraham, *Rhythms: On the Work, Translation, and Psychoanalysis,* trans. Benjamin Tigpen and Nicholas T. Rand (Stanford, CA: Stanford University Press, 1995), and Alexander Freer, "Rhythm as Coping," *New Literary History* 46.3 (Summer 2015): 549–68.
29. Amittai F. Aviram, *Telling Rhythm: Body and Meaning in Poetry* (Ann Arbor: University of Michigan Press, 1994), 10.
30. Vincent Berlatta, *Rhythm: Form and Dispossession* (Chicago: Chicago University Press, 2020).
31. Michael Golston, *Rhythm and Race in Modernist Poetry and Science* (New York: Columbia University Press, 2008); Meredith Martin, *The Rise and Fall of Meter* (Princeton, NJ: Princeton University Press, 2012).
32. Jason David Hall, "Sonic Forms: Ezra Pound's Anti-metronome Modernism in Context," in *Sound and Literature,* ed. Anna Snaith (Cambridge: Cambridge University Press, 2020), 74–91.
33. Jason Rudy, *Electric Meters: Victorian Physiological Poetics* (Athens: Ohio University Press, 2007).
34. Over past years, this tendency has been most powerfully associated with the work of Simon Jarvis. See his "Prosody as Cognition," *Critical Quarterly* 40.4 (December 1998): 3–15. For a fourteenth-century attempt to secure the significance of nondiscursive cognition for intellectual history, see Eric Weiskott, "Early English Meter as a Way of Thinking," *Studia Metrica et Poetica* 4.1 (2017): 41–65.
35. Ewan Jones, *Coleridge and the Philosophy of Poetic Form* (Cambridge: Cambridge University Press, 2014).
36. A representative recent example of this trend is Haun Saussy's *The Ethnography of Rhythm* (New York: Fordham University Press, 2016).
37. Golston, *Rhythm and Race,* 13. For Thaddeus Bolton's familiarity with Spencer, Helmholtz, and others, see the introduction to his *Rhythm* (Worcester, MA: F. S. Blanchard, 1893), 1–35.
38. "Rhythm," in *Princeton Encyclopedia of Poetry and Poetics,* 4th ed. (Princeton, NJ: Princeton University Press, 2012).
39. "While Jacques-Dalcroze's sweeping pronouncements echo many of the observations made by other theorists of rhythm," writes Golston in *Rhythm and Race,* "the difference is the extent to which he recommends 'objectifying' rhythm and utilizing it as a very real tool in projects of socialization, nation building and the creation of a rad-

ically affective psychology. His notion that in the future, the socio-political order of the day will involve uniting integrated individuals into large, racially distinct, 'automatized' social groups, presided over by geniuses who express a nation's soul by uniting its multifarious rhythms[,] . . . is uncannily prophetic" (33–34). This amounts to the direct accusation of Jacques-Dalcroze as an accessory to fascism. Meredith Monk is among numerous artists who testify movingly to the noncoercive pedagogical potential of Dalcrozian gymnastics.

40. "Turning to the German world," writes Golston, "one finds numerous theories of rhythm, centered around issues of race, language, soil, blood, poetry, and music, in place long before the decades of National Socialism" (*Rhythm and Race*, 34). I quite agree; yet to then link Wagner's anti-Semitism to Nietzsche's "racial" declaration that "a German is almost incapable of *presto* in his language" (quoted on 34) seems grotesquely unjust, when Nietzsche manifestly intends immanent cultural critique.

41. See T. V. F. Brogan's diagrammatic representation of these traditions in *English Versification, 1570–1980: A Reference Guide with a Global Appendix* (Baltimore: Johns Hopkins University Press, 1981), 142.

42. Thomas Cable, *The English Alliterative Tradition* (Philadelphia: University of Pennsylvania Press), 1991; Christopher Hasty, *Meter as Rhythm* (Oxford: Oxford University Press, 2007).

43. Derek Attridge, *The Rhythms of English Poetry* (New York: Longman, 1982). The common use of "rhythm" to mark accentual prosody first emerged in consistent form in Edwin Guest's *A History of English Rhythms* (London, 1838).

44. Philip Hobsbaum, *Metre, Rhythm and Verse* (London: Routledge, 1996), 7; Félix Guattari and Gilles Deleuze, *A Thousand Plateaus: Capitalism and Schizophrenia* (London: Continuum, 1992), 314, 313.

1. Stuttering Rhythms

1. Joshua Steele, *Prosodia Rationalis: or, An Essay towards Establishing the Melody and Measure of Speech, to Be Expressed and Perpetuated by Peculiar Symbols* (London, 1779), 67. Subsequent references are cited parenthetically in the text as *PR*.

2. Saint Augustine, "On Music," in *The Fathers of the Church*, trans. Robert Taliaferro (Washington, DC: Catholic University of America Press, 1947), 169–384 (328).

3. Ibid.

4. T. S. Omond, *English Metrists* (Oxford: Clarendon Press, 1921), 76–91; Paul Fussell, *Theory of Prosody in Eighteenth-Century England* (New London: Connecticut College, 1954).

5. For Steele's influence upon linguistics, see David Crystal, *Prosodic Systems and Intonation in English* (Cambridge: Cambridge University Press, 1969), 23–25.

6. James Burnett, Lord Monboddo, *On the Origin and Progress of Language*, 6 vols. (Edinburgh and London, 1773), 3:403.

7. Walter Young, "An Essay on Rhythmical Measures," *Transactions of the Royal Society of Edinburgh* 2.2 (1786): 55–110.
8. John Thelwall, *A Letter to Henry Cline, Esq on Imperfect Developments of the Faculties Mental and Moral, as well as Constitutional and Organic on the Treatment of Impediments of Speech* (London, 1810), 23.
9. Ibid., 36. See also 78–79.
10. Ibid., 231.
11. John Thelwall, *Selections for the Illustration of a Course of Instructions on the Rhythmus and Utterance of the English Language* (London, 1812), 14–16.
12. Julia S. Carlson, *Romantic Marks and Measures: Wordsworth's Poetry in Fields of Print* (Philadelphia: University of Philadelphia Press, 2016), 260–303.
13. George Saintsbury, *History of English Prosody: From the Twelfth Century to the Present Day*, 3 vols. (London: Macmillan, 1906), 3:159.
14. Ibid.
15. James Rush, *The Philosophy of the Human Voice: Embracing Its Physiological History; together with a System of Principles by Which Criticism in the Art of Elocution May Be Rendered Intelligible, and Instruction, Definite and Comprehensive, to Which Is Added, a Brief Analysis of Song and Recitative*, 7th ed. (Philadelphia, 1879), 510. Rush's esteem for Steele did not prevent him from misspelling "rhythmus" as "rythmus" throughout.
16. Ibid., 480.
17. Jonathan Odell, *An Essay on the Elements, Accents, and Prosody, of the English Language* (London, 1806), 44.
18. Ibid., 161.
19. Richard Cull, *Stammering Considered with Reference to Its Cure* (London, 1835).
20. Algernon Sydney Thelwall, *The Reading Desk and the Pulpit* (London, 1861). Thelwall quotes the relevant passage from *Prosodia Rationalis* in full, before declaring that "the principle *here* so clearly enunciated by anticipation, as the result of scientific observation and reasoning, had been discovered, adopted, and acted upon my father in the cure of impediments, before he had ever heard of Steele's name" (29).
21. John Millard, *Grammar of Elocution* (London, 1889), 113; Charles John Plumptre, *King's College Lectures on Elocution, or the Physiology and Culture of Voice and Speech, and the Expression of the Emotions by Language, Countenance, and Gesture, to Which Is Added, a Special Lecture on the Causes and Cure of Impediments of Speech* (London, 1863), 101–14.
22. James Hunt, *Stammering and Stuttering, Their Nature and Treatment*, 1st ed. (London, 1861). Hunt's text absorbs much material from his earlier *Treatise on Stuttering*, which itself had already gone through three editions at the point of publication of this more ambitious work. Hunt helpfully desynonymizes his two titular terms: stuttering sig-

nifies involuntary phonemic repetition, while stammering indicates impeded articulation.
23. These examples occur respectively on ibid., 20n, 71, 66, 65, 66.
24. Ibid., 102.
25. C. S. Bluemel, *Stammering and Cognate Defects of Speech*, 2 vols. (New York: G. E. Stechert, 1917), 2:171.
26. See Shinya Fuji and Catherine Y. Wan, "The Role of Rhythm in Speech and Language Rehabilitation: The SEP Hypothesis," *Frontiers in Human Neuroscience* 8 (2014): 777, http://doi.org/10.3389/fnhum.2014.00777.
27. Marcel Wingate, *Stuttering: Theory and Treatment* (New York: Irvington, 1976), 153–86 (182).
28. Hunt, *Stammering and Stuttering* (1st ed.), 102, 124–25.
29. Ibid., 104.
30. James Hunt, *Stammering and Stuttering, Their Nature and Treatment*, 6th ed. (London, 1870), 52.
31. Hunt, *Stammering and Stuttering* (1st ed.), 167–70. Interestingly, Hunt removed this appendix from later editions, although he incorporated Kingsley's praise into the main body of his text.
32. Ibid., 168–69.
33. James Malcolm Rymer's 1855 novel *The Unspeakable* is dedicated to Hunt: its stuttering protagonist, Charles Theodore Monckton, evinces a thorough knowledge of the burgeoning field of speech therapy, explicitly criticising the rhythm approach of Cull and others; following a course of moral instruction more in line with Hunt's procedures, he finally silences his still-inarticulate homosexual desire. See Riley McGuire, "The Victorian Unspeakable: Stammering and Same-Sex Intimacy between Men," *DiGeSt. Journal of Diversity and Gender Studies* 3.2 (2016): 43–57.
34. George Crabbe, *Tales, 1812 and Other Selected Poems*, ed. Howard Mills (Cambridge: Cambridge University Press, 1967), 135, cited in Molly Desjardins, "John Thelwall and Association," in *John Thelwall: Critical Reassessments*, ed. Yasmin Solomonescu, *Romantic Circles* (September 2011), par. 1; http://www.rc.umd.edu/praxis/thelwall/HTML/praxis.2011.desjardins.html.
35. These instances derive respectively from *The Correspondence of Thomas Carlyle and Ralph Waldo Emerson, 1834–1872* (London, 1883), 47–48; "Prophets Who Cannot Sing," in *The Poems of Coventry Patmore*, ed. Frederick Page (Oxford: Oxford University Press, 1949), 437; and Robert Browning's letter to Elizabeth Barrett Browning on 1 July 1845, where "for I that stammer and answer at hap-hazard with you" serves as a neat summary of the compressed and allusive style of their correspondence more generally (*The Letters of Robert Browning and Elizabeth Barrett Browning, 1845–1846*, ed. Robert B. Browning, 2 vols. [London, 1900]).

36. Walter Besant, *With Harp and Crown*, 3 vols. (London, 1875), 2:118–19.
37. Rupert Brooke, *The Prose of Rupert Brooke*, ed. Christopher Hassall (London: Sidgwick and Jackson, 1956), 106.
38. Oscar Wilde, "The Critic as Artist," in *The Artist as Critic: Critical Writings of Oscar Wilde*, ed. Richard Ellmann (Chicago: University of Chicago Press, 1968), 341–407 (345).
39. James Douglas, *Robert Browning* (London: Hodder and Stoughton, 1903), 23.
40. Stewart W. Holmes, "Browning: Semantic Stutterer," *PMLA* 60.1 (March 1945): 231–55 (231).
41. Ibid., 243–44.
42. Ibid., 234.
43. J. Hillis Miller, *The Disappearance of God: Five Nineteenth-Century Writers* (Urbana and Chicago: University of Illinois Press, 2000), 90.
44. Herbert Tucker, *Browning's Beginnings: The Art of Disclosure* (Minnesota: University of Minnesota Press, 1980), 109.
45. Ibid., 85.
46. Ibid., 110–11.
47. For more discussion of Sordello's background, see Robert Browning, *The Poetical Works of Robert Browning*, ed. Ian Jack and Margaret Smith, vol. 2 (Oxford: Oxford University Press, 1984), 165–71.
48. Ibid., 2:217n. All subsequent references to *Sordello* use this edition and are cited parenthetically in the text.
49. See 2:331, 4:166, 5:304, 762.
50. *Atlas*, 28 March 1840, 203.
51. David Duff, *An Exposition of Browning's "Sordello," with Historical and Other Notes* (Edinburgh and London: William Blackwood and Sons, 1906), 195.
52. Robert Browning, "Caliban upon Setebos; or, Natural Theology in the Island" (23), in Robert Browning, *Selected Poems* (London: Penguin, 1989), 188.
53. Samuel Silas Curry, *Browning and the Dramatic Monologue* (Boston: Expression Company, 1908), 1.
54. Samuel Silas Curry, *Foundations of Expression: Studies and Problems for Developing the Voice, Body and Mind in Reading and Speaking* (Boston: Expression Company, 1907), 32.
55. Curry, *Dramatic Monologue*, 7.
56. Ibid., 214.
57. Samuel Silas Curry, *Mind and Voice: Principles and Methods in Vocal Training* (Boston: Expression Company, 1910), 426.
58. Curry, *Dramatic Monologue*, 215.
59. See the section entitled "Actions of Mind and Voice" (Curry, *Dramatic Monologue*, 147–71).
60. On Browning's broader significance in the North American cultural sphere, see Nancy

Glazener, "The Browning Society in US Public Literary Culture," *Modern Language Quarterly* 75.2 (2014): 171–91.
61. Hiram Corson, *An Introduction to the Study of Robert Browning's Poetry* (Boston, 1888), 92. For a broader discussion of Browning's role in this wider history, see Thomas O. Sloane's "From Elocution to New Criticism: An Episode in the History of Rhetoric," *Rhetorica: A Journal of the History of Rhetoric* 31.3 (Summer 2013): 297–330.
62. George Andrew Lewis, *The Practical Treatment of Stammering and Stuttering, with Suggestions for Practice and Helpful Exercises* (Detroit, 1906), 122–23.
63. Curry, *Mind and Voice*, 110.
64. Yopie Prins, "Voice Inverse," *Victorian Poetry* 42.1 (Spring 2004): 43–60 (48).
65. Ibid., 49.
66. "When we ask what the meter of a poem is, we are not asking how Robert Frost or Professor X reads the poem, with all the features peculiar to that performance. We are asking about the poem as a public linguistic object, something that can be examined by various persons, studied, disputed—univocally" (W. K. Wimsatt Jr. and Monroe C. Beardsley, "The Concept of Meter: An Exercise in Abstraction," *PMLA* 74.5 [December 1959]: 585–98).
67. Sloane claims to trace the afterlife of elocutionary science in I. A. Richards's stipulation "to give the words their full imagined sound and body" ("From Elocution to New Criticism," 321), yet we should note the qualifier "imagined"; in *How to Read a Page: A Course in Effective Reading, with an Introduction to a Hundred Great Words* (New York: W. W. Norton, 1942), Richards explicitly states that reading aloud can generate hermeneutic confusion.
68. Hunt, *Stammering and Stuttering* (6th ed.) 57, 38.
69. Hunt is here referring to De Froberville's article in the *Bulletin de la Société Geographie* (June 1852). The example (they intercalate the syllable, *shill*, or any other, in the middle of each word) does not fit his own formal definition of stuttering as involuntary repetition.
70. Ibid., 29.
71. Josephine Hoegaerts, "S-s-s-syncopation: Music, Modernity, and the Performance of Stammering (ca. 1860–1930)," *Societies* 5.4 (2015): 1–16. Pecuniary circumstances may surely have proved the real reason for this therapeutic aversion. See also Hoegaerts's "'Is it a Habit or Is It a Disease?': The Changing Social Meaning of Stammering in Nineteenth-Century Western Europe," *Terrains & travaux* 23 (2013): 17–37.
72. James Hunt, *Stammering and Stuttering, Their Nature and Treatment*, 7th ed. (London, 1870), 350.
73. Ibid., 351.
74. Ibid., 352–55. Hunt casually lets slip that the "negro girl" may stutter on account of having been kidnapped and sold as a slave in Constantinople.
75. For a broader discussion of the Anthropological Society of London, see Ronald

Rainger, "Race, Politics, and Science: The Anthropological Society of London in the 1860s," *Victorian Studies* 22.1 (Autumn 1978): 51–70. Rainger states that Hunt and Robert Clarke held "diametrically opposite" views on race, which seems to me a little extreme; Hunt's work is unpardonably racist, yet nonetheless retains much of Clarke's conviction concerning the adverse effects of colonialism.

76. James Hunt, "Race in Legislation and Political Economy," *Anthropological Review* 4 (1866): 113–35 (120).
77. James Hunt, *The Negro's Place in Nature* (London, 1863), 23n.
78. Ibid., 22–23; Hunt again cites Clarke to the effect that some "Negro women" prove exceptions to this generalized discordancy.
79. See for example Edward A. Berlin's comparison of Charles Ives's syncopated rendering alongside "straighter" transcriptions, in his excellent *Ragtime* (Berkeley: University of California Press, 1980), 23.
80. The *New York Clipper* remarks that during his performance at Hammerstein's Victoria Theatre, Frank Rogers appeared with "a stammering 'coon' kid" (5 February 1905).
81. The sheet music for "Syncopated Sandy" can be found at https://digitalcollections.nypl.org/items/510d47de-1858-a3d9-e040-e00a18064a99.
82. On this history, see Lyn Abbott and Doug Seroff, "'They Cert'ly Sound Good to Me': Sheet Music, Southern Vaudeville, and the Commercial Ascendancy of the Blues," *American Music* 14.4 (Winter 1996): 402–54.
83. W. F. Gates, "Ethiopian Syncopation: The Decline of Ragtime," *Musician* 7 (October 1902): 341.
84. Craig Dworkin's "The Stutter of Form," in *The Sound of Poetry / The Poetry of Sound*, ed. Marjorie Perloff and Craig Dworkin (Chicago: University of Chicago Press, 2009), offers a helpful overview in this regard.
85. Gilles Deleuze, *Essays Clinical and Critical*, trans. Michael A. Greco and Daniel W. Smith (Minnesota: University of Minnesota Press, 1997), 109.
86. "I hear the stutter as a sounding of uncertainty," Howe notes in an interview with Edward Forster. "What is silence or not quite silenced. . . . A return is necessary, A WAY FOR WOMEN TO GO. Because we are in the stutter. We were expelled from the Garden of the Mythology of the American Frontier. The drama's done. We are the wilderness. We have come on to the stage of Stuttering" (Susan Howe, *The Birth-Mark: Unsettling the Wilderness in American Literary History* [Hanover and London: Wesleyan University Press, 1993], 181).
87. Susan Howe, *My Emily Dickinson* (Berkeley, CA: North Atlantic Books, 1985), 21.
88. In this connection, see Deborah Vlock-Keyes, "Music and Dramatic Voice in Robert Browning and Robert Schumann," *Victorian Poetry* 29.3 (Autumn 1991): 227–39.

2. Idealist Rhythms

1. Janina Wellmann, *The Form of Becoming: Embryology and the Epistemology of Rhythm, 1760–1830*, trans. Kate Sturge (New York: Zone, 2017), 95.
2. Ibid., 22–23.
3. Ibid., 176.
4. Ibid., 308.
5. Ibid., 29, 270.
6. For a broader treatment of the idealist appropriation of rhythm, see David Farrell Krell, *The Tragic Absolute: German Idealism and the Languishing of God* (Bloomington: Indiana University Press, 2005).
7. Friedrich Hölderlin, *Essays and Letters on Theory*, trans. Thomas Pfau (Albany: SUNY Press, 1988), 101–8 (102).
8. Walter Benjamin, "Goethe's Elective Affinities," in *Selected Writings*, vol 1: *1913–1926* (Cambridge, MA.: Harvard University Press, 1996), 297–360 (340–41).
9. Novalis, *Fichte Studies*, ed. Jane Kneller (Cambridge: Cambridge University Press, 2003), 135–36.
10. Ibid., 145.
11. Novalis was certainly being somewhat unfair to Fichte in this regard: from the 1796 edition of the *Wissenschaftslehre*, the latter has ceased to equate "I am I" with Leibniz's "X = X," exhorting the reader rather to "think the I."
12. Novalis, *Schriften*, vol. 2: *Das philosophische Werk I*, ed. Richard Samuel in collaboration with Hans-Joachim Mahl and Gerhard Schulz, rev. Richard Samuel and Hans-Joachim Mähl (Stuttgart, Berlin, Cologne, Mainz: Kohlhammer, 1981). This passage does not make the cut for the recent Cambridge University Press translation of *Fichte Studies*; I therefore translate it from the original here.
13. Friedrich Wilhelm Joseph Schelling, *The Philosophy of Art*, trans. Douglas W. Stott (Minneapolis: University of Minnesota Press, 1989), 117.
14. Tomas Macauley, "Rhythmic Accent and the Absolute: Sulzer, Schelling and the *Akzenttheorie*," Eighteenth Century Music 10.02 (September 2013): 277–86 (278). This is the single quote from Schelling's work to which Macauley refers.
15. Schelling, *Philosophy of Art*, 110.
16. Ibid.
17. Christopher Hasty, *Meter as Rhythm* (Oxford: Oxford University Press, 2007), 22–33.
18. Henry Crabb Robinson, *Essays on Kant, Schelling and German Aesthetics*, ed. James Vigus (London: MHRA, 2010), 98.
19. Schelling, *Philosophy of Art*, 110.
20. Jerome McGann, *The Romantic Ideology* (Chicago: University of Chicago Press, 1983), 40–48.

21. Virginia Jackson and Yopie Prins (eds.), *The Lyric Theory Reader: A Critical Anthology*, (Baltimore: Johns Hopkins University Press, 2014), 3.
22. See the first chapter of Dennis Taylor's *Hardy's Metres and Victorian Prosody* (Oxford: Clarendon Press, 1988), 7–48 (18–29).
23. G. W. F. Hegel, "Who Thinks Abstractly?," in *Hegel: Texts and Commentary*, trans. and ed. Walter Kaufmann (Notre Dame, IN: University of Notre Dame Press, 1977), 117–18.
24. G. W. F. Hegel, *Lectures on Fine Art*, trans. T. M. Knox, 3 vols. (Oxford: Clarendon Press, 1975), 918. Subsequent references are cited parenthetically in the text as *L*.
25. Catherine Malabou, *The Future of Hegel: Plasticity, Temporality, and Dialectic*, trans. Lisabeth During (New York: Routledge, 2004).
26. This account of spirit's leaving and returning itself through the self-cancellation of the beat resembles his later account of the origin of rhyme so closely as to cast doubt upon the privilege of the latter as an index of romantic "interiority" (rhythm being also a recognizably "classical" phenomenon).
27. Isobel Armstrong, "Meter and Meaning," in *Meter Matters*, ed. Jason David Hall (Athens: Ohio University Press, 2011), 26–52 (32). Armstrong treats the Hegelian influence upon Coventry Patmore, although below I will argue that the latter was a more sensitive reader of the former than she allows.
28. Ibid., 31, 34.
29. In this respect, see Simon Jarvis, "Musical Thinking: Hegel and the Phenomenology of Prosody," *Paragraph* 28.2 (July 2005): 57–71.
30. Thomas Maitland [Robert Buchanan], "The Fleshly School of Poetry: Mr. D. G. Rossetti," *Contemporary Review* 18 (1871): 335.
31. Meredith Martin, *The Rise and Fall of Meter* (Princeton, NJ: Princeton University Press, 2012), 69.
32. Yopie Prins, "Patmore's Law, Meynell's Rhythm," in *The Fin-de-Siècle Poem: English Literary Culture and the 1890s*, ed. Joseph Bristow (Athens: Ohio University Press, 2005), 261–84.
33. Joshua King, "Patmore, Hopkins, and the Problem of the English Metrical Law," *Victorian Poetry* 49. 2 (Summer 2011): 31–49 (31).
34. Rudy, *Electric Meters*, 112. Of all the critics surveyed here, Rudy has the most obvious misgivings regarding this immaterialist account of Patmore, as I discuss below.
35. For a fuller treatment of Claudel's relationship to Patmore, see my essay "Coventry Patmore's Corpus," *ELH* 83.3 (Fall 2016): 839–72.
36. John Maynard has written on Patmore, and the *Unknown Eros* in particular, in several contexts; his fullest treatment comes in *Victorian Discourses in Sexuality and Religion* (Cambridge: Cambridge University Press, 1993), 141–270.
37. King, "English Metrical Law," 31.
38. See in particular Hopkins's letter of 24 September 1885, in which he criticizes Patmore's assertion that the wife might enjoy the "vanity" of her body (*The Further Let-*

ters of Gerard Manley Hopkins: Including His Correspondence with Coventry Patmore, ed. C. C. Abbott [London: Oxford University Press, 1956]), 308–10.
39. Coventry Patmore, *The Rod, the Root and the Flower* (London: Grey Walls Press, 1950), 103. Subsequent references are cited parenthetically in the text as *R*.
40. Coventry Patmore, *Coventry Patmore's "Essay on Metrical Law"* (Washington, DC: Catholic University of America Press, 1961), 7.
41. Rudy, *Electric Meters*, 115, 121.
42. Patmore, *"Essay on Metrical Law,"* 9.
43. Ibid., 22.
44. Ibid., 11.
45. Joseph Phelan, *The Music of Verse: Metrical Experiment in Nineteenth-Century Poetry* (Basingstoke, UK: Palgrave Macmillan, 2012), 28–29.
46. Patmore, *"Essay on Metrical Law,"* 9.
47. Ibid., 16.
48. Rudy, *Electric Meters*, 115.
49. Patmore, *"Essay on Metrical Law,"* 18–19.
50. Ibid., 11.
51. Ibid., 31.
52. Patmore, *"Essay on Metrical Law,"* 28.
53. Coventry Patmore, *The Poems of Coventry Patmore*, ed. Frederick Page (Oxford: Oxford University Press, 1949), 19–31. Subsequent references are cited parenthetically in the text.
54. Patmore, *"Essay on Metrical Law,"* 26.
55. Phelan, *Music of Verse*, 33–34.
56. Ibid., 35.
57. Patmore, *"Essay on Metrical Law,"* 31.
58. Richard de Bary, letters to Julian Huxley, 5, 13, and 16 June 1933, in the Huxley Papers, Rice University, Houston, TX. My thanks to Lesley Hall at the Wellcome Library for informing me of this correspondence.
59. W. J. Mander, *British Idealism: A History* (Oxford: Oxford University Press, 2011).
60. A discussion on "Literary Influences on Idealism" is revealingly brief (ibid., 24–27).
61. J. H. Stirling, *The Secret of Hegel: Being the Hegelian System in Origin, Principle, Form and Matter*, 2 vols. (London, 1865), 2:38.
62. G. W. F. Hegel, *The Logic of Hegel*, trans. William Wallace (London, 1874), lxx–lxxii. For an explicit link between German idealism and poetic rhythm, see 100.
63. For a skeptical account, see Menachem Fisch, "Necessary and Contingent Truth in William Whewell's Antithetical Theory of Knowledge," *Studies in History and Philosophy of Science* 16.4 (December 1985): 275–314; for a more affirmative approach to Kant's influence, see Robert E. Butts, "Necessary Truths in Whewell's Theory of Science," *American Philosophical Quarterly* 2.3 (July 1965): 161–81.

64. William Whewell, *The Philosophy of the Inductive Sciences*, 2 vols. (London, 1840), xviii. Subsequent references are cited parenthetically in the text as *PIS*. For an explicit acknowledgment of Kant's influence, see Butts, ibid., 165–67.
65. G. W. F. Hegel, *Science of Logic*, trans. A. V. Miller (London: George Allen and Unwin, 1969), 45–48.
66. Less pleasantly, Whewell likens children in this respect to "very rude savages."
67. Compare to 127, where Whewell's preference for accent over length is clearer.
68. See Whewell's three letters in *Blackwood's Edinburgh Magazine* 60 (1846): 20, 328, 479–80; and "English Hexameters," *North British Review* 19 (May–August 1853): 129–50. Joseph Phelan has written illuminatingly upon this context in *Music of Verse*, 53–64.
69. Theodore Watts-Duncan, "Poetry," in *Encyclopedia Britannica*, 9th ed., vol. 19 (Edinburgh, 1885), 256–73 (257, 262).
70. Ibid., 256–59.
71. Ibid., 262.
72. Alice Meynell, "The Rhythm of Life," in *The Rhythm of Life* (John Lane: London, 1905), 1–6 (1).
73. Ibid., 2–3.
74. Ibid., 6.
75. Prins, "Patmore's Law, Meynell's Rhythm," 277.
76. Ibid., 273.
77. This verse can be found in June Badeni, *The Slender Tree: A Life of Alice Meynell* (Padstow: Tabb House, 1981), 105–6; quoted in Prins, "Patmore's Law, Meynell's Rhythm," 264.
78. Meynell, "Unstable Equilibrium," in *Rhythm of Life*, 26–28 (26–27).
79. Alice Meynell, *Collected Poems of Alice Meynell* (New York: Charles Screibner's Sons, 1914), 94.
80. Ibid., 99.
81. Talia Schaffer, "A Tethered Angel: The Martyrology of Alice Meynell," *Victorian Poetry* 38.1 (Spring 2000): 49–61 (58).
82. Virginia Woolf, *Orlando: A Biography* (New York: Harcourt Brace Jovanovich, 1956), 294–95.
83. Ashley Montagu, *Touching: The Human Significance of the Skin* (London: HarperCollins, 1986), 174.

3. Entraining Rhythms

1. George Eliot, "Notes on Form in Art," in *Selected Poems, Essays and Other Writings*, ed. A. S. Byatt (London: Penguin, 1990), 231–36 (235).
2. Charles Darwin, *The Autobiography of Charles Darwin, 1809–1882*, ed. Nora Barlow (New York: W. W. Norton, 2005), 73.

3. This image originated in Woodward's *Mollusca*. See also Eliot's "Ilfracombe Journal," in *The George Eliot Letters*, ed. Gordon S. Haight, 9 vols. (New Haven, CT: Yale University Press, 1954), 2:238–52.
4. For more on this lineage, see Rosemary Ashton, *The German Idea: Four English Writers and the Reception of German Thought, 1800–60* (Cambridge: Cambridge University Press, 1980).
5. George Henry Lewes, *Sea-Side Studies, at Ilfracombe, Tenby, The Scilly Isles, and Jersey* (London, 1860), 54.
6. Ibid., 189.
7. Ibid., 360–61.
8. Ibid., 32.
9. Ibid., 347. Eliot and Lewes carried out many such experiments, with the former famously writing to Cara Bray in 1867 that "Froggie continues to do better than even he expected without his head *brain* [sic] for months. He dies of starvation at last." These indefensibly cruel experiments should nevertheless be taken in a scientific context where the praying mantis had recently been shown to be able to function without a head.
10. George Henry Lewes, *The Physiology of Common Life* (London, 1859), 331–32.
11. Ibid., 336.
12. Herbert Spencer, "The Social Organism," in *Essays: Scientific, Political and Speculative*, 3 vols. (London, 1891), 1:267–307 (273).
13. Ibid., 2:281–83.
14. James Elwick, "Herbert Spencer and the Disunity of the Social Organism," *History of Science* 41.1 (2003): 35–72 (59–62).
15. Thomas Henry Huxley, "Administrative Nihilism," *Fortnightly Review* 10 (1871): 525–43 (534); quoted in "Herbert Spencer and the Disunity of the Social Organism," 60.
16. Spencer, "Social Organism," 2:276.
17. Ibid., 296–97.
18. Georg Simmel, *The Philosophy of Money* (London: Routledge, 1990); see particularly the final chapter, "The Style of Life" (429–512).
19. Victoria Leong et al., "Speaker Gaze Increases Infant–Adult Connectivity," *Proceedings of the National Academy of Sciences* 114.50 (December 2017): 13290–95.
20. J. E. McGrath and J. R. Kelly, *Time and Human Interaction: Toward a Social Psychology of Time* (New York: Guilford Press, 1986), 89–90; cited in Martin Clayton, Rebecca Sager, and Udo Will, "In Time with the Music: The Concept of Entrainment and Its Significance for Ethnomusicology," *ESEM Counterpoint* 1 (2004): 1–82 (11).
21. Clayton, Sager, and Will, "In Time with the Music," 3.
22. For a concise overview of sympathetic resonance, see *The Cambridge History of Western Music Theory*, ed. Thomas Christensen (Cambridge: Cambridge University Press, 2002), 247–49.
23. Denis Diderot, *Essai sur le mérite et la vertu* (Paris, 1798), 128n; translation mine.

24. Adam Smith, *The Theory of Moral Sentiments*, ed. Knud Haakonssen (Cambridge: Cambridge University Press, 2002), 27.
25. Ibid., 85.
26. Teresa Brennan, *The Transmission of Affect* (Ithaca, NY: Cornell University Press, 2004). This stimulating work offers an early and still-rare treatment of entrainment within a philosophical setting. It is curious, however, that Brennan interprets the phenomenon almost exclusively in terms of smell ("unconscious olfaction" [9]); sound is meanwhile likened throughout to vision (27), as a phenomenon that maintains boundaries between persons.
27. Smith, *Theory of Moral Sentiments*, 82.
28. Ibid., 33.
29. Ibid., 12.
30. Mary Fairclough, *The Romantic Crowd: Sympathy, Controversy and Print Culture* (Cambridge: Cambridge University Press, 2013), 228–29.
31. Charles Dickens, *A Tale of Two Cities* (New York: Barnes and Noble, 2004), 397.
32. Ibid., 56.
33. Ibid., 480.
34. John Gross, "A Tale of Two Cities," in *Dickens and the Twentieth Century*, ed. John Gross and Gabriel Pearson (Toronto: University of Toronto Press, 1962), 189–92 (192).
35. Dickens, *Tale of Two Cities*, 509–19.
36. George Eliot, *Romola*, ed. Dorothea Barrett (London: Penguin, 1996), 279, 230.
37. Herbert Tucker, "Quantity and Quality: The Strange Case of George Eliot, Minor Poet," *George Eliot–George Henry Lewes Studies* 60/61 (September 2011): 17–30.
38. John Morley, "The Spanish Gypsy," *Macmillan's Magazine* 18 (July 1868): 281–87.
39. "The Spanish Gypsy," *Atlantic Monthly* 22 (September 1868): 380–84. For a concise summary of critical response to the work, see Antoine Gerard van den Broek's introduction to *The Spanish Gypsy* (London: Pickering and Chatto, 2008), xxvii–lv. Subsequent parenthetical references to the poem use this edition.
40. See Eliot, *Letters*, 4:463–67.
41. For a still stronger instance of this tendency, see 2:64–80, where "gone" recurs at the end of five lines.
42. *Spanish Gypsy*, 3.
43. For a broad treatment of this phenomenon, see Deborah Epstein Nord, *Gypsies and the British Imagination, 1807–1930* (New York: Columbia University Press, 2006).
44. George Borrow, *The Zincali: or, An Account of the Gypsies of Spain*, 3rd ed., 2 vols. (London, 1843), 2:4–5. I cite here from the edition that Eliot owned.
45. Ibid., 5, 8.
46. Ibid., 9–10.
47. Ibid., 8.
48. Ibid., 13.

49. Ruth Abbott, "George Eliot, Meter, and the Matter of Ideas: The Yale Poetry Notebook," *ELH* 82.4 (2015): 1179–211 (1181).
50. She replaced the line with "Who have no Whence or Whither in their souls" (1:2750); Eliot did not however excise the line that follows shortly after, "Because our race has no great memories" (1:2768).
51. Eliot, *Spanish Gypsy*, 275.
52. See for instance Ewen Calloway, "Fearful Memories Haunt Mouse Descendants: Genetic Imprint from Traumatic Experiences Carries Through at Least Two Generations," *Nature* (9 December 2015), http://doi.org/10.1038/nature.2013.14272.
53. Walter Benjamin, "Toys and Play: Marginal Notes on a Monumental Work," *Selected Writings*, vol. 2: *1927–1934*, trans. Rodney Livingstone (Cambridge, MA: Belknap Press), 117–21 (120).
54. When Fedalma first discovers her Zincali inheritance, she remarks, "Look at these hands! You say when they were little / They played about the gold upon your neck. / I do believe it, for their tiny pulse / Made record of it in the inmost coil / Of growing memory" (1:294).
55. Daniel Dennett, "The Origins of Selves," *Cogito* 3 (Autumn 1989): 163–73.
56. Eliot, "Notes on Form in Art," 235.
57. Lewes's reductionist physiology does contain striking yet undeveloped moments: "In the development of the great series of animal organisms, the Nervous System assumes more and more of an imperial character. The rank held by any animal is determined by this character, and not at all by its bulk, its strength, or even its utility. In like manner, in the development of the social organism, as the life of nations becomes more complex, Thought assumes a more imperial character; and Literature, in its widest sense, becomes a delicate index of social evolution. Barbarous societies show only the germs of literary life. But advancing civilisation, bringing with it increased conquest over material agencies, disengages the mind from the pressure of immediate wants, and the loosened energy finds in leisure both the demand and the means of a new activity: the demand, because long unoccupied hours have to be rescued from the weariness of inaction; the means, because this call upon the energies nourishes a greater ambition and furnishes a wider arena" (*The Principles of Success in Literature* [Boston, 1891], 19). This dynamic understanding of culture contradicts Lewes's insistence, in the passages cited below, that societies cannot be compared to simple organisms.
58. George Henry Lewes, *Problems in Life and Mind*, 2 vols. (London, 1879), 2:31.
59. Hegel, *Science of Logic*.
60. Lewes, *Problems in Life and Mind*, 2:33.
61. W. Tecumseh Fitch, "The Biology and Evolution of Rhythm: Unraveling a Paradox," in *Language and Music as Cognitive Systems*, ed. P. Rebuschat, M. Rohmeier, J. A. Hawkins, and I. Cross (Oxford: Oxford University Press, 2012), 73–95.

62. Henkjan Honing et al., "Rhesus Monkeys (*Macaca mulatta*) Detect Rhythmic Groups in Music, but Not the Beat," *PLoS ONE* 7.12 (2012), http://doi.org/10.1371/journal.pone.0051369.
63. A. D. Patel, "The Evolutionary Biology of Musical Rhythm: Was Darwin Wrong?," *PLOS Biology* 12.3 (25 March 2014), https://doi.org/10.1371/journal.pbio.1001821.
64. Spencer, *Essays*, 2:400–451 (400).
65. Ibid., 413.
66. Ibid.
67. Herbert Spencer, The Life and Letters of Herbert *Spencer*, ed. David Duncan (Cambridge: Cambridge University Press, 2013), 66–67.
68. Charles Darwin, *The Descent of Man and Selection in Relation to Sex* (Princeton, NJ: Princeton University Press, 1981), 333.
69. See Peter Kivy, "Darwin on Music," *Journal of the American Musicological Society* 12.1 (Spring 1959): 42–48 (48).
70. Darwin, *Descent of Man*, 336n. While his amatory explanation of birdsong has historically gained little traction, Richard O. Prum has recently presented a wonderful recovery of "Darwin's forgotten theory," where sexual selection might prove of material use for feminism, among other things. See *The Evolution of Beauty: How Darwin's Forgotten Theory of Mate Choice Shapes the Animal World—and Us* (New York: Doubleday, 2017).
71. Herbert Spencer, "On the Origin of Music," *Mind* 15.60 (October 1890): 449–68 (467).
72. Ibid., 460.
73. Spencer cites Andrew Crosse's 1878 travelogue *Round about the Carpathians* ("Origin of Music," 15.60 [October 1890]: 467). His postscript also cites Emily Gerard's *The Land Beyond the Forest: Facts, Figures, and Fancies from Transylvania* (New York, 1888), another work that features a series of "Gypsy rhymes."
74. Ibid., 455–57.
75. Ibid., 451–54.
76. Richard Wallaschek, *Primitive Music* (London, 1893), 235.
77. Herbert Spencer, "On the Origin of Music," *Mind* 16.64 (October 1891): 535–37 (535). Spencer was responding to Wallaschek's earlier article, confusingly also entitled "On the Origin of Music," published in *Mind* 16.63 (July 1891): 375–86; *Primitive Music* repeats the argument verbatim.
78. Edmund Gurney, *The Power of Sound* (London, 1880), 492.
79. Émile Durkheim, *The Division of Labour in Society*, trans. George Simpson (Glencoe, IL: Free Press 1933), 191–92. Durkheim is citing from Edmond Perrier's *Le Transformisme* (Paris, 1888), 159; though given Perrier's references to Spencer (41–43), he may also have been citing the very authority with which he publicly disagreed. See also Durkheim's *The Elementary Forms of Religious Life*, trans. Carol Cosman (Oxford: Oxford University Press, 2001), 20n. Durkheim elsewhere in this introduction justly

criticizes Spencer's overreliance upon individual experience as a source of collective social categories (15n).
80. Karl Bücher, *Arbeit und Rhythmus* (Leipzig, 1896).
81. Francis Barton Gummere, *The Beginnings of Poetry* (London: Macmillan, 1901), 30. Subsequent references are cited parenthetically in the text as *BP*.
82. Virginia Jackson, "The Cadence of Consent: Francis Barton Gummere, Lyric Rhythm, and White Poetics," in *Critical Rhythm: The Poetics of a Literary Art Form*, ed. Jonathan Culler and Ben Glaser (Fordham, NY: Fordham University Press, 2019), 99.
83. Steve Newman, *Ballad Collection, Lyric, and the Canon: The Call of the Popular from the Restoration to the New Criticism* (Philadelphia: University of Pennsylvania Press, 2007), 196.
84. Virgina Jackson and Meredith Martin, "The Poetry of the Future," *LA Review of Books*, 29 January 2021, http://avidly.lareviewofbooks.org/2021/01/29/the-poetry-of-the-future/.
85. Louise Pound, *Poetic Origins and the Ballad* (New York: Macmillan Company, 1921), 9.
86. Susan Stewart, "Scandals of the Ballad," *Representations* 32 (Fall 1990): 134–56.
87. For a broader treatment of the interrelationship between rigid meter and ideological work (in Macaulay and elsewhere), see Meredith Martin, "'Imperfectly Civilized': Ballads, Nations, and Histories of Form," *ELH* 82.2 (Summer 2015): 345–63.
88. Newman, *Ballad Collection, Lyric, and the Canon*, 196.
89. Child's entry on ballad for *Johnson's Universal Cyclopaedia* (1900) serves notice of these intentions, when he calls the broadside ballads of the sixteenth and seventeenth centuries "thoroughly despicable and worthless" (*Journal of Folklore Research* 31.1/3 [1994]: 214–22 [218]).
90. Francis James Child (ed.), *The English and Scottish Popular Ballads*, 5 vols. (New York: Dover Publications, 1965), 2:156–66.
91. Child, *English and Scottish Popular Ballads*, 2:156.
92. Ibid., 2:159.
93. Ibid., 2:163.
94. Ibid.
95. Ibid.
96. "Nothing could be easier than to give these questions, prevarications, and comments a humorous turn" (ibid., 158).
97. See https://www.youtube.com/watch?v=r5FZtokV9zk.

4. Thermodynamic Rhythm

1. Spencer, *Life and Letters*, 104.
2. Richard Hofstadter, *Social Darwinism in American Thought* (Boston, MA: Beacon Press, 1955).

3. Bruce Clarke cites Tyndall's letter in *Energy Forms: Allegory and Science in the Era of Classical Thermodynamics* (Ann Arbor: University of Michigan Press, 2001), where he concludes that "the notion of energy dissipation . . . plac[ed] a chill on his rosy evolutionary scenario" (67); we hear little of his work from this point on.
4. Spencer, *First Principles*, 316n.
5. For Spencer's elaboration of this concept, see ibid., 359–81. Maxwell was unconvinced, unfavorably comparing the "instability of the homogenous" to William Gibbs's theory on the equilibrium of heterogeneous substances, in a postcard to the physicist P. G. Tait composed on 29 July 1876; this can be found in the Maxwell correspondence held at Cambridge University Library (MS Add. 7655).
6. Maxwell himself would come to believe in the measurability of even this unpredictable motion, through what became known as the Maxwell–Boltzmann probability distribution.
7. Spencer, *Life and Letters*, 430.
8. See Gillian Beer, *Open Fields: Science in Cultural Encounter* (Oxford: Oxford University Press, 1999), 219–41; Michel Serres, *Hermes: Literature, Science, Philosophy* (Baltimore: Johns Hopkins University Press, 1982), 71–83.
9. John Tyndall, *Heat Considered as a Mode of Motion* (Cambridge: Cambridge University Press, 2014), 434. The edition cited above reprints the original 1863 publication; interestingly, Tyndall would remove the passage from later editions, suggesting an equivocation regarding the status of the conservation of force.
10. Friedrich Kittler, *Gramophone, Film, Typewriter*, trans. Dorothea von Mucke (Stanford, CA: Stanford University Press, 1999), 24.
11. Anton Rabinbach, *The Human Motor: Energy, Fatigue and the Origins of Modernity* (Berkeley and Los Angeles: University of California Press, 1992), 68.
12. John Tyndall, *Sound: A Course of Lectures Delivered at the Royal Institution of Great Britain* (London, 1867), 296.
13. Bolton, *Rhythm*, 9.
14. Sidney Lanier, *The Science of English Verse* (New York, 1880), 248.
15. Ibid.
16. Ibid., 250.
17. Ibid.
18. Ibid., 249.
19. Ibid., 250.
20. For more on this topic, see Robin Veder, *The Living Line: Modern Art and the Economy of Energy* (Hanover, NH: Dartmouth College Press, 2015).
21. Henrietta Russell, *The Delsarte Series*, vol. 1: *Yawning* (New York, 1891), 57.
22. Ibid., 61. For a fuller treatment of Russell's involvement with Delsartism, see Carrie J. Preston, *Modernism's Mythic Pose: Gender, Genre, Solo Performance* (Oxford: Oxford University Press, 2011), 69–75, 82–87.

23. Richard Hovey, "Delsarte and Poetry," *Independent* [New York], 27 August 1891.
24. Spencer, *Life and Letters*, 1:306.
25. Bliss Carman, "Personal Rhythm," in *The Friendship of Art* (Toronto: Copp, Clark, 1904), 182–89 (185).
26. Ibid., 182–84.
27. Balfour Stewart and P. G. Tait, *The Unseen Universe, or Physical Speculations on a Future State* (New York, 1875), 48. See 152 for a broader response to the ventriloquized objection that "your doctrine of immortality does violence to that great principle, the conservation of energy"; Balfour and Stewart respond "that when we assert the conservation of energy it is as a principle applicable under special limitations," namely the passage of energy through an "ether" into regions where it cannot readily be detected.
28. Tyndall, *Sound*, 217.
29. Ibid., 218.
30. Ibid., 219.
31. Ibid., 234.
32. Ibid., 240–41.
33. Ibid., 243.
34. Ibid., 235.
35. William Fletcher Barrett, *On the Threshold of the Unseen: An Examination of the Phenomena of Spiritualism and of the Evidence for Survival after Death* (New York: E. P. Dutton, 1917), 39.
36. For a fuller account of his life and work, see Richard Noakes, "The 'Bridge Which Is Between Physical and Psychical Research': William Fletcher Barrett, Sensitive Flames, and Spiritualism," *History of Science* 42 (2004): 419–64.
37. F. W. H. Myers, "M. Renan and Miracles," *Nineteenth Century* 10 (1881): 90–106 (103).
38. F. W. H. Myers, *Human Personality and Its Survival of Bodily Death*, 2 vols. (London: Longmans, Green, 1903), 2:126–27.
39. F. W. H. Myers, "Essay on Virgil," in *Essays Classical and Modern* (London: Macmillan, 1914), 106–76 (134–41). For a recent recovery of Myers's work, see Helen Groth, "Subliminal Histories: Psychological Experimentation in the Poetry and Poetics of Frederic W. H. Myers," *19: Interdisciplinary Studies in the Long Nineteenth Century* 12 (April 2011), http://doi.org/10.16995/ntn.594.
40. Edmund Gurney, "Poets, Critics and Class-Lists," in *Tertium Quid: Chapter on Various Disputed Questions*, vol. 2 (London, 1887), 119–90 (142–52).
41. Ibid., 158n.
42. Ibid., 161–62.
43. Ibid., 163–64.
44. Ibid., 164.
45. See ibid., 153, 154, 155.
46. Ibid., 175.

47. James wrote a tribute upon Myers's death, which was published in the *Proceedings of the Society for Psychical Research* 17 (1903): 13–23.
48. See Henri Bergson, *Mind-Energy: Lectures and Essays,* trans. H. Wilden Carr (New York: Henry Holt, 1920), 75–103.
49. Steven Shaviro, *The Universe of Things* (Minneapolis: University of Minnesota Press, 2014).
50. John Tyndall, "The Sabbath," in *New Fragments* (London, 1892), 1–46 (10).
51. Paul Sawyer, "Ruskin and Tyndall: The Poetry of Matter and The Poetry of Spirit," *Annals of the New York Academy of Sciences* 360 (April 1981): 217–46 (240). Sawyer contrasts Tyndall's equanimity with the apocalyptical visions of Ruskin, with whom he was frequently in public dispute.
52. These musings appeared in the two-volume edition of the *New Fragments* (London, 1879), 2:89–90 (90). Their suppression from subsequent editions is interesting in its own right.
53. Just as he summarily dismisses Herbert Spencer as an uncomplicatedly optimistic social Darwinist, so too Bruce Clarke recurrently dismisses Tyndall as a simple proponent of the first law (*Energy Forms,* 72, 132), which Clarke rejects in keeping with a general preference for entropy over conservation, allegory over the romantic symbol, etc. Yet Tyndall's romanticism was never so simply transcendent or totalizing in the first instance—else how would his work have proven such an inspiration to the subsequent darker visions of Camille Flammarion (a link that Clarke himself demonstrates)?
54. Maxwell's poem is printed in Lewis Campbell and Matthew Garnett's *The Life of James Clerk Maxwell: with a Selection from His Correspondence and Occasional Writings; and a Sketch of His Contributions to Science* (London, 1882), 649–51.
55. William Kingdom Clifford, review of *The Unseen Universe; or, Physical Speculations on a Future State,* by P. G. Tait and Balfour Stewart, *Fortnightly Review* 17 (January–June 1875): 776–93 (790–91).
56. See Gowan Dawson, "Victorian Periodicals and the Making of William Kingdon Clifford's Posthumous Reputation," in *Science Serialized: Representations of the Sciences in Nineteenth-Century Periodicals,* ed. Geoffrey Cantor and Sally Shuttleworth (Cambridge, MA: MIT Press, 2004), 259–84.
57. Algernon Swinburne, *Algernon Swinburne: The Critical Heritage,* ed. Clyde K. Hyder (London: Routledge, 1970), 190. Myers's essay was first published in *Nineteenth Century* 33 (January 1893): 93–111.
58. Ibid., 194.
59. Ibid., 196.
60. Gurney, *Tertium Quid,* 2:147.
61. Ibid., 155–56.
62. Gurney, *Power of Sound,* 553–54.

63. Ibid., 558.
64. Ibid., 129n.
65. Ibid., 557. Gurney is quoting from Allen's *Physiological Aesthetics* (London, 1877).
66. Ibid., 148.
67. Barri J. Gould's *ThermoPoetics* (Cambridge, MA: MIT Press, 2010) proves characteristic in taking Tennyson as the exemplary poet in this context (Swinburne is not present). It does so by associating him with what I have identified as the first response to thermodynamics, which emphasises the conservation of force. Tennyson reflects "the critical shift from *waste* to *vastness*—etymologically linked words sharing the Latin source *vastus*—marks a rethinking of the universe, not as waste space, but as a very large, closed system in which things are never actually lost, but merely diffused" (57). In "'Death Blots Black Out': Thermodynamics and the Poetry of Gerard Manley Hopkins" (*Victorian Poetry* 40.2 [Summer 2002]: 131–56), Jude V. Nixon similarly reads "That Nature is a Heraclitean Fire and of the comfort of the Resurrection" as proof of Hopkins's terror of a closed system tending toward dissolution, which is finally not so closed that God cannot alter its laws.
68. Herbert Tucker, *Epic: Britain's Heroic Muse, 1790–1910* (Oxford: Oxford University Press, 2008), 524. Tucker refers to Swinburne's interest in "the basic elements of existence, whether fresh come from creation or at the spent point of apocalyptic finish or entropic subsidence" (523); it is unclear whether apocalypse and entropy represent different figurative expressions of the same idea.
69. Algernon Charles Swinburne, *Major Poems and Selected Prose*, ed. Jerome McGann and Charles L. Sligh (New Haven, CT: Yale University Press, 2004), xxii. Subsequent references are cited parenthetically in the text as *MP*.
70. Algernon Charles Swinburne, *Under the Microscope* (London, 1872), 1–3.
71. Algernon Charles Swinburne, *The Swinburne Letters*, ed. Cecil Y. Lang, 6 vols. (New Haven, CT: Yale University Press, 1959–62) 2:335. For a consideration of this statement, along with Swinburne's work more generally, according to a less differentiated form of materialism than I attempt here, see Rudy, *Electric Meters*, 145–54.
72. Edward Thomas, *Algernon Charles Swinburne: A Critical Study* (London: Secker, 1912), 13.
73. I am grateful to Herbert Tucker for pointing out that a larger-scale version of this repetition operates in the first and last books of *Tristram*, keyed respectively to Love and Fate.
74. Algernon Charles Swinburne, *Swinburne Replies*, ed. Clyde Kenneth Hyder (Syracuse: SUNY Press, 1966), 22.
75. T. S. Eliot, *The Sacred Wood: Essays on Poetry and Criticism* (London: Faber and Faber, 1967), 17.
76. Ibid., 127.
77. Nicholas Dames, *The Physiology of the Novel: Reading, Neural Science, and the Form of Victorian Fiction* (Oxford: Oxford University Press, 2007).

78. Mary Byrd Davis argues that Swinburne in actual fact took great effort to work together the various source material; yet she is nonetheless forced to confess that the narrative "telescoping," continual flashbacks and total omission of several central narrative strands and secondary characters makes the resulting work "difficult to follow" ("Swinburne's Use of His Sources in *Tristram of Lyonesse*," *Philological Quarterly* 55.1 [Winter 1976]: 96–112 [102]).
79. As Byrd Davis notes (ibid., 99), the libretto to Wagner's *Tristram*—which Swinburne read in 1872 at the latest—is the only source that suggests that Tristan and Iseult were already in love before drinking of the potion. Tucker's claim that the love potion caused their love seems unlikely.
80. Adelaide Crapsey, *A Study in English Metrics* (New York: Alfred A. Knopf, 1918), 21. Crapsey died in 1914, leaving her empirical study of verse incomplete.
81. Ibid., 68.
82. We should read such influence in the broader context of Swinburne's unending interest in ballad form, and his desire to push refrain and repetition to a limit that his own historical context marked more sharply than had the mode's early audiences. See, for example, his early adaptations of Border ballads "The Tyneside Widow" and "The Jacobite's Exile" ("The weary day rins down and dies / The weary night wears through").
83. In his 1867 review of Matthew Arnold's verse, Swinburne writes: "To the lyrics which shall serve as water-springs and pastures I shall have to pay tribute of thanks in their turn; but first I would say something of that strain of choral philosophy which falls here 'as the shadow of a great rock in a weary land'" ("Matthew Arnold's New Poems," in Algernon Charles Swinburne, *Swinburne as Critic*, ed. Clyde K. Hyder [London: Routledge and Kegan Paul, 1972], 56).
84. Compare to Psalm 63:1, which I am sure Swinburne must equally have read and obsessed over: "My soul thirsts for you; my whole body longs for you in this parched and weary land where there is no water."
85. In this respect, the readings that I offer here depart from the imagined interlocutors of Jerome McGann's *Swinburne: An Essay in Criticism* (Chicago: University of Chicago Press, 1972). "Murdoch" and "Karnahan" discuss the lines "Is it with soul's thirst or with body's drought / That summer yearns out sunward to the south?" The former strikes a note reminiscent of T. S. Eliot, asking, "What point does an impossible question like this serve?" Karnahan replies, "Celebration. The question calls a blessing down upon spirit and flesh, summer and winter" (155). Swinburne's "drouth" does indeed serve a point, one that contains, however, other hues than benign optimism.
86. Rudyard Kipling, "Boots," in *The Five Nations* (London: Methuen, 1903), 185.
87. Lewes, *Principles of Success*, 129.
88. Oliver Elton, *A Survey of English Literature, 1780–1880*, 4 vols. (New York: Macmillan, 1920), 4:55.

89. Conrad A. Balliet, "The History and Rhetoric of the Triplet," *PMLA* 80.5 (December 1965): 528–34.
90. Ibid., 532.
91. I won't labour to chronicle the many bad poems and rhyming dictionaries in which "'breath" / "death" and familiar company arise; it is both sufficient and of independent interest to note that Skelton anticipates the "wife" / "strife" rhyme that I will explore below in more detail, at the very moment that *Philip Sparrow* turns to the Tristan legend: "Of Tristram, and King Mark, / And all the whole work / Of Belle Isolde his wife, / For whom was much strife" (641–44).
92. Gregory Bateson, "Cybernetic Explanation," *American Behavioural Scientist* 10.8 (April 1967): 29–37 (37).
93. *OED*, s.v. "waste, n.," https://oed.com/search?searchType=dictionary&q=waste&_searchBtn=Search.
94. The word "strife" occurs twenty-four times in the whole poem; in eighteen of those occurrences, it rhymes with "life."
95. Algernon Charles Swinburne, "The Flogging Block," cited in Yopie Prins, *Victorian Sappho* (Princeton, NJ: Princeton University Press, 1999), 152.
96. Richard Cureton, *Rhythmic Phrasing in English Verse* (London: Longman, 1992).
97. Friedrich Nietzsche, *The Case of Wagner, Nietzsche Contra Wager and Selected Aphorisms*, trans. Anthony M. Ludovici (London: T. N. Foulis, 1911), 5.
98. Jerome McGann, "Swinburne, Wagner, Baudelaire: Poetry in the Condition of Music," *Victorian Poetry* 47.4 (2009): 619–32. In this respect, see also Swinburne's consecutive roundels, "Concord" and "Discord," whose various expressive overlaps suggest a dialectical relation rather than a stark opposition.

Coda

1. Henri Lefebvre, *Rhythmanalysis: Space, Time and Everyday Life*, trans. Stuart Elden and Gerald Moore (London: Continuum, 2013), 21.
2. Ibid., 27–28.
3. A recent empirical study asks participants to articulate a repeated syllable while hearing a regular flow of nonsense syllables. The results demonstrate two clearly divergent groups: some participants entrain their vocal production without prompting to the aural stimulus; others do not. The same study goes on to link such results to differences in brain structure and process (M. Florencia Assaneo et al., "Spontaneous Synchronization to Speech Reveals Neural Mechanisms Facilitating Language Learning," *Nature Neuroscience* 22.4 [April 2019]: 627–32).
4. Joseph North, *Literary Criticism: A Concise Political History* (Cambridge, MA: Harvard University Press, 2017), 107.

BIBLIOGRAPHY

Abbott, Lyn, and Doug Seroff. "'They Cert'ly Sound Good to Me': Sheet Music, Southern Vaudeville, and the Commercial Ascendancy of the Blues." *American Music* 14.4 (Winter 1996): 402–54.
Abbott, Ruth. "George Eliot, Meter, and the Matter of Ideas: The Yale Poetry Notebook." *ELH* 82.4 (2015): 1179–1211.
Abraham, Nicolas. *Rhythms: On the Work, Translation, and Psychoanalysis*. Trans. Benjamin Tigpen and Nicholas T. Rand. Stanford, CA: Stanford University Press, 1995.
Agamben, Giorgio. *The Man without Content*. Trans. Georgia Albert. Stanford, CA: Stanford University Press, 1999.
Aristotle. *Physics: Books III and IV*. Trans. Edward Hussey. Oxford: Clarendon Press, 1983.
Armstrong, Isobel. "Meter and Meaning." In *Meter Matters*, ed. Jason David Hall, 26–52. Athens: Ohio University Press, 2011.
Assaneo, M. Florencia, et al. "Spontaneous Synchronization to Speech Reveals Neural Mechanisms Facilitating Language Learning." *Nature Neuroscience* 22.4 (April 2019): 627–32.
Ashton, Rosemary. *The German Idea: Four English Writers and the Reception of German Thought, 1800–60*. Cambridge: Cambridge University Press, 1980.
Augustine, Saint. *Confessions*. Trans. William Watts. 2 vols. Loeb Classical Library. Cambridge, MA: Harvard University Press, 1912.
———. "On Music." In *The Fathers of the Church*, trans. Robert Taliaferro, 169–384. Washington, DC: Catholic University of America Press, 1947.
Badeni, June. *The Slender Tree: A Life of Alice Meynell*. Padstow, UK: Tabb House, 1981.
Balliet, Conrad A. "The History and Rhetoric of the Triplet." *PMLA* 80.5 (December 1965): 528–34.
Barrett, William Fletcher. *On the Threshold of the Unseen: An Examination of the Phenomena of Spiritualism and of the Evidence for Survival after Death*. New York: E. P. Dutton, 1917.

Barthes, Roland. *The Pleasure of the Text.* Trans. Richard Miller. New York: Farrar, Strauss and Giroux, 1975.

Bateson, Gregory. "Cybernetic Explanation." *American Behavioural Scientist* 10.8 (April 1967): 29–37.

Beer, Gillian. *Open Fields: Science in Cultural Encounter.* Oxford: Oxford University Press, 1999.

Benjamin, Walter. "Goethe's Elective Affinities." In *Selected Writings,* vol. 1: *1913–1926,* trans. Rodney Livingstone, 297–360. Cambridge, MA: Belknap Press, 1996.

———. "Toys and Play: Marginal Notes on a Monumental Work." In *Selected Writings,* vol. 2: *1927–1934,* trans. Rodney Livingstone, 117–21. Cambridge, MA: Belknap Press.

Benveniste, Émile. "The Notion of Rhythm in Its Linguistic Expression." In *Problems in General Linguistics,* trans. Mary Elizabeth Meek, 281–88. Coral Gables: University of Miami Press, 1971.

Bergson, Henri. *Mind-Energy: Lectures and Essays.* Trans. H. Wilden Carr. New York: Henry Holt, 1920.

Berlatta, Vincent. *Rhythm: Form and Dispossession.* Chicago: Chicago University Press, 2020.

Berlin, Edward A. *Ragtime.* Berkeley: University of California Press, 1980.

Besant, Walter. *With Harp and Crown.* 3 vols. London, 1875.

Bluemel, C. S. *Stammering and Cognate Defects of Speech.* 2 vols. New York: G. E. Stechert, 1917.

Bolton, Thaddeus. *Rhythm.* Worcester, MA: F. S. Blanchard, 1893.

Borrow, George. *The Zincali: An Account of the Gypsies of* Spain. 3rd ed. 2 vols. London, 1843.

Brennan, Teresa. *The Transmission of Affect.* Ithaca, NY: Cornell University Press, 2004.

Brogan, T. V. F. *English Versification, 1570–1980: A Reference Guide with a Global Appendix.* Baltimore: Johns Hopkins University Press, 1981.

Brooke, Rupert. *The Prose of Rupert Brooke.* Ed. Christopher Hassall. London: Sidgwick and Jackson, 1956.

Browning, Robert. *The Poetical Works of Robert Browning.* Ed. Ian Jack and Margaret Smith. Vol. 2. Oxford: Oxford University Press, 1984.

———. *Selected Poems.* London: Penguin, 1989.

Browning, Robert, and Elizabeth Barrett Browning. *The Letters of Robert Browning and Elizabeth Barrett Browning, 1845–1846.* Ed. Robert B. Browning. 2 vols. London, 1900.

Bücher, Karl. *Arbeit und Rhythmus.* Leipzig, 1896.

Bukharin, Nikolai. *Historical Materialism: A System of Sociology.* London: George Allen and Unwin, 1926.

Burney, Charles. *A General History of Music: From the Earliest Ages to the Present Period.* 4 vols. London, 1782–89.

Butts, Robert E. "Necessary Truths in Whewell's Theory of Science." *American Philosophical Quarterly* 2.3 (July 1965), 161–81.

Calloway, Ewen. "Fearful Memories Haunt Mouse Descendants: Genetic Imprint from

Traumatic Experiences Carries Through at Least Two Generations." *Nature* (9 December 2015). https://doi.org/10.1038/nature.2013.14272.

The Cambridge History of Western Music Theory. Ed. Thomas Christensen. Cambridge: Cambridge University Press, 2002.

Campbell, Lewis, and Garnett Matthew. *The Life of James Clerk Maxwell: With a Selection from His Correspondence and Occasional Writings; and a Sketch of His Contributions to Science*. London, 1882.

Carlson, Julia S. *Romantic Marks and Measures: Wordsworth's Poetry in Fields of Print*. Philadelphia: University of Pennsylvania Press, 2016.

Carman, Bliss. "Personal Rhythm." In *The Friendship of Art*, 182–89. Toronto: Copp, Clark, 1904.

Child, Francis James, ed. *The English and Scottish Popular Ballads*. 5 vols. New York: Dover Publications, 1965.

Clarke, Bruce. *Energy Forms: Allegory and Science in the Era of Classical Thermodynamics*. Ann Arbor: University of Michigan Press, 2001.

Clayton, Martin, Rebecca Sager, and Udo Will. "In Time with the Music: The Concept of Entrainment and Its Significance for Ethnomusicology." *ESEM Counterpoint* 1 (2004): 1–82.

Corson, Hiram. *An Introduction to the Study of Robert Browning's Poetry*. Boston, 1888.

Crabbe, George. *Tales, 1812 and Other Selected Poems*. Ed. Howard Mills. Cambridge: Cambridge University Press, 1967.

Crapsey, Adelaide. *A Study in English Metrics*. New York: Alfred A. Knopf, 1918.

Crystal, David. *Prosodic Systems and Intonation in English*. Cambridge: Cambridge University Press, 1969.

Cull, Richard. *Stammering Considered with Reference to Its Cure*. London, 1835.

Cureton, Richard. *Rhythmic Phrasing in English Verse*. London: Longman, 1992.

Curry, Samuel Silas. *Browning and the Dramatic Monologue*. Boston: Expression Company, 1908.

———. *Foundations of Expression: Studies and Problems for Developing the Voice, Body and Mind in Reading and Speaking*. Boston: Expression Company, 1907.

———. *Mind and Voice: Principles and Methods in Vocal Training*. Boston: Expression Company, 1910.

Dale, Catherine. *Music Analysis in Britain in the Nineteenth and Twentieth Century*. Aldershot and Burlington, UK: Ashgate, 2003.

Dames, Nicholas. *The Physiology of the Novel: Reading, Neural Science, and the Form of Victorian Fiction*. Oxford: Oxford University Press, 2007.

Darwin, Charles. *The Autobiography of Charles Darwin, 1809–1882*. Ed. Nora Barlow. New York: W. W. Norton, 2005.

———. *The Descent of Man and Selection in Relation to Sex*. Princeton, NJ: Princeton University Press, 1981.

Davis, Mary Byrd. "Swinburne's Use of His Sources in *Tristram of Lyonesse*." *Philological Quarterly* 55.1 (Winter 1976): 96–112.

Dawson, Gowan. "Victorian Periodicals and the Making of William Kingdon Clifford's Posthumous Reputation." In *Science Serialized: Representations of the Sciences in Nineteenth-Century Periodicals*, ed. Geoffrey Cantor and Sally Shuttleworth, 259–84. Cambridge, MA: MIT Press, 2004.

De Bolla, Peter. *The Architecture of Concepts: The Historical Formation of Human Rights*. Fordham, NY: Fordham University Press, 2013.

Deleuze, Gilles. *Essays Clinical and Critical*. Trans. Michael A. Greco and Daniel W. Smith. Minneapolis: University of Minnesota Press, 1997.

Dennett, Daniel. "The Origins of Selves." *Cogito* 3 (Autumn 1989): 163–73.

Desjardins, Molly. "John Thelwall and Association." In *John Thelwall: Critical Reassessments*, ed. Yasmin Solomonescu. *Romantic Circles*, September 2011. http://romantic-circles.org/praxis/thelwall/index.html.

Dickens, Charles. *A Tale of Two Cities*. New York: Barnes and Noble, 2004.

Diderot, Denis. *Essai sur le mérite et la vertu*. Paris, 1798.

Douglas, James. *Robert Browning*. London: Hodder and Stoughton, 1903.

Duff, David. *An Exposition of Browning's "Sordello," with Historical and Other Notes*. Edinburgh and London: William Blackwood and Sons, 1906.

Durkheim, Émile. *The Division of Labour in Society*. Trans. George Simpson. Glencoe, IL: Free Press of Glencoe, 1933.

———. *The Elementary Forms of Religious Life*. Trans. Carol Cosman. Oxford: Oxford University Press, 2001.

Dworkin, Craig. "The Stutter of Form." In *The Sound of Poetry / The Poetry of Sound*, ed. Marjorie Perloff and Craig Dworkin. Chicago: University of Chicago Press, 2009.

Eliot, George. "Notes on Form in Art." In *Selected Poems, Essays and Other Writings*, ed. A. S. Byatt, 231–36. London: Penguin, 1990.

———. *Romola*. Ed. Dorothea Barrett. London: Penguin, 1996.

———. *The Spanish Gypsy*. Ed. Antoine Gerard van den Broek. London: Pickering and Chatto, 2008.

Eliot, T. S. *The Sacred Wood: Essays on Poetry and Criticism*. London: Faber and Faber, 1967.

Elton, Oliver. *A Survey of English Literature, 1780–1880*. 4 vols. New York: Macmillan, 1920.

Elwick, James. "Herbert Spencer and the Disunity of the Social Organism." *History of Science* 41.1 (2003): 35–72.

Fairclough, Mary. *The Romantic Crowd: Sympathy, Controversy and Print Culture*. Cambridge: Cambridge University Press, 2013.

Fisch, Menachem. "Necessary and Contingent Truth in William Whewell's Antithetical Theory of Knowledge." *Studies in History and Philosophy of Science* 16.4 (December 1985): 275–314.

Fitch, W. Tecumseh. "The Biology and Evolution of Rhythm: Unraveling a Paradox." In *Language and Music as Cognitive Systems*, ed. Patrick Rebuschat, Martin Rohmeier, John A. Hawkins, and Ian Cross, 73–95. Oxford: Oxford University Press.

Freer, Alexander. "Rhythm as Coping." *New Literary History* 46.3 (Summer 2015): 549–68.

Frum, Robert O. *The Evolution of Beauty: How Darwin's Forgotten Theory of Mate Choice Shapes the Animal World—and Us*. New York: Doubleday, 2017.
Fuji, Shinya, and Catherine Y. Wan. "The Role of Rhythm in Speech and Language Rehabilitation: The SEP Hypothesis." *Frontiers in Human Neuroscience* 8 (2014): 777. http://doi.org/10.3389/fnhum.2014.00777.
Fussell, Paul. *Theory of Prosody in Eighteenth-Century England*. New London: Connecticut College, 1954.
Glaser, Ben "Polymetrical Dissonance: Tennyson, A. Mary F. Robinson, and Classical Meter." *Victorian Poetry* 49.2 (Summer 2011): 199–216.
Glazener, Nancy. "The Browning Society in US Public Literary Culture." *Modern Language Quarterly* 75.2 (2014): 171–91.
Gleick, James. *Chaos: The Amazing Science of the Unpredictable*. London: Vintage, 1998.
Golston, Michael. *Rhythm and Race in Modernist Poetry and Science*. New York: Columbia University Press, 2008.
Gould, Barri J. *ThermoPoetics*. Cambridge, MA: MIT Press, 2010.
Gross, John. "A Tale of Two Cities." In *Dickens and the Twentieth Century*, ed. John Gross and Gabriel Pearson, 187–97. Toronto: University of Toronto Press, 1962.
Groth, Helen. "Subliminal Histories: Psychological Experimentation in the Poetry and Poetics of Frederic W. H. Myers." *19: Interdisciplinary Studies in the Long Nineteenth Century* 12 (April 2011). http://doi.org/10.16995/ntn.594.
Guattari, Félix, and Gilles Deleuze. *A Thousand Plateaus: Capitalism and Schizophrenia*. London: Continuum, 1992.
Guest, Edwin. *A History of English Rhythms*. London, 1838.
Gummere, Francis Barton. *The Beginnings of Poetry*. London: Macmillan, 1901.
Eliot, George. *The George Eliot Letters*. Ed. Gordon S. Haight. 9 vols. New Haven, CT: Yale University Press, 1954.
Gurney, Edmund. "Poets, Critics and Class-Lists." In vol. 2 of *Tertium Quid: Chapter on Various Disputed Questions*, 119–90. London, 1887.
———. *The Power of Sound*. London, 1880.
Hall, Jason David. "Sonic Forms: Ezra Pound's Anti-metronome Modernism in Context." In *Sound and Literature*, ed. Anna Snaith, 74–91. Cambridge: Cambridge University Press, 2020.
Hasty, Christopher. *Meter as Rhythm*. Oxford: Oxford University Press, 2007.
Hegel, G. W. F. *Lectures on Fine Art*. Trans. T. M. Knox. 3 vols. Oxford: Clarendon Press, 1975.
———. *The Logic of Hegel*. Trans. William Wallace. London, 1874.
———. *Science of Logic*. Trans. A. V. Miller. London: George Allen and Unwin, 1969.
———. "Who Thinks Abstractly?" In *Hegel: Texts and Commentary*, trans. And ed. Walter Kaufmann, 117–18. Notre Dame, IN: University of Notre Dame Press, 1977.
Heidegger, Martin, and Eugen Fink. *Heraclitus Seminar, 1966–1967*. Trans. Charles H. Seibert. Tuscaloosa: University of Alabama Press, 1979.

Hobsbaum, Philip. *Metre, Rhythm and Verse*. London: Routledge, 1996.
Hoegaerts, Josephine. "'Is It a Habit or Is It a Disease?' The Changing Social Meaning of Stammering in Nineteenth-Century Western Europe." *Terrains & travaux* 23 (2013): 17–37.
———. "S-s-s-syncopation: Music, Modernity, and the Performance of Stammering (ca. 1860–1930)." *Societies* 5.4 (2015): 1–16.
Hofstadter, Richard. *Social Darwinism in American Thought*. Boston: Beacon Press, 1955.
Holmes, Stewart W. "Browning: Semantic Stutterer." *PMLA* 60.1 (March 1945): 231–55.
Honing, Henkjan, Hugo Merchant, Gábor P. Háden, Luis Prado, and Ramón Bartolo. "Rhesus Monkeys (*Macaca mulatta*) Detect Rhythmic Groups in Music, but Not the Beat." *PLoS ONE* 7.12 (2012). https://doi.org/10.1371/journal.pone.0051369.
Hopkins, Gerard Manley. *The Further Letters of Gerard Manley Hopkins: Including His Correspondence with Coventry Patmore*. Ed. C. C. Abbott. London: Oxford University Press, 1956.
Howe, Susan. *The Birth-Mark: Unsettling the Wilderness in American Literary History*. Hanover and London: Wesleyan University Press, 1993.
———. *My Emily Dickinson*. Berkeley, CA: North Atlantic Books, 1985.
Hunt, James. *Stammering and Stuttering, Their Nature and Treatment*. 1st ed. London, 1861.
———*Stammering and Stuttering, Their Nature and Treatment*. 6th ed. London, 1870.
———. *Stammering and Stuttering, Their Nature and Treatment*. 7th ed. London, 1870.
Huxley, Thomas Henry. "Administrative Nihilism." *Fortnightly Review* 10 (1871): 525–43.
Jackson, Virginia. "The Cadence of Consent: Francis Barton Gummere, Lyric Rhythm, and White Poetics." In *Critical Rhythm: The Poetics of a Literary Art Form*, ed. Jonathan Culler and Ben Glaser, 87–105. Fordham: Fordham University Press, 2019.
Jackson, Virginia, and Yopie Prins, eds. *The Lyric Theory Reader: A Critical Anthology*. Baltimore: Johns Hopkins University Press, 2014.
Jaeger, Werner. *Paideia: The Ideals of Greek Culture*. 3 vols. New York: Oxford University Press, 1939–45.
Jarvis, Simon. "Musical Thinking: Hegel and the Phenomenology of Prosody." *Paragraph* 28.2 (2005): 57–71.
———. "Prosody as Cognition." *Critical Quarterly* 40.4 (Dec. 1998): 3–15.
Johnson, Samuel. *A Dictionary of the English Language, in Which the Words Are Deduced from Their Originals*. 2 vols. London, 1755–56.
Jones, Ewan. *Coleridge and the Philosophy of Poetic Form*. Cambridge: Cambridge University Press, 2014.
———. "Coventry Patmore's Corpus." *ELH* 83.3 (Fall 2016): 839–72.
King, Joshua. "Patmore, Hopkins, and the Problem of the English Metrical Law." *Victorian Poetry* 49. 2 (Summer 2011): 31–49.
Kipling, Rudyard. *The Five Nations*. London: Methuen, 1903.
Kittler, Friedrich. *Gramophone, Film, Typewriter*. Trans. Dorothea von Mucke. Stanford, CA.: Stanford University Press, 1999.

Kivy, Peter. "Darwin on Music." *Journal of the American Musicological Society* 12.1 (Spring 1959): 42–48.

Krell, David Farrell. *The Tragic Absolute: German Idealism and the Languishing of God*. Bloomington: Indiana University Press, 2005.

Lanier, Sidney. *The Science of English Verse*. New York, 1880.

Laqueur, Thomas. *Making Sex: Body and Gender from the Greeks to Freud*. Cambridge, MA: Harvard University Press, 1992.

Lefebvre, Henri. *Rhythmanalysis: Space, Time and Everyday Life*. Trans. Stuart Elden and Gerald Moore. London: Continuum, 2013.

Leighton, Angela. *Victorian Women Poets: Writing Against the Heart*. Charlottesville: University Press of Virginia, 1992.

Leong, Victoria, Elizabeth Byrne, Kaili Clackson, Stanimira Georgieva, Sarah Lam, and Sam Wass. "Speaker Gaze Increases Infant–Adult Connectivity." *Proceedings of the National Academy of Sciences* 114.50 (December 2017): 13290–95.

Lewes, George Henry. *The Physiology of Common Life*. London, 1859.

———. *The Principles of Success in Literature*. Boston, 1891.

———. *Problems in Life and Mind*. 2 vols. London, 1879.

———. *Sea-Side Studies, at Ilfracombe, Tenby, the Scilly Isles, and Jersey*. London, 1860.

Lewis, George Andrew. *The Practical Treatment of Stammering and Stuttering, with Suggestions for Practice and Helpful Exercises*. Detroit, 1906.

Macauley, Tomas. "Rhythmic Accent and the Absolute: Sulzer, Schelling and the *Akzenttheorie*." *Eighteenth Century Music* 10.02 (September 2013): 277–86.

Maitland, Thomas [Robert Buchanan]. "The Fleshly School of Poetry: Mr. D. G. Rossetti." *Contemporary Review* 18 (1871): 335.

Malabou, Catherine. *The Future of Hegel: Plasticity, Temporality, and Dialectic*. Trans. Lisabeth During. New York: Routledge, 2004.

Mander, W. J. *British Idealism: A History*. Oxford: Oxford University Press, 2011.

Martin, Meredith. "'Imperfectly Civilized': Ballads, Nations, and Histories of Form." *ELH* 82.2 (Summer 2015): 345–63.

———. *The Rise and Fall of Meter*. Princeton, NJ: Princeton University Press, 2012.

Maynard, John. *Victorian Discourses in Sexuality and Religion*. Cambridge: Cambridge University Press, 1993.

Mauss, Marcel. "Techniques of the Body" (1934). In *Incorporations*, ed. Jonathan Crary and Sandford Kwinter, 455–77. New York: Zone, 1992.

McGann, Jerome. *The Romantic Ideology*. Chicago: University of Chicago Press, 1983.

———. *Swinburne: An Essay in Criticism*. Chicago: University of Chicago Press, 1972.

———. "Swinburne, Wagner, Baudelaire: Poetry in the Condition of Music." *Victorian Poetry* 47.4 (2009): 619–32.

McGuire, Riley. "The Victorian Unspeakable: Stammering and Same-Sex Intimacy between Men." *DiGeSt. Journal of Diversity and Gender Studies* 3.2 (2016): 43–57.

Meynell, Alice. *Collected Poems of Alice Meynell*. New York: Charles Scribner's Sons, 1914.
———. *The Rhythm of Life*. London: John Lane, 1905.
Millard, John. *Grammar of Elocution*. London, 1889.
Miller, J. Hillis. *The Disappearance of God: Five Nineteenth-Century Writers*. Urbana and Chicago: University of Illinois Press, 2000.
Monboddo, James Burnett, Lord. *On the Origin and Progress of Language*. 6 vols. Edinburgh and London, 1773.
Montagu, Ashley. *Touching: The Human Significance of the Skin*. London: HarperCollins, 1986.
Morley, John. "The Spanish Gypsy." *Macmillan's Magazine* 18 (July 1868): 281–87.
Myers, F. W. H. "Essay on Virgil." In *Essays Classical and Modern*, 106–76. London: Macmillan, 1914.
———. *Human Personality and Its Survival of Bodily Death*. 2 vols. London, 1903.
———. "M. Renan and Miracles." *Nineteenth Century* 10 (1881): 90–106.
Newman, Steve. *Ballad Collection, Lyric, and the Canon: The Call of the Popular from the Restoration to the New Criticism*. Philadelphia: University of Pennsylvania Press, 2007.
Nietzsche, Friedrich. *The Case of Wagner, Nietzsche Contra Wager and Selected Aphorisms*. Trans. Anthony M. Ludovici. London: T. N. Foulis, 1911.
———. *The Gay Science*. Trans. Josefine Nauckoff. Cambridge: Cambridge University Press, 2001.
Nixon, Jude V. "'Death Blots Black Out': Thermodynamics and the Poetry of Gerard Manley Hopkins." *Victorian Poetry* 40. 2 (Summer 2002): 131–56.
Noakes, Richard. "The 'Bridge Which Is Between Physical and Psychical Research': William Fletcher Barrett, Sensitive Flames, and Spiritualism." *History of Science* 42 (2004): 419–64.
Nord, Deborah Epstein. *Gypsies and the British Imagination, 1807–1930*. New York: Columbia University Press, 2006.
North, Joseph. *Literary Criticism: A Concise Political History*. Cambridge, MA: Harvard University Press, 2017.
Novalis. *Fichte Studies*. Ed. Jane Kneller. Cambridge: Cambridge University Press, 2003.
———. *Schriften*. Vol. 2: *Das philosophische Werk I*. Ed. Richard Samuel in collaboration with Hans-Joachim Mähl and Gerhard Schulz. Rev. Richard Samuel and Hans-Joachim Mähl. Stuttgart, Berlin, Cologne, Mainz: Kohlhammer, 1981.
Odell, Jonathan. *An Essay on the Elements, Accents, and Prosody, of the English Language, etc.* London, 1806.
Omond, T. S. *English Metrists*. Oxford: Clarendon Press, 1921.
Patel, A. D. "The Evolutionary Biology of Musical Rhythm: Was Darwin Wrong?" *PLOS Biology* 12.3 (25 March 2014). https://doi.org/10.1371/journal.pbio.1001821.
Patmore, Coventry. *Coventry Patmore's "Essay on Metrical Law."* Washington, DC: Catholic University of America Press, 1961.
———. *The Poems of Coventry Patmore*. Ed. Frederick Page. Oxford: Oxford University Press, 1949.

———. *The Rod, the Root and the Flower.* London: Grey Walls Press, 1950.
Pechenick, E. A., C. M. Danforth, and P. S. Dodds. "Characterizing the Google Books Corpus: Strong Limits to Inferences of Socio-Cultural and Linguistic Evolution." *PLoS ONE* 10.10 (2015). https://doi.org/10.1371/journal.pone.0137041.
Perrier, Edmond. *Le Transformisme.* Paris, 1888.
Phelan, Joseph. *The Music of Verse: Metrical Experiment in Nineteenth-Century Poetry.* Basingstoke, UK: Palgrave Macmillan, 2012.
Plato. *Laws.* Trans. R. G. Bury. Cambridge, MA: Harvard University Press, 2014.
Plumptre, Charles John. *King's College Lectures on Elocution, or The Physiology and Culture of Voice and Speech, and the Expression of the Emotions by Language, Countenance, and Gesture, to Which Is Added, a Special Lecture on the Causes and Cure of Impediments of Speech.* London, 1863.
Pound, Louise. *Poetic Origins and the Ballad.* New York: Macmillan, 1921.
Preston, Carrie J. *Modernism's Mythic Pose: Gender, Genre, Solo Performance.* Oxford: Oxford University Press, 2011.
Prins, Yopie. "Patmore's Law, Meynell's Rhythm." In *The Fin-de-Siècle Poem: English Literary Culture and the 1890s,* ed. Joseph Bristow. Athens: Ohio University Press, 2005, 261–84.
———. "Voice Inverse." *Victorian Poetry* 42.1 (Spring 2004): 43–60.
Rabinbach, Anton. *The Human Motor: Energy, Fatigue and the Origins of Modernity.* Berkeley and Los Angeles: University of California Press, 1992.
Rankin, J. W. "Rime and Reason." *PMLA* 44. 4 (December 1929): 997–1004.
Richards, Ivor Armstrong. *How to Read a Page: A Course in Effective Reading, with an Introduction to a Hundred Great Words.* New York: W. W. Norton, 1942.
Robinson, Henry Crabb. *Essays on Kant, Schelling and German Aesthetics.* Ed. James Vigus. London: MHRA, 2010.
Rowell, Lewis. "Aristoxenus on Rhythm." *Journal of Music Theory* 23.1 (Spring 1979): 63–79.
Rudy, Jason. *Electric Meters: Victorian Physiological Poetics.* Athens: Ohio University Press, 2007.
Rush, James. *The Philosophy of the Human Voice: Embracing Its Physiological History; together with a System of Principles by Which Criticism in the Art of Elocution May Be Rendered Intelligible, and Instruction, Definite and Comprehensive, to Which Is Added, a Brief Analysis of Song and Recitative.* 7th ed. Philadelphia, 1879.
Russell, Henrietta. *The Delsarte Series.* Vol. 1: *Yawning.* New York, 1891.
Sachs, Curt. *Rhythm and Tempo: A Study in Musical History.* London: J. M. Dent and Sons, 1953.
Saussy, Haun. *The Ethnography of Rhythm.* New York: Fordham University Press, 2016.
Sawyer, Paul. "Ruskin and Tyndall: The Poetry of Matter and The Poetry of Spirit." *Annals of the New York Academy of Sciences* 360 (April 1981): 217–46.
Schaffer, Talia. "A Tethered Angel: The Martyrology of Alice Meynell." *Victorian Poetry* 38.1 (Spring 2000): 49–61.

Schelling, Friedrich Wilhelm Joseph. *The Philosophy of Art*. Trans. Douglas W. Stott. Minneapolis: University of Minnesota Press, 1989.

Seidel, Wilhelm. *Rhythmus: Eine Begriffsbestimmung*. Darmstadt: Wissenschaftliche Buchgesellschaft, 1973.

Serres, Michel. *Hermes: Literature, Science, Philosophy*. Baltimore: Johns Hopkins University Press, 1982.

Shaviro, Steven. *The Universe of Things*. Minneapolis: University of Minnesota Press, 2014.

Simmel, Georg. *The Philosophy of Money*. London: Routledge, 1990.

Sloane, Thomas O. "From Elocution to New Criticism: An Episode in the History of Rhetoric." *Rhetorica: A Journal of the History of Rhetoric* 31.3 (Summer 2013): 297–330.

Smith, Adam. *The Theory of Moral Sentiments*. Ed. Knud Haakonssen. Cambridge: Cambridge University Press, 2002.

Spencer, Herbert. *Essays Scientific, Politic and Speculative*. 3 vols. London, 1891.

———. *First Principles of a New System of Philosophy*. London, 1862.

———. *The Life and Letters of Herbert Spencer*. Ed. David Duncan. Cambridge: Cambridge University Press, 2013.

———. "On the Origin of Music." *Mind* 15.60 (October 1890): 449–68.

———. "On the Origin of Music." *Mind* 16.64 (October 1891): 535–37.

Spiegel, Edward A. "Cosmic Arrhythmias." In *Chaos in Astrophysics*, ed. J. R. Buchler et al., 91–135. New York: D. Reidel, 1985.

Steele, Joshua. *Prosodia Rationalis: or, An Essay towards Establishing the Melody and Measure of Speech, to Be Expressed and Perpetuated by Peculiar Symbols*. London, 1779.

Stewart, Balfour, and P. G. Tait. *The Unseen Universe, or Physical Speculations on a Future State*. New York, 1875.

Stewart, Susan. "Scandals of the Ballad." *Representations* 32 (Fall 1990): 134–56.

Stirling, J. H. *The Secret of Hegel: Being the Hegelian System in Origin, Principle, Form and Matter*. 2 vols. London, 1865.

Sutton, Emma. *Aubrey Beardsley and British Wagnerism in the 1890s*. Oxford: Oxford University Press, 2002.

Swinburne, Algernon Charles. *Algernon Swinburne: The Critical Heritage*. Ed. Clyde K. Hyder. London: Routledge, 1970.

———. *Major Poems and Selected Prose*. Ed. Jerome McGann and Charles L. Sligh. New Haven, CT: Yale University Press, 2004.

———. *The Swinburne Letters*. Ed. Cecil Y. Lang. 6 vols. New Haven, CT: Yale University Press, 1959–62.

———. *Swinburne Replies*. Ed. Clyde K. Hyder. Syracuse: SUNY Press, 1966.

———. *Swinburne as Critic*. Ed. Clyde K. Hyder. London: Routledge and Kegan Paul, 1972.

———. *Under the Microscope*. London: D. White, 1872.

Taylor, Dennis. *Hardy's Metres and Victorian Prosody*. Oxford: Clarendon Press, 1988.

Thelwall, Algernon Sydney. *The Reading Desk and the Pulpit*. London, 1861.

Thelwall, John. *A Letter to Henry Cline, Esq on Imperfect Developments of the Faculties Mental and Moral, as well as Constitutional and Organic on the Treatment of Impediments of Speech.* London, 1810.

———. *Selections for the Illustration of a Course of Instructions on the Rhythmus and Utterance of the English Language.* London, 1812.

Thomas, Edward. *Algernon Charles Swinburne: A Critical Study.* London: Secker, 1912.

Toussaint, Godfried T. "Generating 'Good' Musical Rhythms Algorithmically." *Proceedings of the 8th International Conference on Arts and Humanities, Honolulu, Hawaii, January 13–16* (2010): 774–91.

Tucker, Herbert. *Browning's Beginnings: The Art of Disclosure.* Minnesota: University of Minnesota Press, 1980.

———. *Epic: Britain's Heroic Muse, 1790–1910.* Oxford: Oxford University Press, 2008.

———. "Quantity and Quality: The Strange Case of George Eliot, Minor Poet." *George Eliot–George Henry Lewes Studies* 60/61 (September 2011): 17–30.

Tyndall, John. *Heat Considered as a Mode of Motion.* Cambridge: Cambridge University Press, 2014.

———. "The Sabbath." In *New Fragments*, 1–46. London, 1892.

———. *Sound: A Course of Lectures Delivered at the Royal Institution of Great Britain.* London, 1867.

Veder, Robin. *The Living Line: Modern Art and the Economy of Energy.* Hanover, NH: Dartmouth College Press, 2015.

Vlock-Keyes, Deborah. "Music and Dramatic Voice in Robert Browning and Robert Schumann." *Victorian Poetry* 29.3 (Autumn 1991): 227–39.

Wallaschek, Richard. *Primitive Music.* London, 1893.

Watts-Duncan, Theodore. "Poetry." In *Encyclopedia Britannica*, 9th ed., vol. 19, 256–73. Edinburgh, 1885.

Wellman, Janina. *The Form of Becoming: Embryology and the Epistemology of Rhythm.* Trans. Kate Sturge. New York: Zone, 2017.

Whewell, William. "English Hexameters." *North British Review* 19 (May–August 1853): 129–50.

———. *The Philosophy of the Inductive Sciences.* 2 vols. London, 1840.

Wilde, Oscar. "The Critic as Artist." In *The Artist as Critic: Critical Writings of Oscar Wilde*, ed. Richard Ellmann, 341–407. Chicago: University of Chicago Press, 1968.

Wimsatt, W. K., Jr., and Monroe C. Beardsley. "The Concept of Meter: An Exercise in Abstraction." *PMLA* 74.5 (December 1959): 585–98.

Wingate, Marcel. *Stuttering: Theory and Treatment.* New York: Irvington, 1976.

Woolf, Virginia. *Orlando: A Biography.* New York: Harcourt Brace Jovanovich, 1956.

Young, Walter. "An Essay on Rhythmical Measures." *Transactions of the Royal Society of Edinburgh* 2.2 (1786): 55–110.

INDEX

Abbott, Ruth, 131
Aeschylus, 8–9, 133
Archilochus, 9
Armstrong, Isobel, 77
Attridge, Derek, 18
Augustine, Saint, 21
Autechre, 205
Aviram, Amittai F., 15

ballads, 145–53
Barrett, William, 166
Barrett Browning, Elizabeth, 34, 57, 100, 187
Benveniste, Émile, 8–9
Bergson, Henri, 169
Berlatta, Vincent, 15
Besant, Walter, 35
Bolton, Thaddeus, 16, 159–60
Borrow, George, 128–30, 148
Bowie, David, 64
Brennan, Teresa, 118
British Society for Psychical Research, 166–67, 169
Brogan, T. V. F., 18
Brooke, Rupert, 35
Browning, Robert: and elocutionary science, 50–57; "Flute Music, with an Accompaniment," 67–68; "How They Brought the Good News from Ghent to Aix," 53–56; *Sordello*, 34–50
Burney, Charles, 12

Cable, Thomas, 18
Carlson, Julia S., 26
Carlyle, Thomas, 34
Carman, Bliss, 162–63
catalexis, 83–92
Child Ballads, 147–53
Clarke, Bruce, 171
classical meter: and Greek etymology of rhythm, 8–9, 16; and romance vernaculars, 11–13, 22–24, 76–78
Clifford, William Kingdom, 171–72, 183
Colombat de l'Isère, Marc, 29–33
conceptual history, 13–15, 70–71
couplets, 39–50, 191–99
Crabbe, George, 34, 36
Crabb Robinson, Henry, 74
Crapsey, Adelaide, 182
Crystal, David, 22
Curry, Samuel Silas, 50–54

Dale, Catherine, 11
Darwin, Charles, 109, 138–39, 141–43

De Bary, Richard, 93–94
Deleuze, Giles, 65–66
Democritus, 9
Dickins, Charles, 119–23
Dickinson, Emily, 65–67
Dieffenbach, Friedrich, 29–30
Dryden, John, 192
Durkheim, Émile, 143

Eliot, George, 109, 123–38
Eliot, Thomas Stearns, 177–78
Elton, Oliver, 188
enjambment, 41–45, 126, 179, 189–90
entrainment: and nonhuman animals, 139–42; and resonance, 116–18; and sympathy, 114–23
ethnology, 58–61, 141–44

Fairclough, Mary, 119
fatigue, 159–63, 176–87
Fichte, Johann Gottlieb, 72
Franklin, Aretha, 1–3, 146–47
Fussell, Paul, 22

Golston, Michael, 15–17
Gorman, Amanda, 146
Gumbrecht, Hans-Ulrich, 15
Gummere, Francis Barton, 143–47
Gurney, Edmund, 143, 167–70, 173–74

Hall, Jason David, 15–16
harmony: and rhythm, 8, 30, 117–18, 201
Hasty, Christopher, 18, 74
Hegel, Georg Wilhelm Friedrich, 74–78, 81, 94–95, 133, 139
Heidegger, Martin, 9–10
Helmholtz, Hermann von, 159–61, 174, 183, 188, 201
Hölderlin, Friedrich, 71
Hopkins, Gerard Manley, 80, 174–75

Howe, Susan, 65–66
Hunt, James, 29–33, 58–60
Huxley, Thomas Henry, 112–13
Huygens, Christiaan, 115–16
hypermetricality, 192–95

idealism, 69, 78, 94–96
Isaiah, 185–86

Jackson, Virginia, 75, 145–46
Jacques-Dalcroze, Émile, 17, 205
James, Etta, 64
James, William, 169
Johnson, Samuel, 8, 53

Kant, Immanuel, 10–11, 96–97
Keats, John, 40, 173
Kingsley, Charles, 29, 32–33, 109
Kipling, Rudyard, 187
Kittler, Friedrich, 158

Lamar, Kendrick, 64
Lanier, Sidney, 160–61
Laqueur, Thomas, 14
Lefebvre, Henri, 204–5
Lewes, George Henry, 109–12, 115, 138–39, 187

Macaulay, Thomas Babbington, 148
Malabou, Catherine, 75
Martin, Meredith, 15, 76, 79
maternity, 103–8
mathematics, 97–99
Maxwell, James Clerk, 155–56, 163
Maynard, John, 80, 90
McGann, Jerome, 175, 176
Meynell, Alice, 99–106
mollusks, 109–14
Monboddo, James Burnett, Lord, 22–25
monosyllables, 47, 54, 104, 181–83

music, 11–12, 60–64, 116–18
Myers, Frederic William Henry, 166–67, 172–73

Newman, Steve, 146, 148
Nietzsche, Friedrich, 10, 17, 201
North, Joseph, 206
Novalis (Georg Philipp Friedrich Freiherr von Hardenberg), 72–73

Omond, T. S., 22

Patel, Aniruddh D., 139–40
Patmore, Coventry, 34, 78–94
Phelan, Joseph, 82, 90–91
Plato, 9, 169
Pope, Alexander, 144, 181–82, 192, 196
Pound, Ezra, 37, 56, 106, 162
Prins, Yopie, 53–54, 75, 79, 101–2, 199–200

Rabinbach, Anton, 159
ragtime, 60–64
Rankin, J. W., 9
rhyme and rhythm, 9
Richards, Ivor Armstrong, 57
Rousseau, Jean-Jacques, 11, 22, 77, 140–41, 146
Rudy, Jason, 16, 79
Rush, James, 27–28

Saintsbury, George, 34
Schelling, Friedrich Wilhelm Joseph, 73–74
Scott, Walter, 195
Shannon, Claude, 56, 194
Shelley, Percy Bysshe, 40, 144, 188
Simmel, Georg, 114, 143
Smith, Adam, 118–19

Spencer, Herbert, 10, 112–14, 140–43, 154–56, 160–61
spiritualism, 166–70
Steele, Joshua, 12–13, 21–26
Stewart, Balfour, 163–64, 171
Stewart, Susan, 147–48
Stirling, James, 94–95
stuttering: and race, 58–64; and "the rhythm method," 29–33; and speech therapy, 25–33
Swift, Jonathan, 192
Swift, Taylor, 4
Swinburne, Algernon Charles, 171–201

Tait, P. G., 163–64, 171
Taylor, Dennis, 75
Tennyson, Alfred, Lord, 171, 174
Thelwall, John, 25–27, 34, 95
thermodynamics: and conservation of force, 156–63; and entropy, 154–56, 170–73
Tucker, Herbert, 37, 124, 175
Tyndall, John, 154–61, 163–66, 170–71, 175

Verci, Giambattista, 38
Vossius, Isaac, 11, 143

Wagner, Richard, 17, 143, 201
Wallaschek, Richard, 142
waste, 187–201
Watts-Duncan, Theodore, 99–100
Wellmann, Janina, 70–71
Whewell, William, 95–99
Wilde, Oscar, 35
Woolf, Virginia, 106–8
Wordsworth, William, 89–90

Recent books in the
Victorian Literature and Culture Series

Narrative and Its Nonevents: The Unwritten Plots That Shaped Victorian Realism
CARRA GLATT

Victorian Metafiction
TABITHA SPARKS

Strangers in the Archive: Literary Evidence and London's East End
HEIDI KAUFMAN

Evangelical Gothic: The English Novel and the Religious War on Virtue from Wesley to "Dracula"
CHRISTOPHER HERBERT

Reading with the Senses in Victorian Literature and Science
DAVID SWEENEY COOMBS

Parting Words: Victorian Poetry and Public Address
JUSTIN A. SIDER

The Physics of Possibility: Victorian Fiction, Science, and Gender
MICHAEL TONDRE

Willful Submission: Sado-Erotics and Heavenly Marriage in Victorian Poetry
AMANDA PAXTON

Pirating Fictions: Ownership and Creativity in Nineteenth-Century Popular Culture
MONICA F. COHEN

Mathilde Blind: Late-Victorian Culture and the Woman of Letters
JAMES DIEDRICK

Poetry and the Thought of Song in Nineteenth-Century Britain
ELIZABETH K. HELSINGER

The Antagonist Principle: John Henry Newman and the Paradox of Personality
LAWRENCE POSTON

Personal Business: Character and Commerce in Victorian Literature and Culture
AERON HUNT

Second Person Singular: Late Victorian Women Poets and the Bonds of Verse
EMILY HARRINGTON

The Ghost behind the Masks: The Victorian Poets and Shakespeare
W. DAVID SHAW

Victorian Poets and the Changing Bible
CHARLES LAPORTE

Liberal Epic: The Victorian Practice of History from Gibbon to Churchill
EDWARD ADAMS

Supposing "Bleak House"
JOHN O. JORDAN

Feeling for the Poor: Bourgeois Compassion, Social Action, and the Victorian Novel
CAROLYN BETENSKY

The Science of Religion in Britain, 1860–1915
MARJORIE WHEELER-BARCLAY

Reading for the Law: British Literary History and Gender Advocacy
CHRISTINE L. KRUEGER

The Dynamics of Genre: Journalism and the Practice of Literature in Mid-Victorian Britain
DALLAS LIDDLE

The Fowl and the Pussycat: Love Letters of Michael Field, 1876–1909
EDITED BY SHARON BICKLE

Victorian Prism: Refractions of the Crystal Palace
EDITED BY JAMES BUZARD, JOSEPH W. CHILDERS, AND EILEEN GILLOOLY

Nostalgia in Transition, 1780–1917
LINDA M. AUSTIN

The English Cult of Literature: Devoted Readers, 1774–1880
WILLIAM R. MCKELVY

Artist of Wonderland: The Life, Political Cartoons, and Illustrations of Tenniel
FRANKIE MORRIS

The Material Interests of the Victorian Novel
DANIEL HACK

Behind Her Times: Transition England in the Novels of Mary Arnold Ward
JUDITH WILT

The Circus and Victorian Society
BRENDA ASSAEL

Christina Rossetti: The Patience of Style
CONSTANCE W. HASSETT

Frances Power Cobbe: Victorian Feminist, Journalist, Reformer
SALLY MITCHELL

www.ingramcontent.com/pod-product-compliance
Lightning Source LLC
Chambersburg PA
CBHW021348230426
43666CB00006B/443